TOWARDS A NEW
MYSTICISM

TOWARDS
A NEW
MYSTICISM

Teilhard de Chardin
and Eastern Religions

URSULA KING

The Seabury Press · New York

1981
The Seabury Press
815 Second Avenue
New York, N.Y. 10017

Printed in the United States of America

Library of Congress Cataloging in Publication Data

King, Ursula.
    Towards a new mysticism.
    Bibliography: p. 293
    Includes index.
    1. Religions. 2. Mysticism. 3. Teilhard de
Chardin, Pierre. I. Title.
BL80.2.K56   291.4′2   80-17260
ISBN 0-8164-0475-5
ISBN 0-8164-2327-X pa.

The publishers and author wish to acknowledge the following
publications and publishers:
Aubier Montaigne, Paris (*Lettres Intimes*); Fayard, Paris (*Journal*);
Editions du Centurion, Paris (*Lettres Familières*); Herder &
Herder, New York (de Terra, *In the Field with Teilhard de
Chardin*); Editions du Seuil, Paris (Rivière, *En Chine avec
Teilhard*); Newman Press, New York (Whitson, *The Coming Con-
vergence . . . *); *The Ampleforth Journal*; *Religious Studies*; *Studies in
Religion/Sciences Religieuses*; *The Modern Churchman* and *The Teilhard
Review*.

CONTENTS

EPILOGUE

FOREWORD

by Dr J. Needham

It is a great privilege for me to be invited to write a foreword for the book of my friend Ursula King on Teilhard de Chardin in relation to the religions of Asia, that part of the world in which he himself lived so long. I should say without any hesitation that Father Teilhard was called to be the greatest prophet of this age. That will become more and more clear, I believe, as time goes on. How then did such a man, arising from the relatively narrow environment of provincial Latin Catholic France and yet generating a view which surveyed the infinities of time and space with undimmed theistic conviction, react to the philosophies and religions of the Eastern world far beyond the confines of Christendom? Such a book as Ursula King's has become an urgent necessity, and I think she has made a great success of it. Although many of Teilhard's notes and travel diaries are unfortunately lost, a large amount of material remains, and the author has laid it fully under contribution. She produces a flood of facts hitherto not known — such as Teilhard's meeting with Edgar Snow and his wife, or talking with Living Buddhas, or admiring the numinous quality of Mahayana Buddhist liturgies. Most of us had no idea how much reading he did in comparative religion, especially as regards Asia, nor did we know how active he was in the *World Congress of Faiths*.

From my student days onwards I gradually developed a view of the world which had two principal aspects. On the one hand, following Rudolf Otto and R. G. Collingwood, I became profoundly convinced that man gains true apprehension of the universe only through the exercise of several different forms of experience, science, religion, art, history, philosophy and so on. Even though these forms of experience are liable to contradict each other, no one will do alone, certainly not science which tends to be supreme today. As C. G. Jung said, 'Science should always be man's servant; when it usurps the throne it leads to tyranny'. On the other hand, I was convinced that Christianity must take evolution seriously. Modern knowledge about cosmic, biological and social evolution made it absolutely impossible to maintain any longer the medieval Christian worldviews. In other words, in a way I had become a 'process theologian' without knowing it.

Consequently I ought to have been well prepared to understand Teilhard de Chardin when I met him personally in Paris in 1947 at a time when I was working to establish the Natural Sciences Division of UNESCO. He and I used to dine together from time to time, and I found him a charismatic as well as a lovable person, but I didn't quite understand what exactly he was driving at; and it was only after the appearance of his many books, and after he himself was dead, that I realized we had been travelling on very similar main lines. Actually I have never been able to re-read some of his books, because they move me too much, and I prefer to remain calm and clear-headed though quite conscious of Pascal's frightening infinite empty spaces.

I also had much in common of course with another great friend, Julian Huxley, at that time Director-General of UNESCO, but where I differed from his evolutionary humanism was that I thought the numinous was very important, and I could find it best in my own traditional religion. I had begun as an Anglo-Catholic and an Anglo-Catholic I remained, though deeply attached to Orthodoxy and at the same time by my own confession, an 'honorary Taoist'.

Now I always supposed that Teilhard de Chardin had been very little influenced by the Asian religions. It is admitted that although he lived in China a long time he knew very little Chinese, and in fact inhabited a kind of expatriate colonial milieu, both in Egypt and in China. The impression people got that he was rather hostile to Asian religions probably originated from a distinction which he drew (and which Ursula King discusses on pp. 123 ff.) between 'the Eastern' and 'the Western' modes of spirituality and mysticism. He was against the former because it was too much given to renunciation, the negation of the world of matter, and the belief that the material world was nothing but an illusion of Mara the Tempter. The 'Eastern' way, he felt, was anti-time and anti-evolution; he repudiated the attraction of pure nature-mysticism, and did not like the idea of return or fusion with the One, identification with the universe without the presence of any love. Similarly the 'Western' way for him was a way of convergence including love, of progress, synthesis, taking time as real and evolution as real, and recognizing the world as an organic whole. He sought for a spirituality which feeds social action rather than eschewing it. This was, he felt, a *new* road which religious men could follow, leading to an ultra-personal or supra-personal God to be loved *in* and *through* all things rather than *above* all things.

It seems to have been unfortunate that Teilhard chose 'Eastern' and 'Western' as names for these different ways. A good deal of what he disliked belonged to Hinduism and Buddhism, not at all to Taoism and Confucianism. Both the great Chinese religions were strongly world-affirming. The Tao or 'Order of Nature' could be understood as immanent deity. If Teilhard had been able to get so far as an analysis of Chinese conceptions of time, he would have found that they were not at all cyclical, but much more similar to the one-way time of Hebrew monotheism, a time in which real permanent change can happen and where there can be, for instance, a 'plan of salvation'. But of course he could not expect to have found the evolutionary view of the world in its fullness, because that was a product of modern science, and modern science originated only in the Western world. Still, Teilhard would have been very encouraged if he had been able to get to the foundations of Taoism and Confucianism, because the principle of ethics and ethical love was tremendously there, quite different from any loveless 'fusion with the One' such as might be found in pure nature-mysticism, or in some of the Indian, Platonic or Neo-Platonic forms of mystical experience. A valuable short book by Marie-Ina Bergeron, *La Chine et Teilhard*, complementary to Ursula King's, has explored some of the basic Taoist -Confucian ideas which Teilhard would have appreciated greatly if he could have got access to them.

What was misleading was that by 'Eastern' Teilhard really meant all 'other-worldly spirituality'. The fact is that as a Christian he was bound to the traditions of the 'Peoples of the Book'. As the Great Church says every day, *pistevō eis ena theou patera pantokratora; credo in unum deum patrem omnipotentem* . . . Therefore no non-theistic universe, however immense or glorious, would suffice for such a soul to be one-ed with. At the same time, the knowledge of evolution was a product of modern science and only Europe gave rise to that, so that Teilhard was really a fundamentally post-Newtonian and post-Darwinian theologian. Taoism and Confucianism, however, are only ambiguously non-theistic, in so far as the Tao is the deity immanent in the universe, and remembering that for the Sage, 'Heaven' (non-personal, but not non-theistic) blessed and authorized the ethics which he taught. Moreover, one could go further and say that many currents in Indian religious thought and practice don't agree with the impression one might get from Teilhard that the 'Eastern' road was wrong or imperfect. To mention only one aspect, Tantrism, whether in its Hindu or Buddhist forms, was also world-affirming.

The fact seems to be that Teilhard de Chardin never acquired a detailed knowledge of Asian religious beliefs and practices, although his general acquaintance with the peoples and cultures of Asia was much greater than is usually supposed. It is truly important that his ideas on the religions of Asia should be expounded as thoroughly as Ursula King has succeeded in doing in this present book, for I end as I began with the conviction that Teilhard de Chardin is the prophet of this age, a prophet not for the Western world alone but for all men everywhere, so that his insights will need translation into the idioms of the Eastern nations. I suspect that in the last resort no insights fundamentally true will be irremediably untranslatable. All success to Ursula King's book.

Joseph Needham, FRS, FBA
Director of the East Asian
History of Science Library, Cambridge

President, Teilhard Centre
for the Future of Man, London

PREFACE

During recent years, Eastern religions have attracted increasing attention in the West. And rightly so. Yet many people are confused and do not know how to relate Eastern teachings to their own religious and cultural background. How are we to respond to religious pluralism? Watching the growth of Eastern-inspired cults and groups, some anxiously ask if Eastern religions are going to supersede our own religious traditions. Do they really possess a richer spirituality, a deeper mysticism? Or will all religions ultimately disappear from the modern world? Others, on the contrary, perceive new, exciting possibilities through the closer coming together of the great world faiths, the growth of interreligious dialogue, and of a truly worldwide ecumenism.

Pierre Teilhard de Chardin (1881-1955) first travelled Eastwards well over fifty years ago. He too felt a certain attraction to the East. Although he criticized Eastern religions, it is perhaps less well-known that, from the moment of first encounter, he looked for seeds of religious renewal and inspiration, and for a possible unity beyond existing religious diversity. Yet he lived at a time when interreligious dialogue was in its infancy. The willingness to listen to adherents of religious traditions other than one's own may have existed among certain individuals, but it was not the predominant spirit in the Christian Churches. In his thought, Teilhard ventured beyond the official boundaries of his own Church and, consequently, suffered for being a pioneer. None of his writings on religion and philosophy were allowed to be published whilst he was alive.

Throughout his extensive travels in the East, Teilhard encountered adherents of many different religions, especially from Buddhism, Hinduism, and Islam. At first sight, his writings make little reference to these. Yet as a religious thinker, he was deeply interested in what he called the 'active currents of faith' or what are now referred to as the 'living religions'. What is their role in the modern world? How can the religions of the past help us to solve the problems of the present? What kind of spirituality do we need today, and what is the place of mysticism in religion? It is largely with these questions that the present book is concerned.

Over the last twenty years, several important biographies and studies on Teilhard de Chardin have appeared yet none of them has included a detailed examination of his contacts with the East and its religions. Most writers have interpreted his thought from the perspective of either traditional or contemporary Christian theology but very few have related his reflections on religion and mysticism to the wider study of religion.[1]

More than once Teilhard de Chardin expressed his fascination with Eastern thought. In 1934 he wrote: '. . . my own individual faith was inevitably peculiarly sensitive to Eastern influences; and I am perfectly conscious of having felt their attraction . . .' It appears all the more surprising, therefore, that in spite of many years in the East, his writings seem to value Eastern religions so little and judge them to be in opposition to his own worldview. The passage just quoted continues: '. . . the East fascinates me by its faith in the ultimate unity of the universe; but the fact remains that the two of us, the East and I, have two diametrically opposed conceptions . . .'.[2]

Why did he perceive such an opposition and what did he mean by it? This is an important problem which relates to other questions. What historical, philosophical or theological knowledge of Eastern religions did he possess when comparing them with his own faith? Can the initial impression of his complete ignorance of these religions, assumed by many critics, be shown to be correct? Or will a closer examination of his works require us to modify such an assumption?

To assess Teilhard's statements in their proper context, his knowledge of Eastern religions must be more closely examined. This is less a question of describing any formally pursued course of study than of tracing his experience of the East and its religions. If one accepts the rich texture of lived experience as knowledge in a wider sense, then his extensive acquaintance with several Asian countries and their populations may have provided more influences on his thought than is generally recognized. He was not just an ordinary traveller, journeying Eastwards, but someone particularly receptive to religious insights and therefore likely to reflect more than most on the religious beliefs and practices of the people he met. It must also be remembered that, in the presentation of his thought, he assigns a central place to 'seeing'. This applies to both the visual perception of the many phenomena which constitute the outer world, as well as to the development of an inner vision. One might therefore expect that, although he never systematically pursued a historical or textual study of Eastern religions, he nonetheless acquired a certain amount of knowledge about them as time and circumstances permitted.

The examination of Teilhard's knowledge and experience of Eastern religions has therefore to be understood in a broader sense. In this context, Eastern religions mean some of the major world religions outside the Judaeo-Christian tradition as encountered by Teilhard in Egypt, China, India and elsewhere in Asia. It is not enough, however, to consider only the years spent in the Middle and Far East. Certain formative influences occurred earlier in his life. These permanently influenced his approach to religion and mysticism. Indeed, it is only through these experiences that he became interested in Eastern mysticism at all. To elucidate the web of experiences and influences which shaped Teilhard's ideas on Eastern religions, relevant information has been gathered about his early background, travels and field-trips in the East, as well as his acquaintances, encounters and readings. His contacts and impressions of the East, especially of China, are described here to give something of the flavour of his experiences and relate his thought on Eastern religions and mysticism to the context of his life, in other words, to find the 'Sitz im Leben' of his ideas. Here, as elsewhere, it is true to say that no study of Teilhard de Chardin's works makes sense 'if one does not attempt to retrace the historical conditions of the milieu wherein his personality became conscious of itself'.[5]

It must be stressed at the start that Teilhard's approach to Eastern religions is directly dependent on his understanding of mysticism. This was not primarily theoretical but proceeded from the basis of a personal vision which was grounded in mystical experience. The patterns of this inner realization appear clearly when his writings are studied in chronological order. The basic understanding of mysticism was first expressed in his early essays, written before he went to the Far East. They introduce an important distinction between different forms of mysticism which, in essence, was maintained throughout his life. It is significant, however, that with his stay in the Far East, further references to this distinction almost always include comparisons with Eastern forms of mysticism. Thus, we shall have to discuss his comparative evaluation of Eastern and Western mysticism; in particular, we shall ask what he meant by the 'road of the East' and the 'road of the West', and how far a convergence of these two 'roads' may eventually overcome their former separation.

Teilhard's approach to Eastern religions has very definite shortcomings. However, a sympathetic as well as critical study of his thought reveals a convergent perspective pointing to the possibility of greater unity between East and West. It is certainly worth investigating how a leading Western religious thinker who spent nearly twenty years in the East, reacted to and reflected on Eastern religions and, even more, why he assigned such a central place to a new mysticism.

Few contemporary writers have seen the importance of spirituality and mysticism for today with such great clarity. Teilhard was a man who felt passionately with his age and whose sensibility was groping for a spirituality commensurate with modern man's experience. A prophet of hope, his mystical spirituality was firmly rooted in the Christian tradition. But without doubt the experience of the East and its religions both influenced and enriched his fundamental vision of unity and convergence.

He experienced the world with a great sense of wonder, as

a gift given to man, beckoning him to discover, praise and adore something greater than himself. This experience has been the primary matrix of all poetic vision and philosophic insight, and of man's ongoing religious and scientific quest. Better known and rightly understood, Teilhard's mystical experience and vision may prove a stimulus and challenge to those engaged in the study of religion and the meeting of world faiths, as well as to all those who are searching for new directions in contemporary spirituality.

The writing of this book is due to the convergent nature of several experiences. I was first introduced to Teilhard's thought during my theological studies in France in the early sixties. The first essay I ever read was one of the last he wrote, his spiritual autobiography, 'The Heart of Matter' (1950), still circulating in cyclostyled form at that time. Its vivid pages kindled both my curiosity and enthusiasm without leading to any detailed study. This happened later, during the five years I lived in India where I read and discussed with others many of his philosophical and religious essays. The study of Indian religions and the subsequent teaching of this subject within the wider framework of Religious Studies led to the initial formulation and further development of the ideas contained in this book.

Over several years, Teilhard's published and unpublished writings were analysed in the original French. Correspondence and personal interviews with former friends and family members helped to elucidate this material. It would, indeed, have been impossible to write this book without the collaboration of many people who willingly replied to my questions and letters. Whilst it is impossible to list them all, I would like to record my gratitude and appreciation here. In particular, I thank my former teacher at the Institut Catholique, Professor Paul Henry, SJ, who first inspired me through his lectures on Teilhard's work. Later, help was given by Father Pierre Leroy, SJ, Teilhard's close collaborator and friend, and by Father Henri de Lubac, SJ, who has written extensively on Teilhard's thought.

Dr Claude Cuénot, Teilhard's first biographer, and Mademoiselle Jeanne Mortier, the literary executrix of his papers, answered many of my queries and drew attention to additional material. Madame Béatrice d'Hauteville kindly put at my disposal papers relating to Teilhard's work for the French branch of the *World Congress of Faiths* and also his unpublished correspondence with Madame Solange Lemaître. My thanks also go to Teilhard's youngest brother, Monsieur Joseph Teilhard de Chardin and his wife who so hospitably received me in the family's ancestral homes at Les Moulins and Sarcenat (Auvergne), thereby enabling me to gain a better understanding of Teilhard's background.

I am particularly grateful to Professor E. G. Parrinder for his continuous encouragement and help, to the late Professor R. C. Zaehner for his comments, and to Dr J. Needham for his inspiration, generosity and kindness in writing the foreword.

I would also like to thank the library staff of the Teilhard Centre in London, the Fondation Teilhard de Chardin in Paris, the Jesuit Archives in Chantilly and particularly, the University of Leeds. Without their co-operation this work would have been impossible.

This book is dedicated to my family and the numerous participants in dialogue who, in England, France, and India, inspired and helped me to develop the ideas presented here, and also to all those who, through their work, further a better understanding between East and West.

Ursula King
Leeds
March, 1979

I

Unity of Life
and Thought

A man's vision is the great fact about him.

William James

The greatest success I can hope for in my life —₁
to have published a new vision of the world.

Pierre Teilhard de Chardin

A Fundamental Vision
of Faith

Faith seems to me like a tremendous
mountain range. Tempting from a
distance, when you try to climb it you run
into ravines, perpendicular walls, and
stretches of glaciers. Most climbers are
forced to turn back; some plunge to
destruction, but almost nobody reaches
the peak. Yet the world from on top must
offer a wonderfully novel and clear view.

Albert Speer[1] noted these words in his prison diary after reading Karl Barth's *Epistle to the Romans*. This passage may
imply an understanding of faith which most of us find difficult and austere, yet it well expresses the profound truth
that the immense range of vision gained from the top of a
mountain can transform one's view of the world. It is such
a vision of faith and deep spirituality which characterizes
Teilhard de Chardin's approach to all levels of life, to man's
inner and outer world. In fact, Teilhard is one of the great
Christian mystics of today but he is far too little known or
understood. Particular passages of his works may be quoted
in isolation, approved of, or criticized, but it is generally little
appreciated that what matters most is his overall perspective
and insight linked to a fundamental vision and an ongoing
quest.

The unfolding of this vision of faith can be traced, stage by
stage, in the development of Teilhard's life and the expression
of his thought. There are few whose life and work are so

intrinsically bound up together to form a coherent unity. When he wrote the essay 'My Fundamental Vision' (1948), he presented his worldview in a fairly schematic manner but elsewhere the elements of this vision are expressed in a more personal and autobiographical form, especially in the beautiful late essays 'The Heart of Matter' (1950) and 'The Christic' (1955).[2]

'My Fundamental Vision' is the translation of the French *'Comment Je Vois'* which literally means 'How I See'. It is indeed the importance of 'seeing' which here, as elsewhere, is emphasized in Teilhard's approach. The essay is prefaced by the sentence :

> It seems to me that a whole life-time of continued hard work would be as nothing to me, if only I could, just for one moment, give a true picture of what I see.[3]

The foreword to *The Phenomenon of Man* is also devoted to 'Seeing'. In fact, the entire book is an attempt to let people see more for 'to see is really to become more', a deeper vision 'is really fuller being'.[4] To learn to see in this sense means 'to develop a *homogeneous* and *coherent* perspective of our general extended experience of man'.[5] Many passages in his work emphasize that 'it is essential to see – to see things as they are and to see them really and intensely'.[6] Teilhard uses 'seeing' in an extended sense; to see means to discern, apprehend, and understand, to develop an overall perspective of looking at life and constructing the world. However, for Teilhard it is not merely natural seeing, but a seeing of an altogether different order : 'The perception of the divine omnipresence is essentially a seeing, a taste, that is to say a sort of intuition bearing upon certain superior qualities in things. It cannot, therefore, be attained directly by any process of reasoning, nor by any human artifice. It is a gift like life itself, of which it is undoubtedly the supreme experimental perfection.'[7]

Teilhard's vision of the phenomenon of man embraces at its deepest level the phenomenon of religion and mysticism. What did he see? A universe ablaze with the fire of divine love, suffused with the elements of a presence which beckons, summons and embraces man; a world intimately united with God in all its fibres and phases of development. This world meant the natural and cosmic world as well as the personal and social world, the sphere of human action where the smallest effort contributes something to a higher reality being born. In his earliest writings Teilhard already refers to the experience of the mystic seer, the 'voyant' whose vision constructs the world anew, and in the very last of his essays, 'The Christic', after describing the coherence and beauty of this vision, he movingly asks whether, after all, he is the only person to have seen such a vision, or whether there will be others similarly transformed.

I

Let us recapture some elements of this vision. As Teilhard's life and thought are closely interwoven, both illuminate each other and have to be examined together. This is a difficult task because of the way in which his works have been published. Each volume contains a number of essays selected from the entire span of life. Numerous letters written each year are scattered over several different volumes or remain unpublished. To arrive at a detailed analysis of the development of Teilhard's thought, one has to piece together many fragments from different sources. In this way, a chronological sequence can be reconstructed which reveals the fundamental vision of a man of faith who attempted to chart a new road for contemporary Christian spirituality.

The unfolding of Teilhard's inner vision is linked to certain formative experiences of his life, experiences of a mystical kind which can be inferred from allusions in his letters, diaries, and essays, particularly when read in conjunction with 'The Heart of Matter' (1950). This spiritual autobiography, which has only recently become generally available, is of immense significance for it is here that Teilhard, in his old age, has described in detail the early emergence and growth of a powerful religious vision which sustained him throughout a lifetime. However, for those who can decipher them, there are many clues in earlier writings. Teilhard's earliest attempt to outline some kind of spiritual autobiography goes back as far as 1918, to the first version of 'My Universe'[8] which already sets out the elements of his mystical experience and vision. The experience came first; it provided the nucleus from which he developed a philosophy, a theology, and an integral worldview which included a partly new understanding of spirituality and mysticism. This primacy of experience is also emphasized in an early diary entry which reads: 'The true interest of life does not lie in discovery and knowledge, – but in *realization* . . .'[9]

In 'The Heart of Matter' he relates how, from his earliest childhood onwards, he had decisive inner experiences which made him seek some Absolute, some universal unity and coherence which, at the same time, was tangible and concrete. At first, this search was expressed in a passion for rocks and stones; later, it was the wider contact with nature which developed in him the ardent desire for communion with an All. His father nurtured in him an early interest in science whereas his mother transmitted to him the ardour of a religious faith, deeply nourished by the Christian mystics.

As a child and young adult Teilhard had several mystic experiences which may be described as a realization of cosmic consciousness, an experience where the oneness, the beauty and the divine vibrations running through all of nature were felt with great intensity. Years later, when he was able to describe these experiences in words and reflect upon their significance, he noted that 'all I shall ever write will only be a feeble part of what I feel'.[10]

This nature mysticism, which had its roots in childhood, first came fully to the fore in Jersey where Teilhard spent the years 1901-5. It revealed a pantheistic inclination which was to remain with him all his life but which underwent several important modifications.

Whilst the wide open sea and the lonely rock-strewn shores of Jersey impressed upon Teilhard the beauty and grandeur of nature, it was the strange, exotic features of an Eastern landscape on a vaster scale which led to the full awakening of his mystic search. The first contact with the East was experienced through a stay in Egypt which left a lasting influence and mark on him. During 1905-8, Teilhard taught at a Jesuit school in Cairo. When he had time, he undertook expeditions into the Egyptian desert in order to pursue geological and archaeological field research. There is ample evidence in his later work that the experience of the desert, especially eight days spent with a friend in an expedition to the West of the Nile in 1907, left an indelible impression on his mind. Numerous passages could be quoted where the solitude, the vastness, and the entrancing beauty of the desert are alluded to as the place where the mystic seer is closest to a vision of unity and all-embracing oneness. It was in the desert of Egypt that he 'experienced such sense of wonder'.[11]

Whilst for ever indebted to the positive aspects of this experience, Teilhard nevertheless soon recognized its negative features which he repudiated as a pantheistic temptation, luring the individual away from the world of men in order to be fused with an impersonal All. Teilhard's biographer Cuénot has said that Teilhard underwent his biggest religious crisis in Egypt, meeting there a very subtle and heavy temptation to dissolve himself in nature. If one reflects for a moment on the role of the desert in the history of spirituality, not only as the place of temptation and encounter with God as, for example, in the Christian desert fathers, but also a place of solitude, silence, and emptiness, a motif found in religions other than Christianity, one realizes the crucial importance which the desert experience had for Teilhard's inner development and understanding of mysticism. As a type, the desert experience was later repudiated – it led to a dead point and was what Teilhard subsequently called an 'Eastern vision', a negative road of fusion and escape.

In the following years Teilhard enquired into the mystical experiences of others, both in Christianity and outside it. Immediately following the stay in Egypt, he spent four years studying theology in the Jesuit house in Hastings (1908-12). During this time the strong inclination towards 'cosmic life' and 'the attraction of matter' still predominated. The attraction of nature grew more intensive still through discovering the full meaning of evolution. Under the important influence of Bergson's book *Creative Evolution*, the perception of the greatness and oneness of nature grew overwhelming. The primacy of this experience of nature mysticism is expressed in the following words, written many years later:

All that I can remember of those days . . . is the extraordinary solidity and intensity I found then in the English countryside, particularly at sunset, when the Sussex woods were charged with all that 'fossil' Life which I was then hunting for, from cliff to quarry, in the Wealden clay. There were moments, indeed, when it seemed to me that a sort of universal being was about to take shape suddenly in Nature before my very eyes.[12]

The period at Hastings marked for Teilhard's development the discovery of evolution and its central importance for the reinterpretation of his religious beliefs, particularly for his understanding of the figure of Christ. The cosmic and christic sense which he later described as the two sides of his being, eventually converged into a powerful vision of the universal and cosmic Christ, a symbol of great integrative force, which has its origin in this period.[13] It is a vision intrinsically related to the mystical quality of his nature experiences, but the initial experience of a monistic pantheism had gradually been prolonged and transcended into what Teilhard occasionally referred to as 'panchristic monism', or what one might also call a person-centred theistic mysticism.

Initially, the experience of nature predominated over the experience of an interpersonal world. The difficulty of interpersonal relationships was acutely felt by Teilhard when he described the 'other' as an intruder into one's inner world, breaking the unity and self-contained coherence of the mystic's inner vision. The enriching experience of the personal *Thou* was awakened in him through the love of his cousin Marguerite to whom he became very close, first during his years of study in Paris (1912-14), and later, through their regular correspondence during the First World War. The war itself was a profoundly transforming and maturing experience which brought home to him the complex realities of the social world, the force of human masses in movement and action.

Ordained in 1911, Teilhard performed many pastoral duties at the Front. He preferred to work as a stretcher-bearer attending the sick and wounded as an ordinary soldier rather than to enjoy the relative privileges of an army chaplain. No other period of his life is so closely documented as the war period. We possess the letters to his cousin, entitled *The Making of a Mind*, his diaries, of which only the first volume (1915-19) has appeared so far, and the posthumously published essays *Writings in Time of War* wherein his vision is expressed in a moving and poetic style.

His cousin Marguerite was a major friend and support during these years. She shared and encouraged his literary interests in important ways and was, in fact, the only person who really understood his ideas at that time. One might well describe her as an attendant midwife to the birth of his literary work. Herself a writer, she was the first to receive his essays, and the two friends were mutual critics of each other's achievements.

Teilhard felt now compelled to find an intellectual expression and produce a philosophical elaboration of the pantheistic and mystic experiences he had undergone. Through reading, reflection, and the comparison of his experience with that of others, he was able to formulate what, on one hand, he called his 'vision' and, on the other, he attempted to preach as his 'gospel'. Commentators close to Teilhard's texts are well aware that he felt all his life that he had seen something new. The expression of this vision in literary form began in 1916 and continued until 1955. Studying his works from beginning to end, one cannot but be impressed and enriched by the fundamental beauty, strength and coherence of this consuming vision which he compared to a blazing fire.

The immensity of the war, the daily life at the Front, and face to face encounters with death provided a catalysing influence through which the mystical seer turned writer. One might rightly wonder with one of his friends how, under such adverse conditions, Teilhard was able to reflect at all. But perhaps these circumstances gave Teilhard a compelling sense of urgency without which he might not have launched himself into writing.

The battle of the trenches was experienced as 'a baptism of the real'[14] which brought about the focusing of his vision. With heightened sensibility and extraordinary detachedness he was able, between the battles, to go for lonely walks, reflect in solitude and formulate his ideas. The impressions were so overwhelming that he felt neither the attractions of Egypt nor the stimulating activity of Paris were worth as much as his experience of the mud of the war. It was here, amidst blood, death and terror, that his tremendous vision of mankind belonging together first began to take shape. When Teilhard's war letters were eventually published in 1961, François Mauriac commented: 'The most optimistic view a Christian thinker has ever held of this criminal world, was conceived at Verdun; this frantic cry of hope has been uttered from an abyss . . . The same sort of courage which was necessary to hold out in the trenches of Verdun, was also necessary for conceiving thoughts as joyful as these, so permeated by hope'.[15]

Teilhard's first essay, 'Cosmic Life', written in 1916, was to be his 'intellectual testament' in the event of death. It fully spells out the attraction and abiding influence of a pantheistic vision whilst repudiating at the same time 'the temptation of matter'. The magic appeal of nature echoes through all the war writings but especially through the powerful essays 'The Mystical Milieu' (1917), 'The Soul of the World' (1918), 'The Great Monad' (1918), 'My Universe' (1918), 'The Universal Element' (1919) and 'The Spiritual Power of Matter' (1919).[16] In 1916 Teilhard was for the first time able to articulate his earlier mystic experiences. Yet whilst describing the awakening to the cosmos and the temptation to surrender himself to the appeal of matter, he personally had already overcome this initial attraction and demanded something greater and more transcendent. Through the experience of nature he discovered 'as though in an ecstasy, that *through all nature I was immersed in God'.*[17] He felt that a vigorous effort was required to

> reverse my course and ascend . . . The true summons of the cosmos is a call consciously to share in the great work that goes on within it; it is not by drifting down the current of things that we shall be united with their one, single, soul, but by fighting our way, with them, towards some term still to come.[18]

This polarization of two tendencies in the mystic seeker, expressed in 'Cosmic Life', was to be a lasting feature of Teilhard's approach to the interpretation of mysticism – the choice of reaching ultimate unity either through return and fusion, or through progress and synthesis. In the following years, these two tendencies became explicitly associated with an oversimplified polarization between Eastern and Western mysticism. This emphasis on two types of mysticism, together with the search for a higher unity and new mysticism, will be closely examined later.

'Cosmic Life' is prefaced by a maxim which may be regarded as the recurrent *leitmotif* of Teilhard's entire work. It reads : 'There is a communion with God, and a communion with earth, and a communion with God through earth.' Initially, the 'communion with earth', refers to the experience of monistic pantheism whereas later it stands for any merely immanent or innerworldly attitude of man. 'Communion with God' stands for an excessively other-worldly attitude, an understanding of God and religion as separate from the world. The exclusive or nearly exclusive concern for a transcendent reality, often regarded as the main characteristic of the religious quest, does not place enough importance on the value of human effort and the development of the world. The two attitudes – communion with earth, and communion with God – are regarded as incomplete; what is sought, is the synthesis of both, not as a simple combination of two attractions but as something of a new order altogether. 'Communion with God through earth' symbolizes, so to speak, Teilhard's lifelong attempt to relate God and the world in the most intimate manner, elsewhere expressed through his efforts in seeing science and religion as part of the same quest for ultimate unity, and in relating mystical spirituality to effort and action.

But the synthesis he attempted was little understood. Of the thirteen essays composed during the war, all except one were judged unsuitable for publication. Teilhard realized then how difficult it would be for his ideas to see the light of day 'except in conversation or manuscript form, passed surreptitiously from hand to hand'.[19] Written at the end of 1916, one might regard this as a prophetic statement, for this is exactly what happened for the next forty years. However, we are not following here the vicissitudes of Teilhard's literary career[20] but are mainly concerned with the major stages of his inner development.

II

After the war, Teilhard lived in Paris, first studying and then lecturing until, in 1923, a fellow-Jesuit invited him to come on a scientific mission to China. He greatly welcomed the opportunity to see the Far East which possessed many family associations for him. Little did he know at the time that China would later be a place of exile where he would remain until 1946. The arrival in China completed Teilhard's inner development and brought his mystical vision into full focus. He has unequivocally stated that his pan-christic mysticism matured 'in the two great atmospheres of Asia and the War',[21] finding full expression in two of the most important spiritual writings, 'The Mass on the World' (1923) and Le Milieu Divin (1927) which, together with the much later 'The Christic' (1955), form a kind of mystical triptych.

In the initial contact with China, the experience of the desert was again decisive. This time, it was the Ordos Desert inside the Yellow River bend which Teilhard explored during an expedition to Mongolia. Several times, he likened the Ordos to Egypt which he had experienced more than fifteen years earlier. The period in Mongolia was also like a retreat, which led him 'to the heart of the unique greatness of God'.[22] During the expedition, Teilhard and his companion lived much of the time under a tent, camping in the desert. Under these conditions it was not always possible to say mass and Teilhard continued his habit, begun during the war, to offer the world to God in a prayer which he at first referred to as a 'mass upon all things'. It is from this prayer that the well-known 'Mass on the World' developed, written down in the Ordos Desert, possibly on the feast of the Transfiguration, but finalized at Tientsin, December 1923.[23]

This fervent hymn of praise is autobiographical. It presents a fully formed mystical vision based on a deep personal experience of union and communion with God. It is the offering of the world in all its concreteness to God who is 'the universal *milieu* in which and through which all things live and have their being'.[24] Thus, the world in its fullest extension becomes God's body 'the glorious living crucible in which everything melts away in order to be born anew'.[25] Although not a pantheistic vision, this is a perspective which assumes unto itself monistic and pantheistic aspirations and transcends them. Addressing himself to God, Teilhard recalls his inner development:

> Little by little, through the irresistible development of those yearnings you implanted in me as a child . . . and through the awakening of terrible and gentle initiations by which you made me transcend successive circles, through all these I have been brought to the point where I can no longer see anything, nor any longer breathe, outside that *milieu* in which all is made one.

And he goes on to explain:

> I shall savour with heightened consciousness the intense yet tranquil rapture of a vision whose coherence and harmonies I can never exhaust.[26]

His innermost being vibrates in accord with a single note of incredible richness wherein the most opposite tendencies find themselves united: 'The excitement of action and the delight of passivity; the joy of possessing and the thrill of reaching out beyond what one possesses; the pride in growing and the happiness of being lost in what is greater than oneself.'[27]

The concluding prayer of the poem states unequivocally that for Teilhard everything depended on this fundamental vision of the union of God and the universe. If others proclaim the splendours of God as pure Spirit, he felt it his particular vocation to praise the innumerable prolongations of God's 'incarnate Being in the world of matter', to preach the mystery of God's flesh.

From now on he maintained that the only thing which interested him was 'the universe of the future – the world of living ideas and the mystical life'.[28] He saw mysticism as 'the only power capable of synthesizing the riches accumulated by other forms of human activity'[29] and this mysticism was for him 'the science of Christ running through all things'.[30] 'The Mass on the World' might be said to contain the vision of the world as a cosmic sacrament. In Teilhard's words,

the true substance to be consecrated each day is the world's development during that day – the bread symbolising appropriately what creation succeeds in producing, the wine . . . what creation causes to be lost in exhaustion and suffering in the course of its effort.[31]

This theme was later systematically developed in *Le Milieu Divin* (1927) as 'the divinization of our activities' and 'the divinization of our passivities'. Bearing the subtitle 'An Essay on the Interior Life', the work is now considered to be a spiritual classic. However, the more poetic approach of 'The Mass on the World', further enhanced through its recent setting to music,[32] may have more immediate appeal to many than the more treatise-like structure of *Le Milieu Divin*. The 'divine milieu' is another name for what Teilhard had earlier called the 'mystical milieu'.[33] The mystical vision of communion and union with God gives man access to a new 'milieu', a new environment and centre where everything may potentially become divinized. As is said in the introduction of *Le Milieu Divin*, 'God truly waits for us in things'.[34]

III

Elements of Teilhard's inner vision are dispersed throughout all his essays. Sometimes, especially in the more abstract and scientific essays, it may only be a brief sentence, an allusion, or a short paragraph which refer to his mystical understanding of world and man. The well-known *Phenomenon of Man* is by no means the easiest work through which to find an opening into Teilhard's perspective, at least not from a religious point of view. The work is a kind of *summa* of his comprehensive anthropological perspective in an overall evolutionary framework. As it is addressed primarily to the contemporary scientific temper, questions of spirituality are less touched upon.

The tremendous spiritual vision which illuminated Teilhard's life finds its climax in 'The Heart of Matter' (1950) which celebrates a christo-cosmic vision, a 'Diaphany' of the divine at the heart of the universe. The intimate union of the material and spiritual is affirmed by the maxim of the essay:

> At the heart of Matter
> A World-heart,
> The Heart of a God.

The love of God and the love of the world are inextricably combined, having as their central focus the universal and cosmic Christ. Thus, the essay culminates in a 'Prayer to the ever greater Christ' which is remarkable for its mystical depth and beauty of expression. It is a continuation of all that is most central to Christianity, and reminds one of the hymn of the fourth century Christian writer Prudentius who describes Christ as

> Of the Father's heart begotten
> Ere the world from chaos rose,
> He is Alpha: from the fountain
> All that is and has been, flows;
> He is Omega, of all things
> Yet to come the mystic Close
> Evermore and evermore.

33

Yet even after writing 'The Heart of Matter', Teilhard still felt the need to express his Christ-centred vision once more. He laboured for almost five years to find a more vivid and forceful description of what he had seen. In the essay 'The Christic' (1955), completed a few weeks before his death, he presented his fundamental vision for the last time. This essay is of a very personal, almost confidential nature, a kind of quintessence of the 'Mass on the World', *Le Milieu Divin* and 'The Heart of Matter'. The final testament of Teilhard's panchristic mysticism, it also bears witness to the extraordinary psychological integration which can be achieved through the encounter of religious and scientific insights.

It would be presumptuous to summarize this essay in a few words. It is not an easy work but deserves the most careful and considered attention for it expresses important thoughts which preoccupied Teilhard at the end of his life, as can be seen from his diaries 1944-55. One of the central questions of this period might be stated as 'Is Christianity enough for today's world?'. In 'The Christic' he ponders over the question whether the development of the comparative study of religions has not led to the realization of the relativity of Christianity, bringing about its decline. Here, as elsewhere, he stresses that whilst one has to be open to forces of renewal and insight from other sources, Christianity's specific contribution lies in its belief in the Incarnation of God. Through this belief it has the extraordinary ability to engender an all-transforming dynamic love which embraces both God and the world. The interpenetration of the spiritual and material given through the Incarnation lends Christianity a singular force of attraction and adoration, of worship, of man's access to God via the world. Here is a universal presence, a living God, whose energy animates all matter and levels of life, an ultimate centre where everything finds its consummation. The mystic seer who can perceive such intimate union, sees a new path opening before him.

The last section of 'The Christic' is entitled 'The Religion of Tomorrow'. It makes the important point that only a new religious synthesis can provide the required psychic energy for the evolution of mankind, that is to say, a synthesis which embraces a much wider perspective than in the past and takes into account the complementary insights of other faiths. A personal conclusion expresses the joy of having experienced the wonderful 'Diaphany' of God in and through the world, a vision which transforms everything and makes all things shine anew. The same passage also hints at Teilhard's suffering, doubt, and inner isolation through not being able to share his deepest thoughts with others. Perhaps he was, after all, only the victim of an 'inner mirage'? Why is it that he seems to be the only person to have seen the force of such a cosmic and christic vision?

Teilhard thus questioned his own position, and notes of doubt and self-questioning could be quoted from other essays too. But in 'The Christic' he ultimately concluded by affirming the internal coherence of his vision, the power of an all-embracing love, and the superiority of his new insight over traditional formulas of faith. Hence, the essay finishes on an emphatic note of joy and hope: One day there will be others, similarly 'ablaze' with the vision he saw; the truth has to appear only once to spread like fire.

A new biography of Teilhard,[35] mostly concerned with the external events of his life, begins by relating some folk tales of the Auvergne, his land of birth. These tales speak of the innocent seeker who leaves his land to look for the ultimate secret at the heart of reality, the single truth behind the multiple veil of illusion. In all the tales, the seeker who finds what he is looking for is wounded in the conquest and ends his life alone without being able to communicate his secret to another living soul.

Is this true of Teilhard too, the authors ask? It remains for each of us to answer this question. The new biography is written with the intention to have Teilhard re-examined for he has remained curiously outside the mainstream of contemporary thought; his contribution to the common human heritage has not yet been given full recognition. One might add that in the current situation it is even more important to re-examine his understanding of spirituality and the quest towards a new mysticism. More than a decade ago, Henri de Lubac examined Teilhard's vision of faith[36] but so far, this vision has not been closely linked to his experience of the East, nor has his interpretation of Eastern religions and mysticism been studied in depth. Did Teilhard's ideas about religion and mysticism, after passing through successive formulations, eventually transcend his own tradition and propose something new? If so, what contribution did the experience of Eastern religions make to such a synthesis?

It is with these questions in mind that the following chapters have been written. Beginning with early influences, they present factual information about his knowledge of the East and its religions as it developed through contacts, readings, and travels. Then some key texts are analysed to show how he related his own mystic experiences to an interpretation of mysticism and Eastern religions, followed by a discussion about the relevance of these views for contemporary spirituality.

2

Early Contacts with
the East

Pierre Teilhard de Chardin first began to write on religion and mysticism when he was in his mid-thirties. His reflections were rooted in a primary layer of personal experience yet the formulation of his ideas underwent continuous development linked to important events of his life. Friendships, encounters, travels, and studies all helped to shape his views. How did his attitudes to Eastern religions first develop? Is there any indication that early influences and even his family background kindled a certain interest in the East?

As a child Teilhard was particularly close to his eldest brother Albéric and his sister Françoise, two years senior to him. Both exercised a strong influence on his early life. Before the turn of this century Albéric had joined the French navy and was posted to the Far East for two years. There he spent some time in Shanghai, Peking, and Japan. When Albéric returned, he brought home many souvenirs and to this day, some of these, such as Chinese paintings on silk and rice paper, are kept in the family of Teilhard's youngest brother Joseph. He thinks that Teilhard's interest in the East was first awakened through the travels of his eldest brother.

There is plenty of evidence that these travel reports influenced the elder sister Françoise who expressed a great desire to go to China. After joining a Catholic religious order, the Little Sisters of the Poor, she was eventually sent to a mission house in Shanghai and her regular letters[1] provided another indirect contact with China for Teilhard.

Following his stay in the Far East, Albéric had been posted to Constantinople where he developed a strong interest in the history of Byzantium, a subject about which he lectured extensively on his return to France in 1901-2. It seems that his younger brother Pierre became familiar with this material too. Teilhard's earliest impressions of both the Middle and the Far East were, therefore, mediated through his family. It is impossible to know whether these impressions created more than an initial curiosity or influenced him in any way to seek further Eastern contacts. There is no doubt, however, that the really formative experience of the East occurred when Teilhard, as a young Jesuit, had the opportunity to spend three years in Egypt.

I

The French Jesuit province of Lyons to which Teilhard belonged, was particularly concerned with the missions in the Middle East. A number of schools and educational institutions were in its charge and it was to such a school in Cairo that Teilhard was sent in 1905. There, he taught for three years physics and chemistry to Egyptian boys, many of whom were Muslims. Occasionally, he accompanied pupils home to their families in different parts of Egypt. He thus had an opportunity to get acquainted with the country and become familiar with both urban and rural parts, particularly with the striking landscape of the North African desert, experienced on visits to the classical sites and during several expeditions.

The discovery of the East was for Teilhard always connected with 'the lonesome waste of the desert whose purple plains rose and fell one after another to a vanishing point on the wildly exotic horizon'.[2] The unforgettable experience of magnificent sunsets, the vast spatial expanses of the desert whose calm and tranquillity he later so much missed in Paris, echoed in him for the rest of his life. More than forty years later, he described this experience:

The East flowed over me in a first wave of exoticism. I gazed at it and drank it in eagerly – the country itself, not its peoples or its history (which as yet held no interest for me), but its light, its vegetation, its fauna, its deserts . . .[3]

This passage would suggest that Teilhard's primary interest at this time was in observing nature rather than society. But we know few concrete details about this period of his life which has been little researched so far. Besides allusions in later works, there exist only the rather formal letters sent home from Egypt to his parents. Although they have been described as primarily a collection of natural history, they contain some information about Teilhard's contacts with both the contemporary Islamic, and ancient Egyptian culture. Excursions to the classical sites of Egypt were supplemented by attendance at monthly meetings of the Institute of Egyptology, and repeated visits to the Museum of Egyptian Antiquities. Teilhard expressed his enthusiasm for the beauty of Egyptian art which he preferred to the more abstract Islamic art where he missed the portrayal of life.

Contact with the Arab world was largely mediated through the Muslim pupils at the school. Some of the Jesuits in Cairo specialized in the study of Islam, particularly the later well-known Islamicist, H. Lammens,[4] whom Teilhard saw regularly. Occasionally, Teilhard accompanied his friends in their explorations of the old Arab quarters of Cairo. In his letters, he describes visits to mosques in Cairo and elsewhere; the experience of Ramadan, of meeting Muslim pilgrims returning from Mecca, and reading a thirteenth-century Arab poet. At some stage, he wished to learn Arabic but it remained an unfulfilled ideal although he realized the usefulness of the language in meeting local people who, he felt, enjoyed discussing moral and religious matters.

However indirect it may have been, Teilhard's first contact was with Islam rather than with any other Eastern religion. It is impossible to assess whether or not, during his stay in Egypt, he learnt about Islamic religious belief and practice in any depth and whether, for example, he would have been aware of the existence of Sufi brotherhoods and their teaching. On the whole, his life in Egypt was relatively removed from the life of the indigenous population. Teilhard not only belonged to a Jesuit mission but his social contacts were largely restricted to the expatriate colonial milieu existing in Egypt at the beginning of this century. His scientific interests also reinforced his connections with French scientists and savants working in Egypt at that time. It may be mentioned here that the later experience of China was, to some extent, also mediated through a similar colonial milieu although it contained less of the missionary element. The inherent limitations of his social milieu may have proved an effective barrier for exploring indigenous religious beliefs.

Teilhard never again lived for so long in a predominantly Islamic country. This raises the question how far the relative unimportance given to Islam in his religious thinking, and the negative evaluation of Islam's vitality in the modern world, may in fact be largely due to the experience of a situation of political, social and cultural dependence found in Egypt at the beginning of the twentieth century.

The stay in Egypt also provided an opportunity to encounter several aspects of the Christian heritage, present in its Orthodox, Coptic, Maronite and Catholic forms. It has been said by several friends who knew him well that Teilhard had a good knowledge of Eastern Christianity. Whether it stemmed from this time or from earlier reading in connection with his brother's interest in Byzantium is difficult to say. He certainly assisted at different Christian rites and visited early Christian remains in Egypt. The shrine of the Holy Family near Cairo, mentioned several times in the letters, reminded him of the flight to Egypt, and the excursions into the desert made him think of the early desert fathers.

The lasting influence of the desert on Teilhard's thought has already been mentioned; it later came to symbolize for him a particular aspect of man's religious quest. Analysing the importance of the desert experience for the growth of Teilhard's 'mystic self', Hugh Cairns has written :

In the desert . . . Teilhard returned to memorable psychic experience. In the towns of Egypt he had found the people, the colourful and bustling streets and the atmosphere exotic and exhilarating. Now in the fossil-strewn wastes under the harsh sun and desolate darkness he consciously felt in danger, the psychic danger of a 'vast doubt', a 'night of the soul' and a 'pantheism' in which he felt himself being 'diffused' in the vastness of Nature.[5]

If this is correct, then the experience of Egypt was of crucial importance for Teilhard's inner development. But it was only during the years to come that he was able to evaluate this experience in a wider context and relate it to his interpretation of mysticism.

II

On his return from Egypt, Teilhard continued with his studies. He first spent several years reading theology at Hastings (1908-12) and, after deciding on a research career in science, he pursued palaeontological studies in Paris (1912-14). From the letters written during this period[6] it appears that he found Egypt difficult to forget. However beautiful the countryside around Hastings, it was quite unlike what he had experienced in North Africa. Even after his first year in England, he still felt that part of his heart had been left in the mountains near the Red Sea. After his ordination in 1911, his whole ambition was to return to Egypt.[7] Although the contact with the Middle East was indirect now, it was no less lively. Teilhard corresponded with pupils in Cairo, received occasional visitors from Egypt and kept in touch with the research and expeditions of his former friends.

Through other Jesuits at Hastings, Teilhard also received regular news about the Jesuit missions in China. There was a constant flow of staff and students either going to or returning from China. Shanghai was almost a 'known place' to him as he had met many of the Jesuits who worked there, among them some of his best friends.[8] The contact with China became closer still when his sister Françoise left for Shanghai in 1909. The letters to her parents contain many references to the eldest brother Albéric, his earlier visit to Shanghai, the people he met, and the deep impression he left on all. Similarly, Françoise frequently refers to her brother Pierre, with whom she shared a special bond through their common vocation to the religious life.[9]

Teilhard's letters to his sister have not survived. The family was deeply grieved when Françoise prematurely died of small-pox in 1911, after only three years in China. Unlike Teilhard later on, Françoise so immersed herself in the Chinese milieu that she became fluent in the language. It is important to remember, though, that she went to China as a missionary whilst Teilhard's reason for his later stay in the Far East was first and foremost scientific. However, the influence of Françoise's example was deep and lasting; Teilhard always remembered her. Comparing himself with his sister, he later wrote that whilst the unique importance which the reality of God had assumed in their lives made them fundamentally alike, the difference in their approach to religion was that Françoise 'was following a road where the realities of this world were much more effaced or left behind'[10] than was the case with himself.

Apart from learning about China, Teilhard also gleaned information about India from a friend who had travelled all over the Indian subcontinent. However, references to these conversations in Teilhard's letters are largely restricted to natural history, scientific contacts in Bombay, and the Jesuit missions in North and South India.[11]

More important for his personal development was the meeting with Father Maréchal in Louvain in 1910. Not much older than Teilhard, Maréchal combined a similar interest in science and religion and, from 1908 onwards, had begun to publish articles on the psychology of the mystics. Teilhard consulted Maréchal several times and always took much notice of his advice. It is quite likely that at that time he read Maréchal's study 'On the Feeling of Presence in Mystics and Non-Mystics', published in 1908-9.[12] This article discusses among others Hindu, Buddhist, and Sufi mysticism. It also refers to William James's *The Varieties of Religious Experience* and deals with Bucke's 'cosmic consciousness'. It is probably through Maréchal's work that Teilhard first came across the term 'cosmic consciousness' which so well describes his own experience of nature in Egypt and elsewhere.

Teilhard's own mystical experiences made him enquire into those of others. Probably from 1908 onwards, he became interested in reading about the mystics. The prime motivation for most of this reading was to nourish and develop his own ideas rather than to be merely informed. His enquiry into the nature of mysticism was predominantly a personal and existential, rather than a scholarly quest, born from the need to explicate and communicate an inner vision. It is very difficult, however, to retrace his development during this time in detail. Maréchal's article on mystical experience may well have been an early influence in shaping Teilhard's thought on mysticism. We know for certain that even many years later, in 1945, he consulted Maréchal's work on mysticism and made notes on it.[13]

What other sources of information about the comparative study of mysticism and mankind's religious heritage were accessible to Teilhard at the beginning of this century? It is impossible to point to any single influence with absolute certainty but, given the kind of milieu he lived and studied in, one can make certain conjectures about possible contacts and readings. Teilhard's theological training at Hastings seems to have included a certain amount of teaching on the history of religions.[14] This had probably been introduced on the initiative of Father Léonce de Grandmaison, later director of the Jesuit journal *Etudes* in Paris. Even though Father de Grandmaison left Hastings soon after Teilhard's arrival, the two men kept in touch and Grandmaison's influence in drawing Teilhard's attention towards other religious traditions must not be underestimated.[15]

What the history of religions course at Hastings included is unknown. However, at the beginning of this century important developments occurred in the history of religions as a discipline. Its lively controversies were not only found in scholarly journals but the wider interest in Eastern religions was reflected in French periodicals such as the *Revue des Deux Mondes*,[16] *Le Correspondant*, and *Relations d'Orient* which Teilhard saw regularly.

Father de Grandmaison influenced several Jesuits in becoming actively involved in the study of the history of religions. It was due to his initiative that, in 1910, the Jesuits founded a new journal *Recherches de Science Religieuse*, devoted to research in the comparative study of religions. One of Teilhard's fellow-students, Father Rousselot, became closely associated with this journal whilst another of his friends, Father Huby, edited a textbook on the history of religions entitled *Christus – Manuel d'Histoire des Religions*[17] which can still be found today. First published in Paris in 1913, this book was being planned whilst Teilhard was still a student at Hastings and, according to Henri de Lubac, he 'certainly knew the book *Christus* some of whose main authors were his companions and friends'.[18]

Another of Teilhard's teachers at Hastings, Father Bouvier, attended the History of Religions Congress at Oxford in 1908; in 1912, he founded, together with W. Schmidt, *La Semaine d'Ethnologie Religieuse*[19] at Louvain which became an annually recurring event. Originally, its idea may also have been one of Grandmaison's suggestions. At Bouvier's invitation, Teilhard went to Louvain to attend the first meeting of this conference on religious ethnology during the summer of 1912. The study-week was mainly organized for missionaries in order to acquaint them, according to Teilhard's report, with 'the problems and methods of the history of religions'.[20] Its major themes focused on totemism and questions about the origin and evolution of religion. It was the year of the publication of Durkheim's famous book *The Elementary Forms of Religious Life*. Ideas about religion and magic held by Durkheim as well as Frazer, Marett, Tylor, and Schmidt were intensely debated at the conference. Teilhard, who had already been introduced to Durkheim's ideas through another of his professors at Hastings, reported on the conference for the paper *Le Correspondant*.[21]

These few details about Teilhard's early milieu point to a multiplicity of contacts, a widening of interests, even a certain awareness about discussions on the origin of religion and studies on Eastern religions. What is more important, however, certain formative experiences occurred during this early period which permanently affected the direction of his thought.

In the opinion of one of his superiors who knew him well in later years, it may be that Teilhard's major ideas first emerged during his last years of study at Hastings rather than in the following period where most commentators place them.[22]

III

The years between 1915 and 1923 were central for Teilhard's development; they included the experience of the First World War and the emergence of his literary activity. However, in relation to his contact with the East, this period represents an intermediate stage between the earlier years in Egypt and the later ones in the Far East.

The formative experience of Egypt echoes through all the war writings but it is blended with a new experience, that of the Front. Teilhard worked as a medical orderly in a mixed infantry regiment, consisting largely of Moroccans and Kabyle tribesmen from Algeria, the 'Zouaves'. These troops certainly reminded him of his earlier years in North Africa although it is impossible to know whether an element of choice was involved on his part in being in this regiment. Whether the soldiers knew about his stay in Egypt or not, they certainly expressed their admiration for Teilhard in affectionately calling him 'Sidi Marabout'. Whereas 'Sidi' refers to a North African settled in France, 'Marabout' is the French rendering of the Arabic *murābit*, a man bound to God, sanctified by asceticism, and blessed with divine favour. In fact, 'Marabout' has been described as meaning someone 'tied, bound, fastened to God, like a camel to a post, a ship to a pier, a prisoner to a wall; or more appropriately . . . like a monk to a monastery . . . in some almost intangible sense, attached, bound, tied – perhaps the best word is shackled – to God'.[23]

When Teilhard first joined the regiment, he described his situation as being 'in partibus infidelium' although there was 'no lack of Christians'.[24] Looking after the wounded, he sometimes felt helpless because of the differences in language and mentality. At other times, he described the colourful sights with delight as when he mentioned in one of his letters a performance given to the troops:

. . . one would have to have lost the capacity to be aston-
ished by anything not to be moved by such a scene . . . an
audience of Senegalese, Martiniquans, Somalis, Annamites,
Tunisians and French . . . I brought back from it the very
definite conviction that, among other results of the war,
will be that of mixing and welding together the peoples of
the earth in a way that nothing else, perhaps, could have
done.[25]

It was amidst this mingling of races and the action of the
war that Teilhard first conceived of the human community
as both an organic and spiritual reality, a closely intercon-
nected layer of thought covering the planet earth. It was this
reality, first experienced here, which he came to call later
'the noosphere', of central importance to his understanding of
man.

But amidst all the fighting and clamour of the troops, he
could also recall the entrancing beauty of nature and dream
of the Egyptian desert and its solitude. This is what the visionary, the mystic, seeks – to live apart from the multitude, to be
lulled by passivity, to awaken to cosmic consciousness. But
Teilhard recognized this intoxication of the seeker with his
own isolation as a 'temptation of matter', described in 'Cosmic
Life' (1916) in autobiographical form :

. . . One day, I was looking out over the dreary expanse of
the desert. As far as the eye could see, the purple steps of
the uplands rose up in a series, towards horizons of exotic
wildness; again, as I watched the empty, bottomless ocean
whose waves were ceaselessly moving in their 'unnumbered
laughter'; or, buried in a forest whose life-laden shadows
seemed to seek to absorb me in their deep, warm folds – on
such occasions, maybe, I have been possessed by a great
yearning to go and find, far from men and far from toil
the place where dwell the vast forces that cradle us and
possess us, where my over-tense activity might indefinitely
become ever more relaxed . . . And then all my sensibility
became alert, as though at the approach of a god of easy-
won happiness and intoxication; for there lay matter, and

matter was calling me. To me in my turn, as to all the sons of man, it was speaking as every generation hears it speak; it was begging me to surrender myself unreservedly to it, and to worship it.[26]

This passage recalls the overwhelming impressions left by his earlier mystic experiences, linked to the desert in Egypt, the sea in Jersey, and the woods of Sussex, to which references can be found in other parts of his work.[27] Teilhard always interpreted these experiences in terms of pantheistic monism which he repudiated. Strict monism makes man resolutely cling to the Absolute by rejecting all plurality as merely superficial and ultimately unreal appearances. He characterized his monistic experience as 'the Eastern vision of the blue Lotus',[28] a term recalling a French journal of theosophy which could have influenced him in his usage.

Teilhard's understanding of monism will be examined later but it is important to know that from the beginning, his discussion includes negative references to Eastern thought. The monistic experience is also described as the vision of the Hindu to whom everything appears to be animated whilst 'in reality, everything is materialized . . . Life is understood and experienced as a function of matter'.[29] Teilhard always viewed the monistic experience as succumbing to the 'temptation of matter', as a return to man's original source where matter is felt to be 'eternal, immense, infinitely fertile'. This is 'the God from below', 'pagan, Hindu pantheism', characterized by a distaste for other men because one wants to be alone with nature. It is, therefore, an attitude adverse to society.[30]

The same experience is elsewhere compared to the Buddhist goal of Nirvana: 'Looked at in one way, nature is a drug, lulling us to sleep in the cradle of nirvana and all the ancient pantheisms'.[31] Another passage describes the experience of cosmic feeling, sometimes aroused through the encounter with music or poetry, as leading the soul either 'to lose itself in the lower Nirvana' or 'to unite itself ardently with the great effort towards the higher spheres'.[32] These higher spheres are linked to the search for true mysticism or what Teilhard then called the 'mystical milieu'.[33] Whilst he attempted to spell out its characteristics, he continued to pursue comparative reading as can be seen from his correspondence and even more his *Journal*. Although not a complete guide to his reading, they point to some of the literary sources which influenced his writing on mysticism.

IV

In late 1917, Teilhard read William James's *The Varieties of Religious Experience*.[34] In 'The Soul of the World', written shortly afterwards, he explicitly quotes James as supporting the view that 'the current of "pantheist" (cosmic) mysticism is no stranger to Christianity'.[35] There is more ample evidence, however, for the influence of another book by W. James, his lectures on *Pragmatism*[36] which Teilhard must have read in early 1918.

It is interesting to know that between 1916, when he was working on 'Cosmic Life', and early 1918, the time of 'The Soul of the World', his writings contain no references to either Hindu or Buddhist terms. However, in January 1918, when writing about mysticism, Teilhard mentions against the 'Hindu pantheist path', referring explicitly to W. James's book *Pragmatism*. The diary entry for the 26 January 1918, reads:

I see more and more that I must live and realize my mysticism, – plunge myself into the divine Milieu, and develop it around me. By and large, there are three paths for arriving at an homogeneous Absolute:[37]

a) the Hindu pantheist path which *annihilates all differences* and experimental differentiations (cf. W. James, *Pragmatism*);

b) The Christian path which declares *all earthly differentiations to be in vain*, and discovers a milieu of effort and homogeneous personalization in the *meritorious*, in grace;

c) the Christian path (which I prefer) which seeks to bring together (and to constitute the Homogeneous) by pushing forward the work of heterogeneization along the entire line . . .

Through reading the *Pragmatism* of W. James, I was struck once again by the necessity to adopt path c . . .[38]

As William James is quoted with reference to the 'Hindu pantheist path', it may be mentioned that, in one of his lectures,[39] James speaks at length about the Hindu missionary Vivekananda, who had visited the United States and Europe in the 1890s. Commenting on this 'paragon of all monistic systems',[40] he states: 'Observe how radical the character of monism here is. Separation is not simply overcome by the One, it is denied to exist.'[41] Elsewhere, he speaks of 'Vivekananda's mystic One'[42] and 'Vivekananda's Atman'.[43] In his concluding lecture on 'Pragmatism and Religion', William James has this to say:

Nirvana means safety from this everlasting round of adventures of which the world of sense consists. The hindoo and the buddhist, for this is essentially their attitude, are simply afraid, afraid of more experience, afraid of life.[44]

This negative and rather vague impression of Hinduism and Buddhism is not unlike Teilhard's. One wonders how far the latter's conception of Hindu monism is not primarily due to the discussions found in William James's *Pragmatism* and *The Varieties of Religious Experience*. It was only years later that Teilhard realized the rich diversity of the Indian religious heritage of which monism represents only one aspect.

There are more than a dozen references to William James in the *Journal* and, in spite of criticisms, he recognized James's position as being somewhat akin to his own.[45] Several times Teilhard used James's distinction of monism, pluralism and pragmatism as man's three basic attitudes to the world.[46] He also discussed James's treatment of attitudes to salvation and 'the tough-minded in religion'.[47]

It is clear that *Pragmatism* in particular made a deep impression on Teilhard. This book provided less a direct influence on his thinking, however, than a confirmation of his views on different mystical orientations. Teilhard counted James, together with other writers such as Maeterlinck, Bergson and Wells, among the 'sincere and passionate spirits' of his age. In their books one could discern 'the religion of a near-by, progressive and universal God' who appealed far more to his contemporaries than the traditional Christian ideal.[48]

In 1918, Teilhard's cousin, aware of his strong interest in mysticism, sent him the then popular book of Edouard Schuré *Les Grands Initiés*[49] which deals with various figures of Western and Eastern mysticism. A rather eclectic work, it describes the mysticism of Rama, Krishna, Hermes, Orpheus, and Pythagoras, together with the teachings of Moses, Plato and Jesus. This somewhat motley collection emphasizes the essential affinity of Eastern and Western religions, but presents them as a progressive revelation culminating in the teaching of Jesus. The book criticizes the existing opposition between science and religion and concludes with the hope that a transformation of Christianity and a regeneration of the Eastern traditions may furnish the religious basis for the reconciliation of Asia and Europe.

Teilhard first read the book with enthusiasm but soon he found it rather unreal and out of date. To him the author was at least as interesting as his 'initiates' for, once again, Teilhard found his own experiences confirmed here as he wrote to his cousin :

I've been able to get back to Schuré, from whom I've had a great, but rather complex, pleasure : the joy of finding a mind extremely sympathetic to my own, – the spiritual excitement of making contact with a soul full of enthusiasm for the world, – the satisfaction of realizing that the questions I'm concerned with are indeed those that have animated the deep-rooted life of humanity, – the pleasure of seeing that my attempts at a solution agree perfectly, on the whole, with those of the 'great initiates' without doing any violence to dogma, and (because of the integration of the Christian idea) have at the same time their own very special and original slant. You can readily appreciate that it's a great pleasure and encouragement to me to see so clearly what I can use, and what on the other hand is artificial or unsatisfactory, in Schuré's vision: it makes me twice as strong.[50]

It would be erroneous to regard Schuré's book as a major influence on Teilhard's thought, as one critic has done,[51] yet the references to this work confirm that his reflections on mysticism at this time included the consideration of certain comparative data. The letter just quoted also speaks of 'the mistake of false mystical systems that, confusing the levels, look for mystery at the phenomenal level'. Schuré's treatment was found to be narrow and incomplete. It made Teilhard decide 'to write something on "mystical science", to defend from such abuses and place in its real light (glimpsed by Schuré, but with serious errors in perspective), this science of sciences which is also the supreme art and the supreme work'.[52]

In his work *Evolution in Religion*, R. C. Zaehner describes Teilhard as 'a pantheist by nature' and says that, throughout the First World War, he 'seems to have lived in an almost permanent state of "cosmic consciousness" '.[53] However, Zaehner himself did not look into the way in which this experience was gradually articulated and redefined, nor did he enquire into the literary sources of this 'cosmic consciousness'. Although the influence of Edouard Schuré has been noted before,[54] so far nobody seems to have examined the contact with William James nor the possible influence of Joseph Maréchal on Teilhard's understanding of mysticism. Both these authors discuss the nature of cosmic consciousness, and thus may have helped Teilhard to formulate his own views.

In addition to James, Maréchal, and Schuré, Teilhard read other authors such as Ralph Emerson, Herbert Wells, Maurice Maeterlinck, and Robert Hugh Benson.[55] At the same time, he studied the Christian mystics, especially Tauler and Eckhardt.[56] He must also have been aware of Bremond's famous *Histoire littéraire du Sentiment religieux*. First published in 1916, this work revealed 'to French readers innumerable hitherto unknown mystics'.[57] Father Bremond had been Teilhard's teacher and had earlier guided him to the reading of Newman whose influence on Teilhard was as great as Bergson's. At least in 1923, if not before, he consulted Brémond's work about the mystics.[58] An essay of the same year refers again to the many people who have experienced 'cosmic consciousness', 'the long procession of initiates given to the vision and worship of the All'.[59]

From Teilhard's reading and writing of this period it is abundantly clear that he felt a strong attraction to pantheistic monism, vividly described as the appeal of matter/earth/cosmos or as 'pagan', as 'nature mysticism'. This attraction remained constant throughout his life, but it was held in tension and found its fulfilment in a mysticism suffused with personal love. Eventually, he became firmly convinced that mysticism did not lead into isolation, out of the world, but into it.

During the years following the First World War, Teilhard pursued the discussion on pantheism and mysticism mainly with his friend Father Valensin who introduced him to the philosopher Blondel. In 1919, Teilhard and Blondel exchanged several notes relating to their understanding of mysticism to which we shall refer later.[60] Other philosophically stimulating contacts were the friendships with Edouard Le Roy at the Collège de France[61] and the woman philosopher, Léontine Zanta.[62]

These philosophical contacts, together with the religious and scientific milieu in which Teilhard worked, contributed much to the early dissemination of his ideas. In 1922, he was given the Chair of Geology at the Institut Catholique. This position, previously held by one of his teachers killed during the war, gave him a public platform from where he could expound both science and religion from a new perspective.

The attraction of the East was still in his mind as can be seen from the following reaction to his appointment at the Institut Catholique: 'Rather than this academic post, I should . . . have preferred research work in Beyrouth or Shanghai or Trichinopoly',[63] he wrote to a friend. Soon an unexpected possibility offered itself to realize this wish. In 1923, he was invited to join Father Licent, SJ, in an expedition to North China and Mongolia, sponsored by the Musée de l'Homme and the Institut Catholique in Paris. It would be quite wrong to consider this first visit to China already as an act of exile, imposed on Teilhard for philosophically and theologically unacceptable views.[64] The invitation provided a welcome opportunity to fulfil the desire to see more of the East and to visit some of the places for ever connected with the memory of a dearly loved brother and sister. The expedition opened up new fields of scientific research which were to win him international acclaim in later years.

Earlier, Teilhard had several times expressed the wish to return to Egypt. Although he visited other parts of North Africa in later years,[65] he never saw Egypt again but journeyed much further East instead. Yet it was Egypt which provided the first introduction to Eastern life and thought and thus permanently influenced his attitude towards the Orient. One of his biographers has assessed the importance of this experience by saying: 'The Orient meant for Teilhard the East as a world opposed to the West and, the lure of the exotic once exorcized, the challenge to effect the meeting of these two worlds. This dialogue with the East, more specifically with India and China, was to continue during the whole of Teilhard's life'.[66] Without this experience, his vision would not have encompassed such breadth and universality, and he would not have felt the same compelling need to seek a new road for contemporary spirituality. What form this dialogue took for over twenty years will now have to be seen.

3

East and West:
The Spirit of One Earth

Teilhard's long stay in the Far East can be divided into two periods, from 1923 to 1931, and 1932 to 1946. During the first, his main base was the Chinese city of Tientsin and during the second, he lived in Peking. But until the outbreak of the Second World War, these years also included frequent expeditions and travels in both East and West. This alternating rhythm of living among peoples of different races, cultures and creeds, profoundly shaped his vision. He watched a new world being born which, amidst all its turmoil, was crying out for a new path to the spirit. There are few contemporaries who have lived such an intensive spiritual and mystic life and yet felt so passionately with the present age.

In terms of his literary production, the years in the Far East mark a new phase for he now wrote with vigour and self-assurance. Two of his important spiritual writings were produced during the early years in China and yet, paradoxically, this first period was also the time of his deepest inner crisis when he 'doubted both his religious and scientific vocation'.[1] Few essays refer directly to the experience of the East; most comments are found in the letters[2] and, during the later period, in the unpublished diaries and notes on his reading.

Teilhard left France in April 1923 and, in May, joined Father Licent in Tientsin to assist with excavations in central China. The boat journey from Marseilles to Shanghai included brief stops in Port Said, a visit to Colombo, Penang, Malacca, Saigon, and Hong Kong. On arrival in Shanghai, he spent some time visiting the various Jesuit educational and missionary institutions about which he had heard so much. They included an orphanage, several schools, a university, and a famous observatory.

Without Licent, Teilhard probably would never have set foot in China, and he owed much of his subsequent scientific success in the first instance to him. Almost contemporaries, the two Jesuits had first met in early 1914, just before Licent left for China, and were in correspondence since at least 1921. In his letters, Teilhard expressed great admiration for Licent's work and indicated his interest in collaboration, should circumstances permit him to do so.[3] However, the two men were very different in temperament and outlook. Licent was a solitary explorer working with primitive equipment whose primary objective, even in his scientific work, was always a missionary one. Teilhard, by contrast, soon realized the need for team work and closer collaboration with the Chinese; he also saw the futility of missionary objectives and devoted himself primarily to scientific research.

I

The details of Teilhard's journey to the Far East are picturesquely described in *Letters from a Traveller*. His overall impression is best summed up by the statement that a journey to the Far East represents a 'temptation of the multiple'.[4] This is more fully spelled out in a letter:

My strongest impression at the moment is a confused one that the human world . . . is a huge and disparate thing, just about as coherent, at the moment, as the surface of a rough sea. I still believe, for reasons imbued with mysticism and metaphysics, that this incoherence is the prelude to a unification . . . The fact remains, however, that the multiplicity of human elements and human points of view revealed by a journey in the Far East is so 'overwhelming' that one cannot conceive of a religious life, a religious organism, assimilating such a mass without being profoundly modified and enriched by it . . .[5]

This passage, written shortly after arriving in the Far

East, expresses something of his approach to religion in China. Whilst always considering Christianity as the major 'axis' of development for religion, he also enquired what Eastern religions might contribute to the renewal of Christianity. This is evident from another letter of the same period:

> . . . I feel, more strongly than ever, the need of freeing our religion from everything about it that is specifically Mediterranean. I do not believe . . . that the majority of oriental thought-patterns are anything but outmoded and obsolescent . . . But I do say that by taking these forms, decayed though they be, into account, we discover such a wealth of 'potentialities' in philosophy, in mysticism, and in the study of human conduct that it becomes scarcely possible to be satisfied with an image of a mankind entirely and definitely enveloped in the narrow network of precepts and dogmas in which some people think they have displayed the whole amplitude of Christianity.[6]

However, the initial reaction to China seems to have been one of disappointment, possibly due to the unfavourable impressions gained from the deserted regions through which he travelled during his first expeditions. Later, when he came into contact with the scientific and intellectual circles of Peking, these opinions were considerably modified.

Soon after his arrival in Tientsin,[7] Teilhard and Licent set out for western Mongolia, particularly the Ordos Desert. For many weeks they wandered 'on mule-back across mountains and deserts'[8] and made important geological and palaeontological finds. The work was so successful that Teilhard unexpectedly extended his first visit to China until September of the following year. This gave him the opportunity for several other excursions, especially a major expedition to eastern Mongolia in spring 1924.

These expeditions led him into isolated regions, marked by ancient features both geographically and ethnically. Mongolia struck him 'as a "museum" of antique specimens . . . a slice of the past' giving the impression 'of an empty reservoir'.[9] When not camping under their tent, the two scientists stayed in Chinese inns, Buddhist lamaseries, and, occasionally, Christian mission stations. During these travels they met a mixed population of Mongols, Tibetans, and Chinese Muslims.

It has been said that the first debt which Teilhard owes to the Far East is 'its revelation of the immensity of the earth and of mankind'.[10] The new contact with China, especially the experience of the Ordos Desert, had a decisive impact on him. There is no break, however, no new incision in his inner vision brought about by this first stay in China. There is a deep continuity, an expansion of growth, with new experiences complementing and extending previous insights. The relative isolation of the Ordos Desert stood in stark contrast to the intensity of the war experience; instead of human masses in action, it meant a life of solitariness and the absence of surrounding activity. The letters of this time compare the Ordos with the earlier experience of Egypt as well as that of the war as, for example, the following lines, written in August 1923:

> ... Though I have less leisure than during the war, and perhaps less freshness too ..., in the last two months I have found myself in similar isolation and confronted with realities equally vast. And both these conditions are eminently favourable for meditating on the great All. Now, in the vast solitudes of Mongolia (which, from the human point of view, are a static and dead region), I see the same thing as I saw long ago at the 'front' (which from the human point of view, was the most alive region that existed): one single operation is in process of happening in the world, and it alone can justify our action: the emergence of some spiritual Reality, through and across the efforts of life.[11]

The 1923 expedition to Mongolia lasted four months. During this time, he increasingly realized that 'historical and geographical research is, in itself, empty and deceptive, the true science being that of the future as gradually disclosed by life itself'. He wished to develop this idea in a 'literary fantasy' of his 'impressions of Mongolia'.[12] Collected under the title 'Choses Mongoles', their most often quoted phrase is probably the succinct sentence with which Teilhard summarized his experience: 'I am a pilgrim of the future on my way back from a journey made entirely in the past'.[13]

After relating the external events of the expedition, Teilhard reflected at a deeper level on what he brought back from four months' travel in Mongolia: 'What gain has there been to my innermost being during this long pilgrimage in China? Has the great continent of Asia any profound message for me?' He had come with great hopes but he was disappointed:

. . . when I landed in China, there was one hope I still retained. If . . . the only true knowledge of things lies in foreseeing and building up the future as life gradually brings it into being, then what better opportunity to . . . associate myself with the building-up of the future could I hope for than to go and lose myself for weeks on end in the fermenting mass of the peoples of Asia? There I could count on meeting the new currents of thought and mysticism in process of formation, which were preparing to rejuvenate and fertilize our European world.

But this was a naive assumption comparable to the expectation of 'those simple people of the past who thought that the gods inhabit the hidden places of the world and that long ago they used to reveal themselves to men'. Instead, he found 'nothing but absence of thought, senile thought, or infantile thought . . . Mongolia seemed to me asleep – perhaps dead'.[14]

The same idea is expressed in his comment on a stay in a Buddhist lamasery:

Like all monks everywhere and always, lamas have an infallible instinct in choosing the setting for their dwelling-places, so that it is always a delight for the eye to come upon one of their monasteries suddenly, deep in a most unexpected recess. Gilded flagstaffs glistened in the sun over the geometrical group of red and white rectangular buildings. Now and again a monk went past, in a purple or yellow robe – a sight which delighted the eye and filled the heart with peace. But to admire the lamas and their lamas-eries one has, unfortunately, to see them from a distance. As soon as one draws near, the gleaming façade is seen to be tarnished and the vivid garments dirty and torn. The people who first created these desert retreats were doubtless really great men, prophets who discovered something of great beauty in the world, and beyond the world. Today one scrutinizes the dull faces of their successors in vain to find the most fleeting trace of that long-faded vision.[15]

However, Teilhard realized that he was not in a good position to gain a completely balanced picture. The Christian missionaries he met on the whole reinforced the negative impressions rather than counteracting them. One exception was Father Schram, a missionary from Tibet who, on his return from the Himalayan border, assured Teilhard

that out there there still survived . . . two or three solitaries who nourish their interior life by contemplating the cosmic cycles and the eternal re-birth of Buddha. But a chance passer-by like myself is not in a position to recognize these infrequent heirs of a venerable tradition of thought whose fruit is reserved for some new season. For myself, I have seen nothing in Mongolia to awaken the 'other life' within me.[16]

Distressed at finding nothing 'but the traces of a vanished world', Teilhard finished his impressions on a rather triumphant note about the rise of the West. From the whole of sleeping Asia, it seemed to him, 'there rose a voice which whispered, "Now, my brothers of the West, it is your turn".' However, there is also a faint hint of mutual give and take present when he states:

Our turn. Yes, sleep on, ancient Asia; your people are as weary as your soil is ravaged. By now your night has fallen and the light has passed into other hands. But it was you who kindled this light, you who gave it to us. Have no fear:

59

we shall not allow it to die . . . So long, too, as a few wise
men still have your life (your own life – not a life we would
seek to impose on you) in safe-keeping, it is not extinguished.
Tomorrow perhaps it will shine once more over your
ravaged plateaux.[17]

This can be taken as a pointer that 'within all this shift
of civilizations' and 'beneath the universal turmoil of living
beings' where 'something is being made' at present, Asia may
have its own insights to contribute. This note of hope was
to grow and become more positive in later years, at least
occasionally.

It would in any case be inappropriate to judge Teilhard's
views on China from these first impressions alone. 'Choses
Mongoles' is of no great importance among his literary works;
yet it clearly shows that the unfavourable comparison between
East and West was present from his first encounter with the
Far East. A similar perspective still underlies his explicitly
comparative essay 'The Road of the West' (1932), written nine
years later, when Teilhard's knowledge of China had greatly
increased. As this essay is of greater significance in his work,
it is important to know that some of its ideas were already
foreshadowed in the relatively minor 'Choses Mongoles' noted
down during the first months in China.

It is true that Teilhard's attitude to China always remained
an ambivalent one. On one hand, we find a mixture of negative disapproval and rejection and, on the other, there is also
the more positive search for enrichment and convergence. In
an early letter from the Ordos Desert this is expressed in the
following manner:

When I came to China I hoped to find a reservoir of thought
and mysticism that would bring fresh youth to your West.
I now have the impression that the reservoir is 'blocked'
emptied.
The Chinese are primitive people (beneath their varnish
of modernity or Confucianism); the Mongols are in gradual
process of disappearance, and their lamas are coarse and
dirty monks. The fact remains that in time gone by these

people *saw something*, but that they allowed this light to be lost – and that we can rediscover it. I was positively moved by the serenity and majesty of a Buddha in Peking: we have no finer representation of the Divinity! . . .

Could we not enrich our spirit a little with the heavy sap circulating in their veins, while at the same time bringing them the wherewithal to make them live? Could we not try to complete ourselves by converting them? I haven't noticed that the missionaries have the faintest idea of this.[18]

These are first impressions. As such they must not be given the same importance as Teilhard's more mature literary compositions and yet, they must also be weighed up against some of his more negative comments. The enriching and exuberant aspects of the first encounter with China found a permanent expression in 'The Mass on the World' (1923), a symbolic offering of the world 'in the steppes of Asia'.[19]

One of the finest expressions of Teilhard's mystical vision, this poem has attracted comparisons of which he himself would have been unaware. Mircea Eliade sees this text as proclaiming the possibility that 'cosmic matter as such is susceptible of being sanctified in its totality . . . When Teilhard speaks of the penetration of the galaxies by the cosmic Logos, even the most fantastic exaltation of the bodhisattvas seems modest and unimaginative by comparison – because for Teilhard the galaxies in which Christ will be preached millions of years hence are *real*, are living matter. They are not illusory and not even ephemeral'. Thus, in Eliade's view, Teilhard is '*revealing the ultimate sacrality of nature and of life*'.[20]

Another commentator, Lama Anandagarika Govinda, has pointed out that the Ordos Desert lies in an area which, for centuries, has been under the cultural influence of Tibetan Buddhism. For this reason he has explored similarities between 'The Mass on the World' and the mystical meaning of the Tibetan mantra '*Om mani padme hum*', and also with certain ideas of the seventh-century Buddhist poem *Bodhicharyavatara*. All these works place a similar emphasis on the spiritual transformation of matter, man, and the world when offered up in an act of religious surrender.[21]

II

In 1924, Teilhard had occasion to extend his knowledge of China through further expeditions, especially to eastern Mongolia, and through visits to Peking. Earlier impressions were confirmed and new ones gathered. Reports on his travels are interspersed with observations such as 'The Mongolia of the Gobi is every bit as wild as Central Africa, and the inhabitants are just as primitive. At long intervals you come across a lamasery, and on every prominent rocky peak you find a heap of stones called an obo – at once altar and a landmark – to which the devout Mongol adds a stone as he passes'. Teilhard was truly sensitive to the numinous quality of these tokens of an ancient faith. One of the obos has 'a dozen cairns, each with a branch stuck on top which the wind from the West has blown sideways like the flame of a torch.

'In these silent symbols, these ever-lonely altars, scattered over the wilderness, there is something really mysterious, really wild and impressive.'[22]

In Peking, Teilhard came into contact with the Chinese Geological Survey and especially its director, Dr Ting, who seemed to be closely in touch with the contemporary intellectual leaders of China. During a discussion on Chinese philosophy and the Chinese religious temperament, Dr Ting seems to have stated that the country was undergoing an antireligious phase. The ancient traditions had been severed, and the influence of Western teachers was still too dominant.[23] Teilhard concluded:

Unquestionably the average Chinese is extremely earthbound, and one may well ask oneself in what corner of his soul, or under what unexpected forms, the forces of religion and mysticism lie hidden in him. Even Dr Ting seemed to me to have envisaged the search for a religion in terms of a vast scientific enterprise, whereas the Absolute, as it is only too clear, cannot *'be taken* by force' but should $\begin{cases} \text{'give itself',} \\ \text{manifest itself,} \end{cases}$ to the spirits that await it. What is certain is that if it is to attract the attention, and then the sympathy, of the Far Easterners, Christianity must present itself in a form . . . which amplifies (not minimises!) the mystery, grandeur, interest and problems of the tangible universe.[24]

Yet in spite of seeing China from a predominantly Western and especially Christian point of view, Teilhard did not share the perspective of most Christian missionaries. On one hand, he was aware that he penetrated into distant parts of the country, 'so completely beyond the reach of any missionary';[25] on the other hand, he felt that missionaries were generally too cut off from the contemporary scientific milieu and wider social movements to be able to understand his own worldview. To discuss and explain his vision was perhaps only possible in a particular European setting, and for this reason he sometimes longed to return to France. After having experienced 'at close quarters just what a missionary's life is like, not in the big settlements but in the remote country parts',[26] he came to the conclusion that Europeans in China were often out of touch with the world at large. Thus, he was initially glad to go back to Europe again at the end of 1924. But it was not long before he wrote to a friend : 'I am homesick for China'.[27] He then realized that he preferred staying in Tientsin to being at the Institut Catholique in Paris. This change of attitude was mainly due to the personal difficulties experienced with his superiors.

Given these difficulties, a return to China seemed to be the easiest solution. Teilhard left France before it was finally decided that his connection with the Institut Catholique would be permanently severed. At first, the return to the Far East was perhaps planned for one year but it soon became permanent.

This turn of events led to much questioning and, during the difficult years of 1926-7, strong anti-Church tendencies are expressed in his writings, especially in the letters. A later superior has said of those critical years that Teilhard 'was leaving France under a cloud for an indefinite time, and he saw the momentum of his influence broken just as it was beginning to prove fruitful. The penalty imposed on him seemed unjustified. It was hard for him to "bend". He obeyed in a spirit of faith, but without understanding'[28] when he returned to China.

His cousin Marguerite, fully aware of Teilhard's attraction to Asia, has judged the same events in retrospect more positively:

> In the life of the Far East his mind found a new freedom. The grandeur of nature in a vast new continent, the multiplicity of human types he met on his travels and in the cosmopolitan society of Peking, gave depth and richness to his thought . . . His observation of the great ferment of societies and races, alternated with strict solitude, meditation, and concentration on God.
>
> The trenches of the 1914 war has been for him what the cell is to the monk . . . Père Teilhard now became the wandering hermit of the Asian deserts, a background that facilitated the ascent of his powerful spirit and gave full scope to an outstanding personality and an outstanding destiny.[29]

After his return to Tientsin, in the midst of his deepest personal crisis, Teilhard wrote *Le Milieu Divin* (1927), a spiritual masterpiece wherein he explores a specific approach to Christian mysticism and ascetism.

Le Milieu Divin elaborates the themes on mysticism already familiar from 'The Mass on the World'. The attributes of the 'divine milieu' may externally resemble 'the errors of a pagan naturalism', 'the excesses of quietism and illuminism',[30] but in reality they are at the antipodes of any false pantheism:

> Pantheism seduces us by its vistas of perfect universal union. But ultimately, if it were true, it would give us only fusion and unconsciousness; for, at the end of the evolution it claims to reveal, the elements of the world vanish in the God they create or by which they are absorbed . . .
> Christianity alone . . . saves . . . the essential aspiration of all mysticism: *to be united* (that is, to become the other) *while remaining oneself* . . .
> *We can only lose ourselves in God by prolonging the most*

individual characteristics of beings far beyond themselves:
that is the fundamental rule by which we can always distinguish the true mystic from his counterfeits.
To sum up, one may say that, in relation to all the main
historical forms assumed by the human religious spirit,
Christian mysticism extracts *all* that is sweetest and strongest circulating in all the human mysticisms, though without absorbing their evil or suspect elements. It shows an
astonishing equilibrium between the active and the passive,
between possession of the world and its renunciation, between a taste for things and an indifference to them.[31]

Teilhard always hoped for a publication of *Le Milieu Divin*.
Official censures from his religious superiors prevented the
book from appearing during his lifetime in spite of several
revisions[32] and repeated efforts from his friend Father Charles[33]
in Louvain. However disappointing this lack of recognition was,
he had the satisfaction of seeing his professional services as
geologist and palaeontologist increasingly recognized, especially
by the Chinese. Instead of working primarily for the French,
he was happy to work more and more for the Chinese Geological Survey, and to collaborate with the Chinese University
in Peking. He was convinced of the necessity of 'going over
to the Chinese'[34] but this attitude was not shared by all foreigners.[35] Teilhard preferred to work in an open milieu which
would place at his disposal 'the double and complementary
riches of East and West'.[36] The inherent contrast and tension
of this situation was summed up by his statement: '*Old China,
new China – dead religion, religion being born*'.[37]
Early in 1927, Teilhard wrote about this new China: 'There
is going on here, at this very moment, a human development
of almost geological dimensions; to participate in it would be
a rare chance indeed'.[38] This realization made him perhaps less
regret that he was not returning to Paris. He enjoyed considerable reputation with the Chinese; they referred to him as
'the smiling scientist' and gave him the name 'Father Day-
break Virtue'. Unconventional though this name was, 'to the
Chinese it stood for the man, and was more prophetic than his
unknown donor guessed'.[39]

Teilhard's letters of this period also contain references to the communist movement. During his expeditions, he saw much of 'Chinese China'; he deplored the scourge of militarism and the extent of suffering imposed on the people by the warlords. He welcomed the communist awakening but criticized the movement for its 'internationalization *through hatred*' rather than through sympathy and love.[40] However, he set much hope on the young intellectuals: '. . . one feels that the country's intellectual elite is rapidly casting its skin. In a century the change will have happened. What will it give? A China capable of helping the West in its research, or merely an imitative China? Who can say? . . .'[41]

This expresses quite a different attitude from his earlier appraisal of China. His second stay, unlike the first, made him well aware that a social movement and upheaval were taking place, giving birth to a new China, in fact, to a new Asia, which 'the English forces will not prevent'.[42] He felt that 'nobody knows what will be left of the European establishments (notably the missions) in China in a year, short of very considerable foreign intervention . . . What happens . . . is the modern individualization of Asia . . .'[43] Watching the awakening of Chinese national consciousness, Teilhard was certain in 1931 that the Chinese had now the self-awareness of a modern nation.[44]

At that time, he was friendly with Hu Shih, 'the young well-read philosopher who has behind him the whole of the Chinese undergraduate world'.[45] Often referred to as 'Father of the Literary Renaissance' in China, Hu Shih was well known for his achievements as a writer. He gave Teilhard his autobiography to read which contained the *Credo* Hu Shih was offering to his fellow intellectuals.[46] It proposed 'a framework for a new philosophy of the universe and life' which Teilhard described as 'faith in the world but in a world conceived in a childishly immature and imprecise way . . . [Hu Shih] doesn't see that the cosmos holds together not by matter but by spirit'.[47] Whilst criticizing Hu Shih's *Credo*, Teilhard was nevertheless deeply interested 'to see even Chinese thought, in its own way, taking the same direction as my own and that of my friends',[48] and he recognized an affinity here.

Earlier, Teilhard had expressed the desire to write 'a book of the earth'. This seemed preferable to writing a book on China alone for which, in any case, he did not possess 'the knowledge of the language and the past that would open the hidden treasure'. Yet one question clearly fascinated him in relating his Chinese experience to a global perspective. This was 'to discover the new spirit that is struggling to emerge from the ruins of the old crenelated towns and the old pagodas; to recognize and reveal that specific and essential element which the East must bring to the West so that the Earth will be complete'. Over the years, he became increasingly convinced that the social and political turmoil and the awakening of the new China might be of great importance for the future development of mankind, much more so than, for example, the contemporary events in India. It was in China that Teilhard experienced the immensity of the earth and its peoples. He compared this experience to a voice or song murmuring in him 'not of me, but of the World in me. I would like to express the thoughts of a man who, having finally penetrated the partitions and ceilings of little countries, little coteries, little sects, rises above all these categories and finds himself a child and citizen of the Earth'.[49] He called this 'the Note of China, the Note of the All, joyous and magnificent'. It was a note of universality as well as an indication of the complementarity between East and West. Speaking about his personal experience, he could say that in China 'the West fascinates me: but once west of Turkestan. I . . . dream of the East'.[50] At a deeper level, he always looked out for indications 'as to the possibility of a frank spiritual collaboration between East and West'.[51] It is this note of complementarity and universality which reverberates through the essay 'The Spirit of the Earth' (1931),[52] written to overcome racial, national, and religious barriers, and received with enthusiasm by his friends.

III

The Far East was now Teilhard's permanent home. Outwardly involved in expeditions and research, he still found time for writing philosophical and religious essays which were read by a large circle of friends in China, France, USA, and elsewhere. The years 1931-2 are a kind of watershed. They not only mark an important expedition but also provide a dividing line between the Tientsin period and the subsequent stay in Peking. The Chinese reaction 'to Teilhard's enlightened attitude to co-operation between East and West'[53] was to invite him to become scientific adviser to their Geological Survey. This body was then mainly concerned with the investigation of the palaeontological site at Chou-Kou-Tien near Peking. Teilhard's important association with the work on Peking man (Sinanthropus pekinensis), found in December 1929, brought him worldwide scientific recognition and contacts.[54]

Now at the height of his career, Teilhard spent more time on research and scientific papers than on writing essays. In 1939, this situation was reversed through changed political circumstances. Between 1939-46, it was practically impossible to pursue any scientific work outside Peking because of the city's occupation by the Japanese. Thus, Teilhard lived in considerable isolation and, consequently, devoted most of these years to creative writing and intensive reading. Before 1932, East-West comparisons are mainly found in letters but, after that time, several essays are explicitly devoted to comparisons. The first of these was written after returning from a long expedition to Central Asia. Several encounters during this journey left a deep impression on Teilhard and stimulated him to reflect on the place of religion and mysticism in the modern world.

In the early 1930s, the French firm Citroën organized a large-scale expedition across Central Asia, known as the 'Yellow Expedition'. Consisting largely of Frenchmen, the expedition numbered over forty people, and Teilhard was asked to be the official geologist. The expedition was divided into two groups; the first travelled from China westwards across the Gobi desert to Sinkiang (Chinese Turkestan) whereas the second group started in the West and travelled eastwards via Syria, Persia, Afghanistan, and India, over the Hindu Kush and Pamir Mountains into Central Asia. It was planned that the two groups should meet at the old oasis city of Kashgar[55] at the foot of the Pamir Mountains. However, due to the difficult political situation in China at that time, these plans could not be fully carried out. The expedition lasted for almost a year from May 1931 to February 1932. The journey of the group travelling from Peking westwards covered the breadth of northern China and included many colourful and dangerous adventures, fully reported in the official expedition history.[56] In the words of the leader, it was an 'extraordinary journey across the most inaccessible parts of China, at a time when the most terrible chaos prevailed and there was no law but the law of the strongest'.[57]

Besides Frenchmen, Teilhard's group included an official contingent of Chinese scientists. Apparently, some of these were political agents. Among the eight Chinese representatives was one member of the central committee of the Kuomintang and also a minister of General Tchiang Kai Chek's government.[58] It is a reflection on Teilhard's standing that he was often asked to act as a mediator during the repeated disputes among the Chinese delegation. On arrival at the border of Sinkiang, the Governor refused the expedition entry into his territory until the Chinese delegation had been sent home. But even after that, the French were held prisoners outside the capital of Sinkiang for three months. Through clandestine communication, they eventually learnt that the other half of the expedition, travelling from West to East, had arrived in Kashgar. They pressed for permission to meet up with this second group and, after prolonged negotiations, a small contingent was allowed to establish contact between the two expedition teams by travelling further westwards, but not as far as Kashgar. This small liaison group consisted exclusively of technical personnel except for Teilhard who, thanks 'to his official position in China',[59] was the only scientist to be granted permission to travel further westwards.

It was a similar sign of trust that he was later chosen to accompany a specially selected group led by Joseph Hackin,[60] the director of the Paris Oriental museum, the *Musée Guimet*, to return from Sinkiang via a different route to study ancient Buddhist remains. Even from among this group, only a small party was permitted to visit the actual Buddhist sites in the

Gobi. Besides Hackin, Teilhard, and a mechanic, this party included a photographer and a painter who copied many Buddhist mural paintings. Although they were allowed to take photos of the Buddhist ruins it was explicitly forbidden to take any of the indigenous population. But the painter could record where the camera could not.[61]

Teilhard's report on the results of the expedition[62] explicitly mentions the ancient caves cut into the rock by Manichean and Buddhist monks, and emphasizes that he closely followed Hackin's comparative work on religious iconography. This report includes illustrations of a Buddhist divinity, painted in Tibetan-Mongolian style on a large boulder, and of a Buddhist lamasery where the group stayed. Hackin also invited Teilhard to accompany him on a study-tour of Japan during the following year[63] but this project did not materialize.

The official maps which were later published by the expedition list geographical, geological and botanical information, but also the location of Mongol camps, numerous obo-cairns en route, and some eighteen Buddhist lamaseries. By contrast, only one Chinese temple is shown on the entire itinerary. Most of the lamaseries were met at the beginning of their journey, before they came to the Gobi Desert.[64]

Besides camping, the expedition stayed en route in large Buddhist lamaseries, sometimes in Chinese inns, or occasionally, closer to Peking, in Christian mission stations. They encountered Chinese Buddhists and Muslims, talked to Taoist priests, Buddhist lamas, and various Muslim dignitaries. Unfortunately, they also got caught in a major battle at Hami in the aftermath of the Chinese Muslim revolt of the 1930s.[65]

The details of the contemporary political struggle in China witnessed by the French expedition make fascinating reading but are outside the scope of this book. Of greater interest is the expedition members' stay at the Buddhist monastery Pei Ling-Miao. There, they had the opportunity to assist at a long religious ceremony and engage in discussion with a learned lama, an envoy of the Pantchen Lama. At first the lamas promised to perform one of their famous demon dances but later this proved impossible. However, a day's journey further on, something more exciting happened. It was the Chinese

New Year, and a local prince invited the expedition members to a solemn ceremony where, in the presence of all the dignitaries of the region, the Pantchen Lama himself officiated and gave his blessings.[66]

It seems surprising that we have no description of these details from Teilhard's pen. He was present, though, as we know of a discussion between Teilhard and Hackin on the significance of one of the monastery's wall-paintings, showing a *bhavachakra* or wheel of life. Teilhard was also impressed by the quality of the Buddhist liturgy which he considered as public worship of the first order.[67]

So far, no reference to these experiences has been found in Teilhard's writings. This may be due to several reasons. The tumultuous political situation and general lack of communication did not allow for general correspondence. Thus, the 'Yellow Expedition' is documented by relatively few letters. Moreover, all Teilhard's diaries from China were later lost in the general upheaval following the end of the war. One can also say that, apart from writing letters during travels, he was generally not inclined to giving detailed descriptions of his own experiences.

By February 1932 Teilhard was back in Peking after an expedition of ten months. He felt the after-effects of the sheer physical strain of this journey and regretted the missed opportunities for research, lost through the political situation. The expedition had endured extremes of heat and cold, a harsh winter in the desert with temperatures of -20 to $-30°$ centigrade, and imprisonment, attacks and robbery.[68] Although the scientific results[69] were not as rich as expected, Teilhard had almost doubled his knowledge of the Asian continent and its peoples. He sometimes alluded to their variety and, in the heart of Chinese Turkestan, he felt that

it is a shock to find yourself among people who remind you more of the Near East than the Far East: a negligible minority of Chinese, and a predominance of Arab, Turkish and Persian types. They are practically all Moslems; you see mosques and minarets and hear the muezzin. The men are dignified, grave and bearded.

And further west he wrote:

There are no Chinese any more apart from the adminis-
trators and a few merchants. The men bearded and tur-
banned, trotting on their asses; the women strictly and
becomingly veiled; . . . the loud chant of the muezzins
calling to evening prayer at every corner of little villages.
You begin to see Afghans, Persians and Hindus; it's no
longer the Far East.[70]

In the midst of the enforced stay at the capital of Sinkiang,
Teilhard also mentioned in a letter that two particular themes
preoccupied him, namely, the nature of a 'personalistic
universe', and a work on 'The Conversion of the World', intended as 'a review of the present state of the various religions'.[71] He was fully aware that these plans for new essays
could only be realized later. But such reflections show that
the long journey through Central Asia raised many questions
in his mind as to the religious significance of his rich and varied
experiences. During the 'Yellow Expedition', he came into
contact with different peoples, cultures and religions of the
East. In addition, he was also part of a secular Western 'lay
milieu' represented by the French expedition members of
whom several had completely abandoned religious belief and
practice. Numerous discussions on religious questions reinforced Teilhard's view that Christianity lacked the necessary
openness to contemporary forms of thought and experience.[72]
Thus, he increasingly realized the need for a new approach to
spirituality, and for what he later called a 'new mysticism'.
It is from this perspective that he attempted to present Christianity to the modern world and to formulate some kind of
new 'apologetic' which he outlined in several essays written
in the late 1930s. There he stressed that Christians must above
all 're-think' their own religion.[73]
Another project was realized more immediately. Shortly
after his return to Peking, Teilhard announced that he was
going to write something on 'the fundamental metaphysical
and religious question' of the One and the Many to which he
saw an 'Eastern solution' and a 'Western solution'.[74] This

theme was fully worked out during the following months in 'The Road of the West: To a New Mysticism' (1932),[75] written when travelling on the boat from China to France, and completed at Penang on 8 September, 1932. Scientific reports apart, this is the first major essay after the 'Yellow Expedition' and it is also the first explicitly concerned with a particular comparison between East and West. Thus, it may in some way be seen as the outcome of Teilhard's reflections during that long journey across China, and we shall later return to its major ideas.

From 1932 on, Peking became Teilhard's permanent residence. Several expeditions led him to other parts of the country, especially to southern China, western Honan, and up the Yangtze River. The discovery of the Chinese south in particular was a new experience about which he wrote: '. . . every moment showed me a China more Chinese than the north. The pagodas are more brilliant and more mannered, hats are wider and more pointed, the whole countryside more like the China we know in books'.[76] Again, we possess only occasional references to the impressions left on him by these various expeditions. A more detailed account of some journeys, shared with George Barbour, are found in the latter's book *In the Field with Teilhard de Chardin*.[77] There he reports some of the discussions he had with Teilhard during their expeditions. At the end of day, when their scientific work was done, Teilhard would launch 'on an analysis of the various religions which developed one after the other throughout history; he sought to discern what contribution each might have made towards a better understanding of the structure of the universe and towards a deeper comprehension of God'.[78] This is only a brief reference, but it proves again that the abstract ideas of Teilhard's essays are but the distillations of his lived experience which supplied the raw material for all his reflections. This experience was further enlarged through contacts with Eastern countries outside China, particularly through visits to India, Indonesia, and Burma.

IV

In 1935, he was invited to visit both India and Indonesia. At first, he was not greatly excited about the idea of going to India where he was to join an expedition led by the German scientist Helmut de Terra. Yet afterwards he admitted that he had spent 'four really exciting months'[79] and that he 'was delighted with India'.[80] The main reason for the journey was again scientific; in retrospect, the experience proved a great addition to his knowledge of prehistory and yet, at a deeper level, it gave him 'only moderate satisfaction'. He summed up this contrast in a letter to his brother: 'As a purpose in life, my science (to which I owe so much) seems to me to be less and less worthwhile. For a long time now, my chief interest in life has lain in some sort of effort towards a plainer disclosing of God in the world. It's a more killing task but it's my only true vocation and nothing can turn me from it.'[81]

Teilhard arrived in Bombay in September 1935. He spent a few days in the city and then went by train to Rawalpindi. From there he travelled by car to Srinagar, accompanied by the British scientist T. T. Patterson.[82] They joined de Terra on a houseboat and spent a week on field-work in Kashmir. Subsequently, they moved to western Punjab, living in Rawalpindi and elsewhere. Together they visited the prehistoric drawings in the Indus Valley and the excavations at Mohenjo-Daro which left a deep impression on Teilhard. They also had an opportunity to visit the regions of Sind and Baluchistan. Later, their search for prehistoric material took them for a fortnight to the Narbada valley in central India. Teilhard ended his three months' stay in India with a week in Calcutta and from there he embarked for Java.

Travelling by camel or car in the Salt Range of western Punjab, now part of Pakistan, the semi-desert country reminded him of Egypt and also of Ethiopia which he had visited a few years before. This is not only expressed in *Letters from a Traveller*[83] but also in Helmut de Terra's vivid account of their visit to India. In his book *Memories of Teilhard de Chardin* he mentions that the landscape of the Sind Desert 'reminded Teilhard so vividly of the Nile Valley and of Cairo where he had worked as a teacher, that he felt as though he had been suddenly transported to Egypt. Here, as there, rivers threaded the desert with the luxuriant valley pastures to which the ancient civilizations had owed their wealth – yet how different had been their respective fates!'[84]

Reflecting on the desert as a place of religious experience which has stimulated 'the spiritual and visionary sides' of 'men of destiny', de Terra particularly remarks that Teilhard 'fitted so well into the wilderness'.[85] He loved the 'wonderful luminosity' of the north Indian countryside but he commented more harshly on its population.[86] It must be remembered that Teilhard's first and most extensive contact with Indians was mainly with Muslims whom he considered backward in their customs. About Hindus he wrote: 'So far as I have been able to form an opinion of them, the Hindus have been a disappointment to me. In them, too, the creative power seems in a pretty poor way, and you have to go to India to realize the numbing and deadening effect of a religion obsessed by material forms and ritualism'.[87] However, when he met the Hindu upper classes in Lahore and Calcutta, he found them 'highly civilized'. He thought Indians charming as individuals but judged the country as a whole then still incapable of self-government. He was fully aware, though, of the general dislike of the English among the local inhabitants who 'want independence at all costs'.[88]

Teilhard also saw something of Indian religious life. According to de Terra, they watched a Hindu village festival in honour of Shiva in central India. People danced and chanted all night, offering *puja* and floating little oil lamps on the river:

With its groups of palms and venerable mango trees, the whole place seemed to have been transformed into a setting for some oriental 'Midsummer Night's Dream' . . . Apparently, the god had visited their fields a few days ago in the guise of a flood, leaving behind numerous symbols of his procreative power in the shape of some longish pebbles, which were regarded as an especial mark of divine favour. From the temple, where festivities were in full swing, came the sound of flutes and drums and the nasal incantations of the priest . . . The whole village seemed to be involved in the festival. In several houses we glimpsed old men seated . . . by candle-light, holding their hands before their foreheads in prayer . . . and chanting continuously from books with such devotion that for a moment we felt ourselves carried back in time to the far-off days when the Vedic hymns still formed part of daily worship.[89]

Teilhard's more negative impression of Hinduism may be related to other experiences, such as the following, again described by de Terra :

Then there were the fakirs squatting beneath the broad branches of mango trees, their naked torsos smeared with ash and their long matted hair piled turban-like atop their ascetic faces – hideous caricatures of human beings whom Teilhard regarded with compassion, likening them to 'spirits of the underworld'. Just as the fakirs reminded him of the human bondage caused by religious fanaticism, so he was disgusted by the caste-mark tradition.[90]

It was de Terra's opinion that if there were any foreigner 'who could have roused ancient India to new life, it was Teilhard. In this superstition-ridden Indian world, he seemed like a new species of human being'.[91] Yet it has also been remarked that, unlike other visitors to the country, Teilhard was neither impressed by the religious fervour of the people nor did he appreciate the Hindu assertion 'of a cosmic unity, which was in many ways analogous to his own ideas',[92] at least he did not realize it then.

After leaving India, Teilhard paid a brief visit to Rangoon where he spent Christmas 1935. He returned to this city again for a longer period two years later. After the stay in Rangoon, he travelled for about a month all over Java. His scientific work kept him too occupied then to visit any of the famous sites. But he was proud to have lived 'in the Javanese kampongs among the gentle and graceful natives'. Although it was the rainy season, conditions were favourable and he 'revelled in the exoticism of this marvellous country'.

However, Java was overpopulated; apart from its high peaks and some remnants of jungle, 'it is nothing but one immense village; but the huts are so small, so scattered and so lost in the vast sea of green, that all you see is a forest of palms enclosing rice-fields, the whole dominated by a series of volcanoes, each as big as Etna'.[93]

On his return journey to China he wrote down his travel-notes but these do not seem to have survived. Few details are known about this or the subsequent visit to Java, undertaken in April 1938. The scientific work of the second visit has been described at some length by Helmut de Terra, from whom one can also gather that they visited the island's interior and saw some of Java's splendid attractions:

From Bandung we travelled to Surakarta, ancient seat of the Javanese princes, where we watched dancers rehearsing for a performance in the palace. It was like some old oriental fairy-tale, with young dancing-girls in heavy brocaded costumes gliding beneath the mango trees in the palace courtyard to the strains of a gamelang orchestra . . .[94]

Unfortunately, neither this nor any other sightseeing was recorded by Teilhard. Slightly more information is available on his subsequent visit to Burma, lasting from December 1937 to March 1938.[95] He stayed as long in Burma as in India but he took more to this Buddhist country than to Hindu India. He commented with delight on Burmese life and wrote from Pagan, the old temple city:

I overlook the Irrawaddy, fringed by low mountains and held in a ribbon of green, exactly like the Nile in Upper Egypt . . . the surroundings are simply one great forest of pagodas . . . The population is very much of a mixture. First the Burmese, all grace and beaming smiles . . . dressed in dazzling colours, with an extraordinary proportion of orange-robed monks. Towards the Arakan-Yoma you meet the 'Chins', small men, with moustaches, almost Mongol. To the east the black-turbanned Shans and a chequer-board of small groups of strange ethnic types . . . A few days ago we were at Pagan, the ancient capital . . . of the Burmese kings. Now it is simply a village lost in palms, banyans, mangoes and mimosa, but surrounded by over a hundred pagodas, some of them in ruins that may well date back to the twelfth century. Nothing really artistic or grand (all brick-built) but about the whole, particularly when the sun is setting, there is something most fantastic and unreal. I am becoming very fond of this radiant country, three-quarters covered with bush or jungle, in which the most insignificant inhabitant is as graceful and colourful as a flower.[96]

According to Helmut de Terra, Teilhard's host and colleague during this expedition, it was hard to finally take leave of Burma with its 'idyllic river landscape, the wild expanses of tropical mountain forest, the Buddhist traditions of the country's graceful inhabitants, the colourful splendour of village festivals'.[97] In the wilderness of the jungle, de Terra also noted that he 'could always sense, in Teilhard's company, something of the mystical empathy with Nature'.[98]

On their return journey, they called at various ports, including Malacca, on the Malayan coast, half-way between India and China, well-known for its Jesuit missionary associations. Long ago, St Francis Xavier regarded the Malacca mission as a springboard for the conversion of China and Japan to Christianity. This vision of a religious conquest of Asia has been described as 'a Napoleonic idea in religious terms'[99] and Teilhard considered it as something well belonging to the past.

Other journeys to and from China provided an opportunity to get acquainted with places en route such as Ceylon, Penang, Singapore, Saigon, Hanoi, Hong Kong, and Hawaii. Here again, little detailed information is available except for brief descriptions in Teilhard's correspondence, particularly the *Letters from a Traveller*. Even less known are the details of his three brief stops in Japan during 1931, 1937, and 1938. Apart from the industrial centre of Kobe, Teilhard visited at least the ancient cities of Kyoto and Nara, well known for their famous Buddhist and Shinto temples. In Kyoto, he saw 'a whole series of classical temples, more sombre in colour than the Chinese but very clean, built of a most magnificent wood and nestling in such a wonderful green background of tall dark-foliaged trees'.

To his regret, he had a missionary as guide so that he could not linger on as long as he would have liked 'in front of the gilded altars, *without* idols'.[100] Father Leroy, who accompanied Teilhard on one of the subsequent visits to Japan, has said[101] that, on seeing these temples, they both realized the vitality of Japanese religious life in comparison to that of China. The activity in Japanese temples stood in stark contrast to the neglected Confucian temples, for example. In view of this difference, it seems surprising that Teilhard himself never commented on this experience.

De Terra found it equally surprising that, given the grandeur of Teilhard's ideas, he never assumed the role of a religious preacher or prophet. Instead, his primary concern was with the study of man in all its aspects, seeking an all-embracing, universal perspective which, he felt, science had so far left out of its purview. In the opinion of this fellow-scientist, Teilhard was wittingly or unwittingly 'the founder of a new kind of anthropology, although he would have been hard put to find it a home in existing academic institutions'.[102] This comment is as true today as it was then. Teilhard's new anthropological and universalist perspective found expression in numerous essays but particularly in his major work *The Phenomenon of Man*, written in Peking between 1938-40. However, Teilhard considered this work to be a synthesis of forty years of studies, experience, and reflections. Yet in spite of multiple revisions, this book suffered the same fate as *Le Milieu Divin* did earlier: permission to publish it was always withheld during his lifetime. Yet cyclostyled copies of the book were soon circulating among a number of personal friends and scientists.

The Phenomenon of Man, primarily addressed to fellow-scientists, carries few explicit references to religion except for its epilogue on 'The Christian Phenomenon'.[103] But the third section of the book, dealing with the rise of thought and the emergence of the modern world, includes a short part on 'the rise of the West'[104] which is of special interest here. In a very general manner, Teilhard considers the gradual 'confluence' of civilizations. He sees the movement of history as a rhythm of conflict and harmonization between dominant 'currents', summarily illustrated by five major civilizations of the past including, among others, Chinese and Indian civilization. Whereas ancient China remained static and unchanged, early India was drawn into metaphysics: 'India – the region *par excellence* of high philosophic and religious pressures: we can never make too much of our indebtedness to the mystic influences which have come down to each and all of us in the past from this "anticyclone" '.[105]

Here as elsewhere in Teilhard's work, there is an explicit recognition of India's central position in the development of mysticism. However, this took place in the far-away past, and Teilhard goes on to point out its shortcomings:

But however efficacious these currents for ventilating and illuminating the atmosphere of mankind, we have to recognize that, with their excessive passivity and detachment, they were incapable of building the world. The primitive soul of India arose in its hour like a great wind but, like a great wind also, again in its hour, it passed away. How indeed could it have been otherwise? Phenomena regarded as an illusion (Maya) and their connections as a chain (Karma), what was left in those doctrines to animate and direct human evolution? A simple mistake was made – but it was enough – in the definition of the spirit and in the appreciation of the bonds which attach it to the sublimation of matter. Then step by step we are driven nearer to the more western zones of the world – to the Euphrates, the Nile, the Mediterranean – where an exceptional concurrence of places and peoples was, in the course of a few thousand years, to produce that happy blend, thanks to which reason could be harnessed to facts and religion to action.

. . . we would be allowing sentiment to falsify the facts if we failed to recognize that during historic time the principal axis of anthropogenesis has passed through the West. It is in this ardent zone of growth and universal recasting that all that goes to make man today has been discovered,

or at any rate *must have been rediscovered* . . .
In truth, a neo-humanity has been germinating round the
Mediterranean during the last six thousand years . . .
. . . from one end of the world to the other, all the peoples,
to remain human or to become more so, are inexorably
led to formulate the hopes and problems of the modern
earth in the very same terms in which the West has formulated them.[106]

Although one may agree with Joseph Needham[107] in judging
Teilhard's history to be out of focus here, it would be a mistake to regard these paragraphs as merely an ethnocentric
statement, based on the naive assumption of Western suprem-
acy in all developments of life. However unsatisfactorily
presented, this particular passage as well as *The Phenomenon
of Man* as a whole, is concerned with a problem of historical
genesis: how and where did our modern world originate in
the form we know today?[108] This is followed by a consideration of the collective issue of man's survival, and the unity
of the human family, requiring 'the confluence of thought'
and a 'convergent spirit' among mankind. In the area of religion and mysticism, this implies that the West is not only
indebted to the East for the origin of certain mystical insights
but, what is more, without a 'confluence' and mutual interaction of the different religious traditions from now onwards,
a full understanding of the phenomenon of man as a whole
cannot emerge. Such a convergent perspective applies to the
earth as a whole and not to West or East in isolation. The
human community, though deeply torn apart, is increasingly
feeling the need to think of itself as interdependent and one.[109]
It was the Chinese milieu which provided the background for
the emergence of this universalist perspective of the spirit of
one earth. Let us, therefore, briefly consider some further
encounters Teilhard had in Peking and Shanghai.

V

In Peking, Teilhard was more in touch with an international
scientific, artistic and diplomatic milieu than with a traditional

Chinese one. He knew the élite of the country, that is to say, leading Chinese scientists and intellectuals rather than political revolutionaries. Yet through his wide and varied contacts, he was informed about what was happening elsewhere.[110] Here only two particular incidents, generally little known, will be mentioned as they illustrate Teilhard's awareness of certain political and religious developments at that time.

Between 1933-36, Teilhard counted among his friends Edgar Snow, the journalist and famous author of *Red Star over China*.[111] According to Helen Snow, Teilhard was one of the first Westerners to learn about the experience on which this book is based, namely Snow's visit to Mao Tse-Tung and the Chinese communist movement in 1936. Supporting evidence for this comes from another member of the Peking circle[112] who writes that Edgar Snow, on his return from visiting the communist headquarters in Yenan, in western China,

> brought photographs and information about the life and conditions there. As he was one of the first journalists to visit the Communists his reports were of the greatest value, and Père Teilhard questioned him from every angle as this new phenomenon was of much interest to him, as were all large manifestations of human energy.[113]

Apparently Teilhard read the *Red Star over China* with great fascination and together with the Snows they discussed 'the new controversial subjects – fascism, Marxism, socialism, communism, and isms for which we had not even any common language then'. Through Mao Tse-Tung's Marxism, an element of Western thought and ethics reached for the first time the majority of Chinese villagers never before touched by Western missionary influence. In Helen Snow's opinion, Mao Tse-Tung's influence and presence, more than anything else, were an example of Teilhard's thesis of the evolution of man. Apparently, Mrs Snow told Mao personally in 1937 about Teilhard's own vision and thought.[114]

Whether this actually happened or not, the story illustrates that Teilhard knew more about the rising forces of communism in China than one would generally suspect. He had for a long time been aware of the compelling attraction of Marxism[115] and many of his essays refer to the inner strength and activating power of the Marxist belief in the development of man and the world. He shared this belief to a great extent but he criticized it for its lack of transcendence.

The longest account of Teilhard's later years in Peking comes from Claude Rivière who headed the French radio station in Shanghai during the war. In her book *En Chine avec Teilhard de Chardin*,[116] she describes their long discussions on Chinese religion and society. Amidst the indescribable misery and suffering of China where the extremes of poverty, hunger and cold exceeded anything ever seen in India, Teilhard could maintain an attitude of hope and unparalelled dynamism. Rivière thinks this was only possible because of the strength of his inner vision which she describes as a deeply mystical one: 'To convince oneself of the authenticity of the mystical . . . nature of [his] faith . . ., words were unnecessary. It was enough to see him . . . at the end of a retreat or after his Mass with a transfigured face, suffused with radiant joy'.[117] She also mentions that Teilhard left the contemporary world the irreplaceable contribution of a 'sense of the Divine which all the great mystics have' and 'a visionary intuition of the sacred'[118] which radiates through his entire work.

With regard to Teilhard's encounter of Eastern religions, Claude Rivière reports one incident, not documented elsewhere. At the end of 1942, Teilhard and his friend, Father Leroy, visited Claude Rivière in Shanghai. At that moment, a conference of leading Buddhists from all over Asia was taking place in order to discuss the spiritual influence of Buddhism in the Far East. The participants included two well-known 'living Buddhas', Lama Lo-Song from Outer Mongolia, and Lama Awangishi from Tibet.

Claude Rivière, in her capacity as broadcaster, interviewed the two Lamas in the Temple of the Great Jade Buddha in Shanghai, and Teilhard was present. She mentions that he specifically asked the Lamas about the current state of Buddhism and also about its foreseeable future. After a lengthy discussion, the Tibetan Lama is reported to have ended by saying that Teilhard was a great 'living Jesus' of the West.

One day he would be famous and many people would be nourished by his message.[119]

These visits initiated long discussions about the state of religion in China. Generally speaking, Chinese Buddhism was at a low ebb during Teilhard's time although a growing movement of renewal was then spreading through the country.[120] During his expeditions, he frequently stayed in or near various Buddhist temples; yet he had had little opportunity to get closely acquainted with the great monasteries where ancient Buddhist and Taoist traditions were still alive. The beautiful old temples in the Western Hills near Peking, which he knew well, had so few pilgrims that 'the priests rented some of the courtyards and rooms to foreigners who used them as country retreats' and gave parties there.[121]

Teilhard's encounter with Buddhist monks, his earlier meeting with the Pantchen Lama, and his experience of Buddhist liturgy are only a few examples which show that he came into contact with some aspects of living Buddhism at a time when, apart from scholarly specialists, relatively few Western people had the opportunity to do so. Not all critics will realize this as Teilhard's essays do not allude to these experiences at all.

During the years 1939-46, travel became virtually impossible. Apart from the visit to Shanghai, Teilhard remained wholly confined to Peking and its immediate neighbourhood. In 1940, Teilhard and Leroy founded the 'Institut de Géobiologie' from where they published a Bulletin and various scientific papers with the idea of launching a new perspective in anthropological studies. The realization of this ambition was greatly curtailed, however, through the circumstances of the war.[122] The enforced leisure of these years made Teilhard write more than ever before and many philosophical and religious essays date from this time.[123] His ideas were mainly expressed in writing, but much less in personal communication. Father Leroy, who was in daily contact with him, knew little of Teilhard's innermost thought; in fact, he did not realize its full thrust until much later on.[124] This must have applied to a number of Teilhard's friends in Peking. Whilst Teilhard mixed easily with people socially, he is also known to have been a solitary thinker. It is not surprising that he experienced serious nervous depressions during 1939-40 and also later, in 1947-48.[125] Thus, the popular image of Teilhard as an over-optimistic and untroubled thinker is far from the truth. On the contrary, a close study of his life and works reveals the depth of suffering and pain experienced again and again at various stages of his life.[126] Apart from the opportunity for regular writing, the war period in Peking also provided him with time for intensive reading and study. This is well documented through the careful notes and comments found in his unpublished *carnets de lecture* and diary entries.[127] These contain material of particular interest in relation to his knowledge of Eastern religions and, therefore, deserve special mention.

Teilhard's reading during the last years in China covers a wide range of works from such different fields as philosophy, theology, literature, archaeology, biology, physics, sociology, and anthropology.[128] Books on religious topics include titles on ancient Greek religion, Zoroastrianism, Christian thought (especially the theologians Troeltsch and Barth),[129] on mysticism and Indian religions.

The notes on mysticism are a proof of his continued interest in a topic central to his thought since the early days of his writing. The closer study of Indian religions, however, is more surprising as we do not know about such detailed reading in earlier years. Of particular interest are the notes he made on Joseph Maréchal's book *Etudes sur la Psychologie des Mystiques*, and on Pierre Johanns's two-volume study *Vers le Christ par le Vedanta*.[130] The five pages of notes on Maréchal's work are concerned with pantheistic monism, and include comments on the difference between monistic and theistic forms of mysticism. The distinction between different forms of mysticism is a lasting concern of Teilhard's writings. Maréchal deals with this in a general manner whereas Johanns's study pursues the comparative theme in great detail. He deals in depth with Indian religious thought, expounding the different forms of Vedanta and comparing the ideas of the great Vedanta theologians about God, man, and the world with those of Christianity. Teilhard's ten pages of notes include his own criticisms of both Indian and Christian ideas, in the form presented by Johanns.

Although Teilhard often equated Hinduism with Vedanta monism, the comments on Johanns's book show that, at least since reading this work, if not before, he became aware of the internal differences and complexity of the Hindu religious tradition. He realized that Christianity was by no means unique in its worship of a personal God, and that such personal devotion was an important strand in Indian religious thought.

His interest in other aspects of Indian culture is apparent from the brief references to Dravidian India, a mention of the Indian gods Shiva and Kali, comments on contemporary political developments in the Indian subcontinent,[181] and a diary entry quoting Rabindranath Tagore's famous work *Gitanjali*. Further reading on Indian history and religion was pursued in the following years, after Teilhard had returned to the West.

During the last year in Peking, he also studied Aldous Huxley's *Perennial Philosophy*, published in 1945. Teilhard was well acquainted with Huxley's literary works but, usually, these are simply listed by their titles in his notes. For this work, however, he added some brief, but significant, excerpts. He noted down Huxley's concern with three issues: Man requires a faith as a basis for his life; the ultimate reality is not a personal God but a spiritual Absolute, a 'God-without-form'; man's union with the One is conceived as a return of the many to the One. Thus, the final state of deliverance does not incorporate any increase or achievement on man's part.[182] As will be seen later, these are precisely the themes which preoccupied Teilhard, and with which he takes issue in his interpretation of mysticism.

Other notes criticize Roger Bastide's book *Le Problème de la Vie Mystique*[183] which, in Teilhard's view, presents mysticism quite wrongly as an isolated and exceptional phenomenon. It thereby overlooks the extraordinary importance of mysticism for people today. This was a theme of primary interest to Teilhard, and he listed other titles on mysticism for further consultation,[184] presumably in order to clarify his own ideas.

Teilhard's *carnets de lecture* and diary entries express a constant search for additional insight, gained in critical dialogue with other works. Seen from this perspective, his philosophical and religious essays appear as the final product of a long process of assimilation and reflection, based on a wide range of experience and sources to which he seldom explicitly refers. Thus, his work presents a tremendous synthesis without disclosing the myriad elements employed in its making.

In 1946, after seven years' confinement, Teilhard's Peking period came to an end. Earlier in 1943, a clandestine BBC broadcast had wrongly announced that he had been killed by bandits on the Chinese-Tibetan border.[185] Yet his life was not to end in China although he still died in exile elsewhere. The stay in the East came to an end when he returned to France in 1946. However, he still maintained an interest in reading, reflecting, and writing about Eastern religions, especially in relation to the role of mysticism and spirituality in the contemporary world. If anything, these themes gained further prominence throughout the following years.

4

The Ongoing Quest

Teilhard's last years were spent in the West. It is true to say however, that even when he lived in the Far East the West was always with him; throughout the years of exile it remained his true intellectual and spiritual home. After being back in France for several years he publicly admitted, however, that a good part of his heart had been left in China and that he would return to work there, should conditions allow him to do so.[1]

It is certain that, without the experience of the East, his thought would not have developed in the way it did. It would never have reached the same perspectives of unity, universality, and convergence, searching for a spirit of one earth which ultimately transcends both East and West.

The last period of Teilhard's life is divided between the years spent in Paris (1946-51) and the years in New York (1951-55), interrupted by two study tours to South Africa (1951 and 1953) and brief visits to Argentina, Brazil and Trinidad.

After returning to the West, Teilhard's life was characterized as much by uncertainty and misunderstanding as during his earlier years in China. Some people think that these last years add nothing new to his work and that the essays written during this period repeat only what was said earlier. But only a superficial reading can lead to this impression. If one studies his works in their chronological sequence, one is struck by the fundamental thrust of his vision and the immense coherence of his central themes from 1916 to 1955. And yet new questions were asked, new insights added, the creative surge forward continued until the day of death on Easter Sunday 1955.

Teilhard's mind remained open to new ideas until the end. He was interested in the latest developments in science, psychology, sociology, and religion, and for ever questioned both scientific and religious orthodoxies. On one hand, he upheld the highest demands for exact standards in scientific research, pressing for a further advance in the human effort to seek knowledge and understanding but, on the other, he saw this as part of the same fundamental quest for unity which elsewhere found expression in spirituality and mysticism. Science, religion, and mysticism are part of one and the same longing in the hearts and minds of men. To see this, Teilhard felt, it is necessary to break the boundaries of a narrowly understood science and remove the fetters of outworn creeds.

This is forcefully expressed throughout the last years of his life, particularly in his unpublished diary,[2] but also in letters.[3] The pages of Teilhard's diary are the most convincing proof of the versatility, range and depth of his mind, vigorous, creative, and open to the last. They never relate external events or personal occurrences but, up to three days before his death, are packed with ideas and critical reflections. This last period was also one of intensive literary activity; in terms of the sheer quantity of titles it outnumbers any other[4] although the essays of this time tend to be shorter than before.

I

In Paris, Teilhard was at home with the capital's intellectual and social élite.[5] He found a congenial milieu meeting philosophers, scientists, artists, and Orientalists. It was particularly the contact with this last group which gave him an opportunity to discuss his experience of the East, reflect on its significance, and extend his reading on Eastern religions.

Yet Teilhard was in a very delicate personal position. The Jesuit order did not wish to draw further attention to his thought, nor did they want to incur its official censure by higher religious authorities. For these reasons, they asked him not to write or speak publicly on any philosophical or religious topic but to restrict himself exclusively to scientific activities. In deference to this request, Teilhard expressed his ideas only when talking to close friends or to small informal groups which met privately. Yet it was on occasions like these or when writing letters that he voiced his deep disappointment. Thus, he mentioned to one correspondent how humiliating it was not to be allowed to lecture publicly about his new understanding of Christian mysticism at a time when an Indian Swami was given an important platform at the Sorbonne in order to diffuse what Teilhard considered a rather 'nebulous' mysticism.[6]

But even his scientific activities were curtailed. In 1948, it was proposed to elect Teilhard, in recognition of his scientific achievements, to the Collège de France. To seek the necessary permission from the relevant religious authorities, Teilhard made his first and only visit to Rome. But unfortunately, permission to go ahead with the election was withheld and none of the restrictions on his work were lifted. Thus, the visit was hardly a happy one. Describing his impressions, he wrote home: 'Rome has not given me nor will it give me, I feel, any shock, either aesthetic or spiritual. I was expecting this. So far as the past is concerned, I am immunized; and as for the picturesque, there is nothing more to surprise me — after the great East'.[7] Deeply suffering from the lack of recognition of his thought and the restricted opportunities for work, he remembered with regret that, before 1940, 'it was so convenient . . . to be able to return for some time to China in order to be forgotten . . .'[8]

During his years in Paris Teilhard maintained close contact with the French branch of the *World Congress of Faiths*. His work for this movement is little known[9] but it provides evidence of his continued interest in Eastern religions and, even more, his support for the closer coming together of different religious traditions.

Sir Francis Younghusband founded the *World Congress of Faiths* in London in 1936. From the beginning, several French Orientalists showed an interest in this movement which aims at building bridges between the world faiths. For various reasons, however, a French branch did not come into existence until 1947. Before that, a group of individual Frenchmen had informally followed the activities of the *World Congress of Faiths* in England and, according to one of the founders of the French branch, after the war this small group mainly regained its vitality 'thanks to the presence of Teilhard' who, as guest and adviser, stimulated the members with his enthusiasm.[10]

Teilhard certainly knew of Sir Francis Younghusband;[11] whether he was aware of his interfaiths movement is difficult to say. Interestingly enough, one of the diary entries of the Peking period already mentions a 'congress of religions' in 1945: 'True structure of a congress of religions: to proceed through selected groups, composed of people who are *already converging* in the religion and mysticism of evolution — =nucleus of the religion *foreseen* for tomorrow'.[12] Shortly after his return to Paris, another diary entry of 1946 mentions the suggestion of 'an association for the sympathy and synergy of religions', built on a mutually shared concern for contemporary issues.[13]

The French branch of the *World Congress of Faiths*, first called 'Le Congrès Universel des Croyants' and subsequently 'Union des Croyants', was founded in 1947 by René Grousset, Louis Massignon, Georges Salles, Charles Puech, Paul Masson-Oursel, and Dr Loriot. The philosophers Edouard Le Roy, Etienne Gilson and Gabriel Marcel also gave their support.[14] Teilhard was asked to provide the inaugural address for the first meeting of the movement. As he himself was not permitted to speak publicly, this address on 'Faith in Man' (1947)[15] was read out in his absence by the well-known Orientalist René Grousset.

'Faith in man' is seen as a necessary 'elementary, primordial faith', providing the basis from where one must begin to work towards the summit of the spirit. Such a commonly shared basis is required as 'the general atmosphere in which the higher, more elaborated forms of faith which we all hold in one form or another may best (indeed *can only*) come together'.[16] Looking at the development of the French branch of the *World Congress of Faiths* fifteen years later, Louis Massignon called this address in retrospect 'an outstanding text'[17] which from the start gave a definite direction to the work of this interfaith movement in France.

But Teilhard was personally present at some smaller meetings during the following years. This is evident from a long discussion on religion and mysticism[18] in which he took part with Louis Massignon, René Grousset, Aldous Huxley, and Gabriel Marcel. During 1949 and 1950, he also gave three talks to small groups of the movement meeting privately in members' houses. In addition, he drafted two pages stating the aims of the French branch of the *World Congress of Faiths*.[19]

In his understanding, it is not the object of the *World Congress of Faiths* to proclaim the essential sameness of all religions, nor should it reject out of hand any purely humanistic creed. Rather, the movement should attempt to bring closer together all those who believe in a future for man and the world. The possibility of such a future depends now on the union of all individuals, races, and nations. Although conditioned by technical and social progress, this union can ultimately only be achieved through sharing a common vision : a supreme centre of attraction and personalization is required. The different type of scientific thought and religious faith have to be in much closer contact; only then can a convergent vision emerge. Religions on their own cannot achieve human unity but they have an essential contribution to make for, without the central insights of the great religious traditions, human efforts towards creating greater sympathy, understanding, and union cannot find their true centre.[20]

Because of his officially precarious position, Teilhard was never a publicly prominent member of the French branch of the *World Congress of Faiths*; yet it is known that he took an active part in many committee meetings.[21] Among the adherents of other faiths present on the committee were an Iranian Sufi, a Confucian, and Swami Siddheswarananda from the Ramakrishna-Mission with whom Teilhard had discussions on yoga and meditation.[22]

Swami Siddheswarananda, who had been in Paris since 1937, was particularly interested in the comparison between the mysticism of St John of the Cross and Vedanta. Although Teilhard did not agree with his interpretation, the two men seem to have had much sympathy and understanding for each other. This is confirmed by a comment from Swami Siddheswarananda's successor who wrote that the Swami 'met Père Teilhard de Chardin, and was impressed by the personality of the man. In a private letter he commented on de Chardin's capacity of listening to the other; and how Swami Siddheswarananda felt that he himself should acquire the same trait'.[23]

Teilhard was particularly friendly with the secretary of 'Le Congrès Universal des Croyants', Madame Solange Lemaître, with whom he remained in close contact until his death. His correspondence with her, which remains unpublished so far, represents an important exchange of ideas bearing on many aspects of religion and mysticism.[24] It is probably through her that he first learnt about the plan for founding a French branch of the *World Congress of Faiths*.

Solange Lemaître was then working at the Oriental museum in Paris, the Musée Guimet,[25] in close collaboration with René Grousset. Earlier, she had worked for many years for the Association 'Amis de l'Orient'. The study of Eastern religions was her particular interest; she had published in this field and, in subsequent years, she became well known through her three volume anthology *Textes mystiques d'Orient et d'Occident*.[26] This selection of mystical texts through the ages from both East and West was discussed in detail with Teilhard when she was preparing the book. His ideas are to some extent reflected in this work as are those of the Orientalists Jacques Bacot and Louis Massignon.[27] The contemporary section of the anthology includes an extract of Teilhard's essay 'The Mass on the World' (1923), published here before it was available anywhere else. It is prefaced by a short introduction on Teilhard, known to have been written by himself.[28]

Even when he had left France, he maintained a continuous interest in the work of the French branch of the *World Congress of Faiths* as can be seen from his correspondence. In 1952, he wrote that the work of this movement, however modest, may be important in bringing about the transformation of religious thought, provided that 'it is not dominated by too "oriental" a notion of the relations between matter and spirit'.[29] In his last letter to Solange Lamaître, written one month before his death, he mentions that the required religious and mystical transformation may be stimulated by the work of the 'Union des Croyants'.[30] Although he personally still understood this transformation too narrowly as occurring within a predominantly Christian framework, these references express a greater awareness of the need for religious unity and a world ecumenism on Teilhard's part than is generally recognized. Mme Lemaître confirms this when she relates that, on his last visit to Paris in 1954, Teilhard especially told her to look after the 'Union des Croyants' because it would be 'the summit movement of tomorrow'.[31]

II

On his return from China, Teilhard also developed a close friendship with another member of the 'Union des Croyants', the Orientalist René Grousset.[32] His conversations stimulated further reading on Teilhard's part and to some extent helped him to modify his approach to Eastern religions.

According to Cuénot, Teilhard 'spent some time studying Far Eastern art and philosophy at the Musée Guimet' although it is impossible to obtain any precise information about this.[33] The contact with Orientalists and the intensive reading of this last period in Paris certainly provided an opportunity for Teilhard to reflect on his experiences in the East and led him to appreciate more than before the specific insights of Eastern religions. This found its reflection in 'The Spiritual Contribution of the Far East' (1947)[34] which is, incidentally, the only essay referring to the East in its title.

It seems that before writing this essay, Teilhard clarified certain details about Eastern metaphysics in discussions with his friend René Grousset.[35] His influence is also evident from Teilhard's diary. It contains several references to Grousset's book *Le Bilan de l'Histoire* (1946), which includes two chapters on 'The Contribution of Asia' and 'The Contribution of India' to the history of human civilization. Thus, the book may well have suggested to Teilhard the choice of his own essay title 'The Spiritual Contribution of the Far East', written during the following year. His diary includes extracts and comments from Grousset's book, dealing with aspects of Hinduism,

Amida and Zen Buddhism as well as Taoism.

The continuing interest in Eastern religions is also documented by other titles. Olivier Lacombe's book *'L'Absolu selon le Vedanta*[36] dealing with the great Hindu theologian Ramanuja, is quoted by Teilhard as evidence that Hindu thought freed itself from extreme monism and comes close to theism.

During 1947, he read through the unpublished letters of the writer Romain Rolland to Mademoiselle Jeanne Mortier.[37] These deal with several aspects of Indian thought, especially the comparison between Indian and Western mysticism. The letters cover over twenty years, including the time when Romain Rolland was working on his well-known biographies of Ramakrishna and Vivekananda. They also refer to Rolland's correspondence with Rudolf Otto and Otto's work in the comparative study of mysticism. It was planned to publish this correspondence and Teilhard wrote a brief introduction to it but, together with the letters, it remains unpublished so far.

In his biography, Cuénot notes that Teilhard attended the Orientalists' Congress in 1948 without mentioning any further details.[38] This certainly came about through Teilhard's close contact with French Orientalists, especially with René Grousset. The XXI International Orientalists' Congress took place in Paris, with Jacques Bacot as president and René Grousset as general secretary, and Teilhard is listed in the published proceedings as a member of the honorary Congress Committee.[39]

More intriguing is the fact that during the autumn of the same year, 1948, whilst on his visit to Rome, Teilhard was reading about Indian history and religion. The Rome diary quotes extracts from George Dunbar's two-volume work on the *History of India*,[40] dealing with the main developments of Indian civilization. Teilhard's notes refer to the Indus valley civilization, Aryan and Dravidian elements in Indian culture, classical Hindu scriptures, the development of the major divinities and the caste system. They also deal with Buddhism and Jainism, the expansion of Buddhism overseas and its extinction in India; the rise of Islam and the Moghuls, especially Akbar; and the coming of the early Western explorers and Jesuits to India. Whilst Dunbar's work is primarily a political history, it obviously refers to events of general cultural and religious importance and it is interesting to see that Teilhard's notes deal mainly with this last aspect, i.e. the development of religion in India. He also criticizes Dunbar for his mistaken view about the late appearance of *bhakti* in India, that is to say, the movement of fervent religious devotion to a personal God. Teilhard rightly points out that Dunbar fails to recognize the early origin of this movement in ancient India as well as its influence on certain developments in Buddhism.[41]

More important still, at the very heart of Christendom and at a time when Teilhard was drafting the first plan for his spiritual autobiography, 'The Heart of Matter',[42] he explicitly refers to Radhakrishnan's book *The Hindu View of Life*, noting down in English: 'A *central Reality* which is one with *the deeper self* of Man'. This is obviously a shortened version of a quotation from Radhakrishnan found in Dunbar's work. Teilhard added to it a comment in French which says: 'That is the whole question: to define the central self: identification or union'. In brackets he noted 'Essence: Road of the East'. A second comment reads: '=The whole question (is): where to place *this Centre*: $\genfrac{}{}{0pt}{}{\text{of convergence through tension.}'^{43}}{\text{of relaxation}}$

At the beginning of the following year, Teilhard enquired from his friend Solange Lemaître whether she could advise him on the best book on Taoism for the non-specialized reader, and also, where to find information about Chu Hsi, the Chinese 'Spencer'.[44] Again, there exists no information about the reply of his correspondent nor is it known whether Teilhard followed up these references and for what purpose they were required.

It is in any case impossible to reconstruct Teilhard's entire reading for this or any other period of his life. References to books occur at random but they cannot all be mentioned here. We shall return to some later when we discuss the interpretation of Eastern religions and mysticism. For the present suffice it to say that these references reveal a greater interest and familiarity with certain aspects of Eastern thought than one would expect from reading Teilhard's essays. Yet at the same time it must be stressed that he never studied Eastern religions in their own right, as presented from within, by their own adherents. In fact, he did not read these works primarily from a perspective of scholarly enquiry but mainly from one of a deep personal commitment. Thus, it is not surprising that his attention was often drawn to specific works through particular friendships or in search for a confirmation of his own thought.

It was through such a personal contact that Teilhard learnt about Sri Aurobindo's magnum opus *The Life Divine* which Jacques Masui,[45] editor of a journal on comparative spirituality and a series of Eastern religious texts in translation, lent to him in either 1953 or 1954. Teilhard understood Sri Aurobindo mainly as a 'modernist' and, after reading some chapters, he apparently returned *The Life Divine* saying, 'This is comparable to my own work, but for the Indian tradition'.[46] Such a remark no doubt refers to Aurobindo's and Teilhard's shared attempt to integrate a modern evolutionary perspective with the traditional insights of their religion.

Other titles read during these last years deal with wider aspects of religion and culture. As examples may be mentioned here E. Brunner, *Christianity and Civilizations*; M. Eliade, *Le Mythe de l'Eternel Retour*; J. Huxley, *Religion without Revelation*; C. Jung, *Modern Man in Search of a Soul*;[47] J. Needham, *Order and Life*, and *Time: The Refreshing River*; F. C. Northrop, *The Meeting of East and West*.[48]

All these works indicate his wide range of interests. From his essays and letters it is clear that he emphasized above all the importance of central Christian insights for the contemporary world. At the same time he stressed the present need for a transformation of Christianity. However, such a transformation cannot come about without a movement of convergence which must include the contribution of Eastern religions. But these ideas were hardly worked out in a systematic form.

III

When Teilhard read about J. Casserley's book *The Retreat of Christianity from the Modern World*,[49] he felt almost jealous about the author's reference to a 'Christianity which surpasses itself'. It so coincided with his own perspective that he wished he had found this 'perfect expression' himself. The book convinced him that 'in the non-Roman branches of Christianity a spirit of religious invention is finally manifesting itself which is the sole possible agent of a true ecumenism : not the sterile and conservative ecumenism of a "common ground" but the creative ecumenism of a "convergence" . . . on to a common ideal'.[50] However, he had also been convinced for some time that 'the great theologians of Rome' did not facilitate a 'convergence of religions' nor did they grasp what such a phenomenon implied.[51] Although Teilhard himself did not fully map out the implications of such an approach, he sensed the importance of certain insights from the East.

Among the many tentative suggestions in his diary, one of the most puzzling and least expected is the reference to the Indian god Shiva and to 'Christ-Omega/Shiva' in 1948.[52] Most intriguing is an extract from a letter to 'Mg'.[53] After referring to the overpowering forces of the cosmos which can neither be tamed nor appeased, he says that '. . . It is not enough to refuse or ridicule Shiva : for *he exists*. What is necessary, is to christify him. Christ would not be complete if he did not integrate Shiva (as a component), whilst transforming him'.[54] Not only the immense organic structure of the universe, but also its apparent indifference to the sufferings of man and the blind inhumanity of its forces of destruction may illuminate certain aspects of the Divine for man. It is these which must be integrated into our image of God, he thought.

Teilhard's reflections occur within the context of further quotations from René Grousset's book *Le Bilan de l'Histoire*, mentioned before. The earlier extracts, dating from 1946, also refer to Shiva's cosmic dance and the contradictory aspects associated with his nature.[55] Grousset depicts the great Indian god Shiva as a figure embodying the untamed forces of nature; he represents the powers of destruction as well as those of periodic renewal, for in him are integrated the forces of joy, suffering and energy which pulsate through the universe. This ambivalence of Shiva appealed to Teilhard who saw the cosmos as animated by divine energy, filled and alive with 'christic' elements, and it is precisely this cosmic dimension of God which traditional Christianity has never fully explored.[56]

Here again, as so often, Teilhard briefly perceived but never explored in depth an enriching Eastern insight which might transform and enlarge the Christian concept and experience of the Divine. However, whereas his vision of the cosmos and his increasingly ecumenical view of humanity made him 'most anxious to integrate Eastern thought',[57] his emphasis on the unique nature of personhood made him also strongly repudiate other aspects of Eastern religions. Several times he emphatically underlined the difference of his vision from that of Hinduism, for example, so much so that he has been accused of a deep misunderstanding of this religious tradition. For him, the Christian view of man's relation to God cannot be expressed in Hindu terms, at least not in those of Vedanta monism. Thus he wrote to a correspondent: 'If you only knew how much I mistrust Hindu mysticism – it is based not on union, which generates love, but on identification, which excludes love'.[58]

It is quite surprising, therefore, that one of the earliest books on his thought, published during his lifetime, placed his views among those of 'the existentialists and Hinduisers'. In contrast to this opinion, Teilhard was at pains to point out that these two groups were in fact his *bêtes noires*.[59] He felt so concerned about this criticism that, on the one occasion when he stated his intellectual position in public by giving a newspaper interview, he strongly repudiated the false interpretation of his thought as either 'totalitarianism' or 'hinduising pantheism' which seeks the spiritual in the direction 'of an identification of beings with an underlying common ground'.[60]

At the same time, he became aware of the growing interest in Indian religions in the West, due especially to the spiritual emptiness left by the Second World War. In the intellectual climate of the postwar period some embraced atheism and existentialism whilst others turned to Eastern gurus for direction. Teilhard learned about the teachings of these gurus through some of his friends who became closely involved with Indian religions. For example, his diary refers to the guru of one of his former acquaintances from China, Ella Maillart, with whom he shared the knowledge and love of Chinese Turkestan.[61] He noted down what Ella Maillart's guru had to say about the nature of man's true self, and he commented again on the necessary distinction of whether the higher self is found through identification or convergence.[62]

Two other friends in New York belonged to a group directed by a Hindu Swami. Teilhard described the spirituality of this circle as 'terribly vague',[63] just as the mysticism preached by another Swami appeared to him to be 'infra-Western'.[64] However, he was also prepared to admit that, for many Western people, Indian religions may hold the answer to their spiritual quest, for at present, it is so difficult to pierce through the hardened forms of religion which Christian theologians propound as 'orthodoxy'.[65] Too often, their teaching presents a 'religion without mystery' where 'everything is clear, everything certain, everything "revealed" '.[66] Some of the best Western minds may be religiously uprooted not for a lack, but for an excess, of religious desire, a thirst which remains unquenched.[67] The dynamic forces which animate neo-Hindu, neo-Buddhist and, even more, neo-humanist movements make traditional Christianity appear tame and 'underdeveloped' at times. It is from this spirit of dissatisfaction and the growing realization of the need for renewal that Teilhard increasingly searched not only for a Christian, but a 'trans-Christian' God whose image corresponds to man's growing need for adoration. As this need is no longer fully met in Christianity, people in the West join centres and groups *where the religious quest is still open*'.[68]

Although Teilhard expressed such views only in private and not in public, his influence was nevertheless judged to be too great in France. In 1951, the offer of a research post in anthropology from the Wenner-Gren Foundation in New York led to his residence in the United States; once more he was practically in exile.[69] The stimulating experience of different intellectual horizons, a renewed contact with field-work in South Africa as well as a brief return to France in 1954, could not compensate for the fact that these last years were extremely difficult and lonely. Teilhard's isolation and depression were enhanced by the feeling of being misunderstood by his own order, his 'beloved family' which contained some of his closest friends.[70] Father Leroy has described the difficulties of these last years with much sensitivity, emphasizing Teilhard's suffering and 'inner martyrdom'. This agony and struggle unto the last has also been well brought out in the most recent biography by Mary and Ellen Lukas.[71] It is all the more extraordinary and moving that the two great essays 'The Heart of Matter' (1950) and 'The Christic' (1955) were produced during these years. A fundamental affirmation of Teilhard's deep faith and hope, they bear permanent witness to the compelling force of a lifelong inner vision and are a proof of the tremendous psychic energy which sustained him in the face of all opposition.

Father Leroy has depicted his friend as frequently silent and withdrawn during the last months of his life. However, one of the surprising utterances reported from this period is Teilhard's avowal, 'I now live permanently in the presence of God'.[72] It is precisely this experience of living in God's presence which radiates through the last pages of his work. They may be considered as the culmination of his creative power and are written with a fervour and intensity only found in his earliest essays.

Throughout his life, Teilhard was a wanderer between different worlds. His life and thought are interwoven like the parts of an immense symphony with ever new variations on a basic theme. This theme is the supreme adventure of man's ascent to the spirit, and the continuous breakthrough of God's presence in the world of matter and flesh. Teilhard's vision, like that of other seers before him, was one of consuming fire, kindled by the radiant powers of love. It was a mystical vision deeply Christian in origin and orientation; yet it broke through traditional boundaries and grew into a vision global in intent.

In this process of growth and expansion, the experience of the East, its peoples, cultures and religions, played an indispensable part. As he himself admitted, the invitation to come to China proved to be 'the decisive event of his destiny' for until then, he had felt the attraction of the earth without really understanding the greatness of its phenomena.[73]

His vision of convergence, of the complementary religious insights of East and West, and of the need for a new understanding of Christianity, emerged in China; it impressed itself upon his mind with even fuller force and urgency on his return to the West. Today, the attraction of Indian religions to many Westerners is greater still than it was during Teilhard's time. The questions which he asked then are even more important now although they may have to be asked in a different way. But in spite of differences in detail, the basic orientation of his search and the open-endedness of his quest, particularly in later years, may well point beyond Christianity as we know it. At a time when few Western contemporaries were aware of and alive to the problems of modern spirituality, Teilhard was already seeking insights in the East and stressing the central importance of mysticism for religion today.

We have traced some of the events and contacts which influenced Teilhard in his approach to Eastern religions. Now we shall discuss some central texts which show his comparative evaluation of Eastern and Western religions, always undertaken from the perspective of a mystical quest. More than that, these texts reveal an ongoing search for a new approach to mysticism in a new era of human consciousness.

II

Eastern and Western
Religions
in a Converging World

The revival of inwardness may prove to be a
revolutionary act in relation to the objectified
world; it may prove to be a revolt against
determinism or, in other words, a spiritual
permeation of the world in order to inspire and
transfigure it.

Nikolai Berdyaev

I believe the mystical is less different, less
separated from the rational than one says, but I
also believe that the whole problem which the
world, and we in particular, are presently facing,
is a problem of faith.

Pierre Teilhard de Chardin

5

The Search for Unity:
From Monistic Pantheism
to Mysticism

In the formulation of his religious thought Teilhard came to distinguish gradually, but early, between monistic pantheism and mysticism. This distinction is absolutely fundamental for his approach to Eastern religions. For Teilhard, pantheism and mysticism are distinct but not unrelated. Their different characteristics were mainly elaborated in the early writings, during the years which have been called 'the mystical period'.

It must be borne in mind that Teilhard's interpretation of mysticism was not primarily theoretical or speculative; rather, it proceeded from the experiential basis of a personal vision. The pattern of this inner realization unfolds clearly on reading his works diachronically in the order in which they were conceived. The early essays, written after the formative experience of Egypt, but before the prolonged contact with the Far East, introduce an important distinction between different forms of mysticism which, in essence, was maintained throughout later writings. However, with the stay in the Far East, further references to this distinction, especially in essays written after 1932, almost always include comparisons with Eastern religions.

I

Before we examine these texts, it may be helpful to comment briefly on Teilhard's method. As already mentioned, his thinking was always rooted in a primary layer of religious experience. This must be understood in the widest sense for it includes certain 'peak experiences' as well as his continuous adherence to the Christian faith and to religious practices such as daily prayer, celebration of the Mass, regular retreats, and so on. It would be wrong, however, to consider this religious experience in isolation from his total life experience, and especially, to separate it from his experience of scientific work. It is the reflection on the entire range of his experience which led Teilhard to formulate certain key ideas, recurring like 'leitmotifs' throughout his work. Prolonged scientific training and research deeply influenced his expression so that his ideas and vocabulary are strongly marked by biological patterns of thought. This is particularly true of the generalized use of evolutionary categories, including such themes as organic growth, complexity and synthesis.[1]

Already at an early stage Teilhard was conscious that he had a method of his own which linked the particular to the universal, the cosmic-natural-scientific dimension to the universal-personal-religious sphere, and the immanent to the transcendent.[2] Apart from the transference of scientific terms to philosophical and religious thought, his method also includes the use of typology, particularly when interpreting historical data.

This typological approach to history means that 'Teilhard understands every phase of history in terms of an overarching paradigmatic pattern'.[3] This pattern is often represented through the image of a spiral, a synthesis of the circle and the straight line. A cyclical interpretation of history implies a fundamental recurrence of events whereas a linear interpretation leaves room for novelty. Through the image of the spiral, history is interpreted in terms of ascending levels in which patterns recur together with an element of novelty. This typological method of interpretation is evident in Teilhard's approach to the development of human societies and civilizations. It is also apparent in his approach to religions where specific 'types' of development are singled out and compared. At the neglect of a wealth of historical detail, these 'types' tend to emphasize certain patterns and key developments.

When reading Teilhard's essays, one must not only keep in mind this scientific and typological orientation but also remember the general nature of his writings. It is important to distinguish between the frequently revised, final versions of books and essays destined for publication, and the many briefer notes which he left as summaries or lecture-outlines. The shorter essays are often only variations of a theme more extensively dealt with elsewhere, whereas the major essays were always carefully planned and only written down after considerable reflection. A particular piece of writing may thus have taken several months or even years to reach its final form.

Teilhard was a prolific writer. Apart from the many volumes of scientific, philosophical and religious writings, he maintained an enormous correspondence and kept a diary for forty years. This is not a diary in the ordinary sense of the word but a series of notes, jotted down in exercise books which contain, in the words of Father Leroy, 'any comment of a philosophical, scientific or religious nature he thought worth preserving. These notes . . . with no apparent connecting thread, will enable students of Père Teilhard's thought to follow day by day . . . the workings of a ceaselessly active mind'.[4]

When one compares the entries in Teilhard's diary where he first noted down the idea of a new essay, followed later by its detailed plan and title, with the letters and essays of the same period, one can follow the unfolding of his ideas step by step. Thus, one discovers how his thought emerged, grew and matured until it found its definite expression in a specific essay.

To understand Teilhard's thought on a particular theme and assess its full meaning, it is necessary to compare all available texts and to study his writings in their chronological order. This, however, is an especially difficult task as the published volumes of his writings do not follow each other chronologically. With the exception of a few titles, each book represents a collection of essays chosen from the entire span of his life. This manner of publication, perhaps the only one possible at the time, can easily give a misleading impression of Teilhard's thought and has in no way facilitated the understanding of a notoriously complex and subtle thinker.

II

Most early essays found in *Writings in the Time of War* include a discussion of pantheism, monism, and mysticism[5] but we shall look in particular at two of special significance. These are 'Cosmic Life' (1916)[6] and 'The Mystical Milieu' (1917)[7], studied together with contemporaneous entries in the *Journal* and the important later essay 'Pantheism and Christianity' (1923).[8]

The particular attraction of pantheism lies in the fact that it represents an all-embracing unitive experience, for it implies the fundamental oneness of all phenomena. For Teilhard, this experience is closely linked with man's response to nature. The natural world which surrounds man is both infinitely attractive and repellant; with the variety and immensity of its phenomena it seems so much greater than man himself. The experience of nature may produce states of anxiety and alienation in some people but it can lead others to an awareness of 'cosmic consciousness', that is, a feeling of expansion and fusion. Teilhard wrote in 'Cosmic Life' that man's first impulse in this experience of cosmic consciousness is *'to allow himself to be rocked* like a child by the great mother in whose arms he has just woken'[9] and feel cradled in deepest security.

Nature's attraction lies particularly in the great and mysterious unity of her phenomena, 'les grands homogènes', as Teilhard called them:

> Entranced by those great homogeneous systems – ocean, air, desert – man, poised over emptiness and silence, locked up within himself, envies the intimate fusion of the drops of water in the sea, of the molecules in the atmosphere; and he glimpses the bliss there would be in becoming continually more intermingled with Another, in sinking deeper and deeper into it, like smoke that vanishes, like the sound that dies away in space, like the stone that slips gently down to the bottom of the sea.[10]

This is a strictly monistic experience, typical of all forms of pantheism which remain naturalistic and immanent and lead

man to worship the divine around him. Teilhard asked himself:

> And why, indeed, should I not worship it, the stable, the
> great, the rich, the mother, the divine? Is not matter, in its
> own way, eternal and immense? Is it not matter whose
> absence our imagination refuses to conceive . . . Is it not
> the absolutely fertile generatrix, the *Terra Mater*, that
> carries within her the seeds of all life and the sustenance
> of all joy? Is it not at once the common origin of beings
> and the only end we could dream of, the primordial and
> indestructible essence from which all emerged and into
> which all returns . . . All the attributes which a philosophy
> of the spirit posits as lying outside the universe, do they
> not in fact lie at the opposite pole? Are they not realized
> and are they not to be attained in the depths of the world,
> in divine matter?[11]

This appeal of matter, of the divine in nature, is everlasting. On
one hand, Teilhard emphasized man's intimate relation to
nature, to cosmic life, and recognized the appeal of a monistic
pantheism but, on the other hand, he also outlined the possibility of a different kind of pantheism, leaving room for a
transcendence beyond nature. Thus, he distinguished 'non-
Christian pantheisms' and 'paganism', which allow only a
'communion with earth', from a possible Christian pantheism
based on a 'communion with God through earth'. For a naturalistic, immanent pantheism

> everything in the universe is uniformly true and valuable:
> so much so that the fusion of the individual must be effected
> with all, *without distinction and without qualification*.
> Everything that is active, that moves or breathes, every
> physical, astral, or animate energy, every fragment of force,
> every spark of life, is equally sacred; for, in the humblest
> atom and the most brilliant star, in the lowest insect and
> the finest intelligence, there is the radiant smile and thrill
> of the *same Absolute*.[12]

This fundamental equivalence without distinction of everything that exists, 'at the expense of conscious and personal
life, for the benefit of the rudimentary and diffuse modes of
being', is for Teilhard the basic characteristic of what he first
called the 'Eastern vision of the blue Lotus'. From his sources
and later characterizations it is clear that he identified this
form of experience with Eastern, and especially Hindu,
monism.

This monistic pantheism is a very basic and powerful experience; it constitutes the permanent 'temptation of matter',
consisting of a search for fusion and identity with an initial
source. He equated such an attitude with effortless enjoyment,
inertia, and 'the tendency to follow the line of least resist-
ance'.[13] In his diary, this experience is described as *pagan,
naive pantheism . . .* which envisages only the fusion with
the original All: thus, there are no real grades in being, no
progress, . . . *no failures*'. For Teilhard, however, this powerful experience had to be prolonged and ultimately transcended.

Man's quest for the All, his passion for unity, cannot be
adequately satisfied through fusion with a common ground or
nostalgia for the past. To seek return, whether to primal
matter or the time of origin, proves a futile quest. The more
the seeker advances, the more he realizes: ' "*The world is
empty*", that is to say, by remaining on the mere level of
experience, one goes around the world without penetrating it
. . .' Teilhard asked himself: 'Why does the pantheistic feeling so often take its origin from emptiness (sea, desert, stellar
spaces, the past . . .)?' In his experience, these phenomena did
not possess the fullness he sought: 'The past, the far-away
distance are empty and give access to nothing'. This remark
shows that the magic spell of the cosmos was already shattered for him; the fulfilment of nature's promise had to be
found elsewhere.

'Where do we seek the secret? — in the desert? In the far-
away past? In secret matter? It is to be found in the future
and its increase (*unforeseeable* because not open to experience
yet . . .)'.[14] The ultimate term is still to be achieved through
a maximum of energy and effort; it is a union to come, a goal
in the future. Through it alone will the pantheistic yearning

for oneness be stilled.

Teilhard's powerful nature experiences together with his theistic faith and the realization of the fundamental importance of the personal and social world, made him search for a synthesis between the immanent and transcendant aspirations of man's mystical quest. Early in 1916, he noted in his diary:

> If I write anything, if I become intellectually active, it must be, it seems to me, *in order* to bring together, to reconcile (in a sense) God and the world, that is to say, to show that God eminently fulfils our immanent and pantheistic aspirations (i.e. God and matter; 'the divine matter' (=amazing realization of this in our Lord Jesus Christ).[15]

This intention was put into practice in 'Cosmic Life', written soon afterwards. The essay is preceded by the words: 'There is a communion with God, and a communion with earth, and a communion with God through earth . . .'[16] The mere 'communion with earth' refers to the experience of monistic pantheism whilst 'communion with God' stands for an excessively other-worldly attitude, linked to a view of God and religion as separate from the world. The exclusive concern for the transcendent, often regarded as the main characteristic of a religious quest, does not place enough importance on the value of human effort and the development of the world.

These two attitudes – communion with earth and communion with God – are regarded as incomplete; only the synthesis of both is acceptable. This synthesis of 'communion with God through earth' is not simply a combination of two different attractions but something of a new order altogether. The initial experience of 'cosmic consciousness', the love of the earth and all its realities, is prolonged and transformed through the experience of God as both an immanent and transcendent presence. Strictly speaking, therefore, one cannot say that monistic pantheism is rejected by Teilhard although, linguistically, expressions of rejection are found. Rather, this form of pantheism is judged to be insufficient; it finds its fulfilment only in a fully developed theistic mysticism. The letter, in turn, is not exclusively spiritual but assumes unto itself, in an ascending order, the various levels of reality, material as well as spiritual. Unlike Zaehner in his book *Mysticism Sacred and Profane*, Teilhard does not see a break between 'sacred' and 'profane' mysticism; on the contrary, the former is a continuation of the latter.

Teilhard referred to himself as a 'naturally pantheistic soul'.[17] He initially experienced the appeal of the Absolute through the contact with nature whose unity and homogeneity appeared to contrast starkly with the plurality of human beings and their scandalous 'heterogeneity'. The presence of another person seems to interrupt the unity of the world, to pluralize it for the seeker of ultimate unity. The problematic aspect of interpersonal relationships was acutely felt by Teilhard when he described the 'other' as an intruder, as someone who breaks the unity and coherence of the mystic's inner vision and disturbs his solitude. In his diary he wrote: 'Who says person, says contingent, artificial, fragmentary . . .'[18] and his intrinsic difficulty with 'the other' is more forcefully expressed in the much later *Le Milieu Divin*:

> But 'the other man', my God — by which I do not mean 'the poor, the halt, the lame and the sick', but 'the other' quite simply as 'other', the one who seems to exist independently of me because his universe seems closed to mine, and who seems to shatter the unity and the silence of the world for me — would I be sincere if I did not confess that my instinctive reaction is to rebuff him?[19]

Thus, the realm of the persona! appeared at first problematic to Teilhard. He realized this particularly through the profoundly disturbing experience of the war. At the same time, the close friendship with his cousin Marguerite made him see the great enrichment found in personal relationships. Ultimately, the mystic quest must lead to a reality which embraces the cosmic as well as the personal, the human and the divine. For Teilhard, the only reality which answers to this is the vision of Christ which brings together the universal and the personal.

III

Teilhard's movement from monistic pantheism or nature mysticism to a person-centred mysticism is fully described in the essay 'The Mystical Milieu' (1917). Written more than one year after 'Cosmic Life', it presents the progress of mystical experience in a series of expanding circles, an approach which has been compared to that of St Teresa's *Interior Castle*.

The first three circles are seen as those of presence, consistence, and energy; they stand for the homogeneity of the universe, for its fundamental oneness. Teilhard describes the 'seer', another name for the 'mystic', as 'immersed in a *universal Milieu*, higher than that which contains the restlessness of ordinary, sensibly apprehended life: a Milieu *that knows no change*, immune to the surge of superficial vicissitudes – a *homogeneous* Milieu in which contrasts and differences are toned down'. But this experience may lead him to 'be lost in naturalistic mysticism, or take the degraded form of godless pantheism'.[20] Nevertheless, the passion for unity and universality remains the most basic mystic intuition. The mystic finds the incorruptible principle of the universe and this extends everywhere: '*the world is filled* and filled with the Absolute. To see this is to be made free'. But the mystical effort to see must give way to '*the effort to feel and to surrender*'.[21] The vision must lead to a communion with the essence of the universe which is creative action, pulsating energy: 'The mystic was looking for the devouring fire which he could identify with the Divine that summons him from all sides: science points it out to him. *See, the universe is ablaze!*'[22] The reference to science may at first seem odd here. Yet it is through the evolutionary insights of science that the universe comes more alive than ever before. That science can stimulate a mystical quest and vision has recently again been demonstrated by Fritjof Capra's exciting exploration of the parallels between modern physics and Eastern mysticism in his book *The Tao of Physics*.[23]

For Teilhard, the mystic is plunged into an 'ocean of energy' from which he draws 'undiluted joy':

In very truth, it is God, and God alone whose Spirit stirs up the whole mass of the universe in ferment.

. . . . . .

The fact is that creation has never stopped. The creative act is one huge continual gesture, drawn out over the totality of time. It is still going on.[24]

The circle of energy is a transitional phase leading into the 'Heterogeneous', the 'circle of the spirit' and, at its summit, the 'circle of the person'. This is a dialectical development which stands in contrast to the first three circles. There, the mystic was immersed in some universal Divine and lived in 'a sort of *higher dream* in which the distinctions of practical life seem of minor importance and are blurred'.[25] In the two succeeding circles, the experience of the Divine as merely immanent is surpassed. Now the seer turns from his own interiority to the multitude of other beings which, at first, had seemed 'an infliction hard to bear'.[26] The Divine itself is experienced as both transcendent to the cosmos and yet interwoven with it at all levels. The seer realizes that action and communion are neither situated in the divine or created sphere alone, 'but in a special reality born of their mutual interaction. The mystical milieu *is not a completed zone* in which beings, once they have succeeded in entering it, remain immobilized. It is a *complex* element, made up of *divinized created being* . . . We cannot give it precisely the name of God: it is his Kingdom. Nor can we say that it *is*: it is in the process of *becoming*.'[27]

The mystic now becomes the 'supreme *realist*' who fights the battle for the light, who moves forward to the real by searching to know, to love, and to fulfil it. For Teilhard, the mystical milieu gradually assumes a form at once divine and human which culminates in the person of Jesus. The last part of the essay invokes his name after each paragraph, and reads like a Jesus-prayer. The end of 'The Mystical Milieu' also states that this is only an introduction to mysticism for Teilhard did not feel qualified to describe the most sublime mystical states but only wished to emphasize their natural and cosmic roots without which no mystical experience can grow and be nourished. He recognized the need for contact with matter in the widest sense in order to sharpen man's sensibility and spoke of 'the vast cosmic realities that give God his tangible and palpable being here below'. In his view, the great Christian mystics cannot even be understood unless one realizes 'the full depth of the truth that *Jesus must be loved as a world*'.[28]

The aspirations of a naturalistic pantheism thus find their culmination in a rightly understood Christian pantheism. In this vision, a transcendent reality over and above the universe is acknowledged but at the same time, the Divine is experienced as the most intimate, and universally present, element of all realities in the cosmos. This 'universal element' is, by virtue of the Incarnation, found in Christ.[29] It is the 'christic element' present everywhere, but eminently so at the level of personal life and interpersonal encounter. The monistic experience of cosmic life and consciousness is crowned by the vision of the cosmic and universal Christ in whom all beings converge.[30] It is the same powerful and unitive experience which made the poet Gerard Manley Hopkins say that 'the world is charged with the grandeur of God' and that 'Christ plays in ten thousand places, lovely in limbs, and lovely in eyes not his to the Father through the features of men's faces'.[31]

Teilhard elaborated this unifying vision of mystical experience into a philosophical theory of 'creative union' which represents his answer to the problem of the one and the many.[32] For him, union always implies both unification and differentiation, and this theory is fundamental for his approach to all spiritual and material realities, for his understanding of personal relationships, and for his concept of God. Although Teilhard's vision of unity has been described as that of a 'christomonist',[33] he himself preferred to speak of 'pan-Christism', a term taken from Blondel, or of ' "pan-Christic" monism' and ' "pan-Christic" mysticism'.[34]

The deeply coherent vision of a union between God and the world found poetic expression in the title of other war essays, such as 'The Soul of the World' (1918)[35] and 'The Great Monad' (1918).[36] The 'mystical milieu' was later simply renamed 'divine milieu': a milieu suffused and charged with divine presence, a centre which draws man into intimate union and communion with God. At its roots, the mystical experience is always embedded in a natural and cosmic dimension but this is animated throughout by divine elements. The world has an activating centre from where all life and energy radiates.

The permanent value of the experience of pantheism lies in the fact that it may progressively lead into deeper forms of mysticism. There can be a progression from naturalistic, monistic pantheism to theistic and pan-christic mysticism. Rightly understood, pantheism can be seen as close, and even necessary, to Christianity. For Teilhard, this was the 'true pantheism', to be distinguished from any form of 'false pantheism'.

The difference between pantheism and mysticism was a fundamental one and permanently influenced his approach to Eastern religions. Teilhard arrived at this distinction through reflection on his own monistic experiences but one must not forget that these mainly occurred in Egypt. It is for this reason that his descriptions of pantheism frequently include references to the desert.

IV

Teilhard's approach to pantheism and mysticism can also be illustrated from his exchanges with Valensin and Blondel.[37] During the summer of 1919, Teilhard visited his friend Valensin in Jersey when the latter was working on an article about pantheism. Teilhard criticized his friend's work 'for dismissing too summarily "living pantheism"' and for understanding it in a too purely negative way. He tried to persuade Valensin 'to go beyond the refutation of pantheistic thought-systems by incorporating a second, constructive study' which would present a synthesis of the Christian faith. Valensin seems to have followed his friend's advice to some extent by revising his work. Yet in Teilhard's judgment, Valensin's approach to pantheism resulted more from the desire to construct a philosophy than from the need to revere an omnipresence in the universe.[38]

The extraordinary experience of this omnipresence rings

through Teilhard's own composition 'The Spiritual Power of Matter' (1919),[39] written during the same summer in Jersey. It culminates in the stirring 'Hymn to Matter' whose stark realism and radical concreteness can be easily misunderstood:

Blessed be you, harsh matter, barren soil, stubborn rock: you who yield only to violence, you who force us to work if we would eat.
Blessed be you, perilous matter, violent sea, untameable passion: you who unless we fetter you will devour us.
Blessed be you, mighty matter, irresistible march of evolution, reality ever new-born . . .
Blessed be you, universal matter, immeasurable time . . . : you who by overflowing and dissolving our narrow standards of measurement reveal to us the dimensions of God.
Blessed be you, impenetrable matter: you, who, interposed between our minds and the world of essences, cause us to languish with the desire to pierce through the seamless veil of phenomena.

. . . . . .

I bless you, matter, and you I acclaim: not as the pontiffs of science or the moralizing preachers depict you, debased, disfigured – a mass of brute forces and base appetites – but as you reveal yourself to me today, *in your totality and your true nature.*

. . . . . .

I acclaim you as the divine *milieu*, charged with creative power, as the ocean stirred by the Spirit, as the clay moulded and infused with life by the incarnate Word . . .[40]

This hymn concludes a story where a man is walking in the desert. He there comes upon the vision of an immense living heart moving palpably beneath the surface of things. This image symbolically expresses Teilhard's conviction that matter has a 'heart', a centre, and it is no coincidence that, more than thirty years later, 'The Spiritual Power of Matter' and its concluding 'Hymn to Matter' were appended to the autobiographical essay 'The Heart of Matter'.

When the philosopher Blondel read this and also the two versions of 'My Universe' (1918 and 1924)[41] and 'Pantheism and Christianity' (1923),[42] he objected to some of the details and argued that it was necessary 'to detach oneself from the illusory realism of the intellect and the senses'. According to Blondel, it is necessary to distinguish clearly :

> True pan-Christism sharply disassociates itself from anything having to do with physicism and pantheism. This means that it is important not to be a 'visionary', and the real seer is one who, contemplating in darkness, has the sense of the infinite richness of the mystery, one who never stops, as required by the masters of the mystical life, even at visions which are truly supernatural in character – less still, at symbols of his own invention.[43]

Although Teilhard had earlier declared his intention that 'the Church's mystical practice' should be 'the basic foundation' of his thinking,[44] he felt nevertheless that Blondel's approach to mysticism was 'more traditional' and 'orthodox' than his own and regretted that the philosopher lacked a certain 'cosmic sense'.[45] Whereas Blondel thought that the experience of the world was a phase to be left behind, and that Teilhard perhaps misrepresented the Christian mystics, especially St John of the Cross, Teilhard, on his part, expressed the view that he had already gone beyond the stage where Blondel was now. The 'communion with God through earth', which he had proposed in 'Cosmic Life', did not exclude the mystical journey through 'the night' but rather introduced and justified it.[46]

Blondel, as others after him, may have been shocked by the realism of Teilhard's pantheism. He did not appreciate the full implications of a simultaneous love of the world and love of God. Whilst for most theologians and spiritual writers, the word 'mystical' is interpreted in a minimalist sense, implying little organic or physical meaning, Teilhard argued against a presentation of the spiritual as 'an attenuation of the material'; for him the spiritual is in fact 'the material carried beyond itself: it is super-material'.[47] Man's fundamental passion for the All and the deeply unifying experience of the cosmos represent a 'natural mysticism of which Christian mysticism can only be the sublimation and crowning peak'.[48]

To reveal the Christian soul of pantheism or the pantheist aspect of Christianity is the stated aim of 'Pantheism and Christianity' (1923). This essay, written a few months before Teilhard's first visit to the Far East, discusses pantheism in general terms without explicit reference to Eastern monism. On one hand, there have always been naturally pantheistic souls who experienced cosmic consciousness but, on the other, this sense of the All, this 'passion for the Whole' seems at present 'to be going through a real crisis of awakening' and is highly peculiar to our own time.[49] The 'worship of the world' which 'dominates modern religious history' has developed on a scale unknown before because of the newly discovered dimension and complexity of the universe: 'The present religious crisis derives from the antagonism between the God of supernatural revelation on one side and the great mysterious figure of the universe on the other'.[50] And yet, looking at the sources of the Christian tradition, 'has any evolutionist pantheism, in fact, ever spoken more magnificently of the All than St Paul did in the words he addressed to the first Christians?'[51]

The religion of the All has hitherto been primarily expressed in terms of paganism and anti-Christianity. Discussing the reasons for this, Teilhard wrote:

Whether because the Christian God seemed useless and distant, . . . in comparison with the powerful evolution immanent in things – or whether because philosophic thought believed that it found its perfect expression in a monism which united beings to a degree at which all distinction was lost – the fact remains that the great mass of those who follow the religion of the All have abandoned Christianity.[52]

Man's need for worship is seeking new forms of expression, and this accounts for 'the present proliferation of neo-Buddhism, of theosophies, of spiritualistic doctrines'. Few

Christians would have admitted this in the 1920s and stressed the need for a 'Christian transposition of the fundamental pantheist tendency'. In Teilhard's view, Christianity 'must directly confront the spellbinding grandeur that is revealing itself – overcome it, take possession of it, and assimilate it'. Only by adopting such an attitude, can Christianity satisfy the legitimate pantheistic aspirations of men and, at the same time, provide the necessary environment wherein 'Christian dogma and mysticism . . . can develop freely'.[53]

Teilhard's primary concern was with such a development of Christian mysticism. But from the beginning of his reflections he was also acutely aware of introducing a new element into the understanding of mysticism, not seen by spiritual writers of the past. There exists perhaps no more insightful discussion of Teilhard's Christian mysticism than in the works of Henri de Lubac, especially his study *The Religion of Teilhard de Chardin*.[54] De Lubac has stated more than once that anything Teilhard ever wrote about the 'mystical milieu' and the 'divine milieu', makes sense only in the context of the Christian faith. However, it is possible to understand this in a minimalist sense – the Christian faith as traditionally practised – or, alternatively, in a much more open-ended way where it acquires a more searching meaning. The comparative aspects of Teilhard's understanding of mysticism have so far been little explored but they add a new dimension related to his experience of the East.

Let us for the present sum up the meaning of pantheism. For Teilhard there can be a genuine Christian pantheism for, rightly understood, Christianity can satisfy both pluralistic and monistic tendencies. Throughout his works, he maintained the possibility of a 'true pantheism' which he distinguished from all 'false pantheisms'. According to de Lubac, Teilhard is hardly ever prepared to condemn pantheism as such 'without any exact qualification', of which he lists as examples 'ancient pantheism', 'common pantheism', 'the Hindu type of pantheism', 'the pantheisms of East and West', as well as 'humanitarian neo-pantheisms'.[55]

In his lexical study of Teilhard's language, Claude Cuénot has found 28 contexts in which the term pantheism is used, each qualified by a different adjective or noun.[56] Basically, however, this wide-ranging usage relates to only two major types, of which the second one can be further subdivided:

I *Pantheism of diffusion*   II *Pantheism of convergence*
a) pantheism of unification
b) pantheism of union

The first type implies the loss of consciousness and the dissolution of the person at a lower level. Its major synonyms in Teilhard's works are pantheism of expansion, dissolution, or identification. This form of pantheism is also equated with the lower forms of monism, ancient and false forms of pantheism.

The second type is by its very nature a more complex form. The Absolute is here perceived as a centre, formed through the gathering up of all beings into itself, maintaining their difference whilst uniting them. This implies a higher degree of consciousness and a progressive personalization. This form of pantheism represents a continuum ranging from a merely external unification of all elements (II a) to the deepest personal union, effected through love (II b). In Teilhard's writings, the major synonyms for this form (II b) are pantheism of love, tension, or differentiation. The latter is ultimately identified with Christian, or true pantheism.

These two major types represent two antipodal forms whose fundamental difference Teilhard always maintained. In a conversation, recorded as late as 1954, he expressed this difference rather schematically as follows:[57]

| I Pantheism of diffusion identification | attitude *without* love | God is All |
| II Pantheism of convergence differentiation | essentially effect of love | God is All in all (St Paul) |

It would be wrong, however, to see these two types as exclusively opposed to each other. From the early writings onwards, it is evident that there is continuity as well as discontinuity between these forms: monistic pantheism finds its prolongation and true fulfilment in a person-centred, theistic mysticism based on love. Man's search for ultimate unity can proceed along many different paths which Teilhard grouped into two major types with not too sharp a break between them. Mysticism is seen as different and more complex than monistic pantheism. Yet at the same time it must not be forgotten that the mystic experience remains always rooted in a cosmic matrix and, what is more, that it may develop towards new dimensions. Man's search for ultimate unity may well lead to the discovery of new forms of religious experience.

As will be shown later, not only the presence of love but its dynamic, transforming capacity is, for Teilhard, the truly differentiating factor between pantheism and mysticism as well as between different types of mysticism. Presently, the polarity between two existing 'types' of pantheism must be linked to yet another polarity, summarily expressed by the 'road of the East' and the 'road of the West'. It relates to two fundamental religious orientations and was formulated by Teilhard after living for considerable time in the Far East.

6

Two Roads to Unity:
'Road of the East' and
'Road of the West'

Soon after arriving in the Far East, Teilhard wrote that he hoped to find 'a reservoir of thought and mysticism that would bring fresh youth to our West'.[1] From the beginning of his stay in China he compared the East with the West, particularly in letters to his friends. But the comparison of Eastern and Western mysticism occurs only much later, in an essay of 1932 which refers for the first time to the 'road of the East' and the 'road of the West'. These expressions seem to be Teilhard's own invention and one wonders whether he would ever have chosen them, had he not lived in the East for so long.

The comparison between two different 'roads' was first introduced in 'The Road of the West: To a New Mysticism' (1932).[2] The main theme of this essay was subsequently expressed in a variety of ways; specific comparisons between Eastern and Western religions, although generally brief, can be found in many later essays.[3]

The idea of two different 'roads' for achieving ultimate unity is linked to the difference between monism and mysticism but it expresses this earlier distinction in a different and more accentuated manner. After 1932, references to the two 'roads' are found in many essay and diary entries, with a marked preponderance of the 'road of the West'. As Teilhard's understanding of Eastern religions is nearly always linked to this fundamental dichotomy, we must explore why he emphasized the existence of two 'roads', what he meant by them, and for what reason he linked the 'road of the West' with the idea of a 'new mysticism'.

I

The theme of 'The Road of the West' was first announced in a letter of March 1932, written after the return from the 'Yellow Expedition' which had left a deep impression on Teilhard : '. . . at the first possible opportunity, I propose to write something new on the fundamental metaphysical and religious question : "What is the Multiple, and how can it be reduced to Unity ?" (the Eastern solution, and the Western solution)'.[4] The opportunity to deal with this question came soon for the essay was completed at the beginning of September 1932. From then onwards, the dichotomy between the 'road of the East' and the 'road of the West' was used intermittently to refer to two different kinds of spirituality, represented by two antipodal ways of man's search for the Absolute. Although their contrast may on occasion have been forced, Teilhard took great pains to explain what he meant by this dichotomy in order to exclude false interpretations. Thus, he frequently also used more general, and less geographically dependent, terms to express this fundamental difference of man's religious quest.

The comparison between the two 'roads' relates primarily to the understanding of mysticism for, in Teilhard's view, the phenomenon of mysticism and the relentless quest for absolute unity underlying it, represents the central core of all religion : 'Without mysticism, there can be no successful religion : and there can be no well-founded mysticism apart from faith in some unification of the universe'.[5] Whilst many traditional mystics may be described as being primarily either soul- or God-centred, Teilhard's approach to mysticism is intrinsically related to the world surrounding man, to the experience of multiplicity and organic complexity found in both nature and society. In this sense, his view may be characterized as 'extrovert' rather than 'introvertive' mysticism. The threefold, interdependent relationship between man-world-Absolute introduces a different degree of complexity into the understanding of mysticism, and much of Teilhard's interpretation hinges on this pivotal difference.

'The Road of the West: To a New Mysticism' discusses

what sort of unity is sought in different types of mysticism. The essay intends 'to show how, in continuity with (and at the same time in opposition to) ancient forms of mysticism (particularly Eastern), mankind today, the child of Western science, is even now – for all its appearance of sceptical positivism – pursuing along a new road the persistent effort which since time began seems to have been driving life towards some plenifying unity'.[6] This intention should be borne in mind when one reads some of the subsequent characterizations of the 'road of the East' and the 'road of the West'. Basically, the passage just quoted implies already four themes which are more fully developed in the essay : 1. It states the ancient origin of Eastern mysticism from which Western mysticism itself was initially derived; 2. the interrelatedness of Eastern and Western mysticism can be expressed in terms of both continuity and partial opposition; 3. the development of modern science, too, is an expression of man's continuous search for unity; 4. contemporary man pursues this search in a new situation, on a 'new road', leading to a new form of mysticism which will ultimately transcend the ancient ones. Before the meaning of this 'new road' can be understood, it is important to ask what is really meant by the 'ancient forms of mysticism' which Teilhard particularly associates with the East? In other words, what does he mean by the 'road of the East'?

Teilhard was the first to admit that he was speaking in 'over-simplified terms' when he briefly sketched the characteristics of the 'road of the East' or the 'Eastern solution' to man's quest for ultimate oneness. The search for meaning underneath the manifold reality of experience has led throughout history to various conceptions of unity and absolutes among men. In Teilhard's thought, the 'road of the East' stands for a path whereby the ultimate One is totally opposed to the many. Unity can only be achieved by a return to the One, that is to say, through the suppression or negation of the multiple. This is a 'unity by impoverishment' rather than enrichment, a unity of simplicity and not of complexity. The most important practical consequence of such an absolutist religious and philosophical attitude is the implicit denial that the achievements of human life have an intrinsic value of their own. It is the 'total death of constructive activity: the fundamental emptiness of the experimental universe'.[7]

Which Eastern religions did Teilhard associate then with this characterization of the 'road of the East'? He assumed that a search for ultimate unity achieved through release or return, through identification with an underlying ground rather than union with a higher centre, was typical of both Buddhist and Brahmin thought: it was an attitude which, at one time, affected all Asian mentality right up to Japan.

These sweeping generalizations can and must be criticized for their negativity towards the East. However, it would be a mistake to judge them in isolation. They must be placed in a wider context relating to Teilhard's thought on religion and mysticism as a whole. He was emphatic to point out that the incomparable greatness of the religions of the East lies in their being second to none in vibrating with a passion for ultimate unity. The mystical search for oneness in Eastern, especially Indian religions, is historically primary in the sense that it was the first type of mysticism to appear in time, and also in that various features of Eastern mysticism found their way to the West and influenced certain religious developments there. One can say that the characteristics of the 'road of the East' are not only Indian but equally Neo-Platonic and, through the writing of Pseudo-Dionysius, impressed their lasting stamp on much of Christian mysticism.

Although Teilhard later acknowledged the 'extreme polymorphism' of Indian religious thought, he always equated the essence of Indian spirituality with a very particular conception of unity which, in his opinion, gives even Hindu theism 'in whatever form it may be expressed, a colouring and flavour that are immediately recognizable'.[8] This emphasis on a particular understanding of unity seems to derive mainly from his acquaintance with Indian monistic views, particularly as found in the teachings of Vedanta.

Elsewhere, it becomes even more apparent that the 'road of the East' is mainly equated with certain forms of Hindu monism. What Teilhard finds especially unacceptable in this 'road', is the exaggerated feeling of the final unreality of all phenomena, the teaching that the world is ultimately illusion,

Maya. The 'road of the East' implies for him the denial of the existence of matter; it characterizes an attempt to escape from matter and its confusing multiplicity, encountered in both the natural and social world. The appeal of this 'road' can be summarized as 'renounce the earth, its passions and cares, and the effort it demands'. Logically, this is 'a doctrine of passivity, of relaxation of tension, of withdrawal from things' in order to achieve an identification or fusion with an ultimate One. Expressed in theistic rather than impersonal terms, it would mean that God is arrived at by a negation of the world rather than by its completion and fulfilment.[9]

This fundamental religious orientation understands the primary task of man as one of renunciation and detachment from the world. The goal of religious activity is considered to be contemplation rather than action. Such contemplation or absorption leads to a 'mysticism of identification' of man with the Absolute or, to use Indian terminology, an identification of *Atman* with *Brahman*. For Teilhard, such a spirituality implies 'simplification'; it incurs the risk of evading the responsibilities of human life. Perfection or salvation is sought by man's direct vertical rise to the Absolute without a corresponding horizontal connection with his surrounding milieu. Comparable to the earlier characterization of naturalistic or monistic pantheism, the 'road of the East' is seen to lead to a fusion of the individual – without distinction or qualification – with an original All, leaving no room for man's progress or failure: '*In strict logic*, the Indian sage cannot concern himself with anything the life of the world has been, is, or will be'.[10]

Teilhard reacted negatively to such a 'road' of onesided, exclusive detachment. In fact, he criticized all exclusively contemplative life, whether in East or West. The 'road of the East' was seen as one of 'dehumanizing spirituality', leading to a 'dissolution of personality' rather than to its perfection and fulfilment. Such statements, however, must not be understood literally as applying to Eastern religions as they are frequently practised today. Other passages show that Teilhard was to some extent aware of the reformist tendencies in contemporary Hinduism and Buddhism. He referred to the modern 'renaissance' of Eastern religions which has so much influenced certain people in Europe that some have even suggested 'that the monist serenity of the East might well convert the confused pluralism of the West',[11] a statement not written today, but in 1932.

However, it is obvious that Teilhard did not share the opinion, much more common since then, that the difficulties and especially the materialism of the West might find a ready remedy in the spirituality of the East. European disciples of Eastern religions may well be subject to 'a vast misunderstanding' here. In his view, they are neither aware of the logical implications of an extreme monism nor do they realize its practical consequences, apparent only to someone who has had a prolonged personal contact with Eastern societies. This is more pungently expressed in another essay :

> . . . . we turn to the imposing mass of Hindu and Eastern mystical systems. The East, the first shrine, and, we are assured, the ever-living dwelling place of the Spirit. The East, where so many from the West still dream of finding shelter for their faith in life . . . Let us take a closer look at those mighty constructions; and, without even venturing into the temple to savour what sort of incense still burns within it, let us, not as archaeologists or poets, but as architects of the future, examine the solidity of its walls. The very moment we came into fundamental contact with Asia there can be no question of doubt. Those impressive columns are utterly incapable of supporting the drive of our world in these days.[12]

In Teilhard's opinion, Western followers of Eastern religions may be a long way from realizing the full implications of certain forms of traditional Eastern thought. However, the societies and religions of the East have been in close contact and interaction with Western thought for well over a century at least. This has led to a revival and new vigour of Eastern religions, and they may well have an important contribution to make to the contemporary search for an adequate spirituality for modern man.

Seen in this light, the discussion about the 'road of the East' is of a largely theoretical nature. The characteristics of this 'road' are not to be understood as descriptions of an empirical state of affairs. Teilhard's statements about this 'road' are hedged in by a number of qualifications[13] which must not be overlooked. The frequent use of quotation marks for the 'road of the East' also indicates a non-literal meaning of this term. It is emphasized that 'the "Eastern" solution certainly exists *in theory*', but it is only put forward 'to make plain the exact nature and originality of Western neo-mysticism'. The latter is a new kind of mysticism emerging only now 'in a diametrically opposite direction' to the 'road of the East'.[14]

However, the characteristics of the 'road of the West' are sketched in an equally brief form. This new 'road' is seen as opposed to the 'road of the East' mainly because of its different attitude to the world. In terms of the mystical quest this means that unity is achieved through unification, union, and ultimate convergence of the many in the One. Thus, the One is not opposed to the multiple, but partially born from it.

Such a view presupposes that the universe is considered as an organic whole, formed of interlinked elements which are coming more closely together. Unity is created through the union of all elements effected over time. The multiple is no longer reduced to an underlying, common ground but, on the contrary, a new, higher form of unity is emerging through the gradual transformation and convergence of multiple elements. All parts of reality, whether impersonal or personal, are transformed and united into a higher centre. Instead of escape from, there is transformation of matter. At the same time, transcendence is gained through effort rather than release. Instead of emptiness, this 'road' is characterized by fullness. The world itself is being experienced as filled with the divine Absolute. Its omnipresence radiates through all levels of reality and, therefore, each element possesses an intrinsic value of its own.

Religiously speaking, this means that 'heaven is not opposed to the earth but it is born from the conquest and transformation of the earth'. Expressed in theistic terms, 'God is reached, not by draining away of self, but by sublimation'.[15] It is this effort to reach *beyond* and *not below* consciousness, to seek a higher form of personalization and not to dissolve personality in general cosmic consciousness, which Teilhard saw as the most distinctive feature of the 'road of the West'.

However, one must not look for an 'explicit formulation of this doctrine' or make the mistake of equating the 'road of the West' with Christianity. Teilhard repeated over and over again that the 'road of the West' is a new 'road' representing the 'great religious discovery' of modern times. This 'road' consists for him in a new synthesis of two traditionally exclusive concerns, namely man's search for the One, and his relation to the many. One could also say that it represents a combination of 'other-worldly' and 'this-worldly' attitudes, a synthesis already partly hinted at in the maxim of 'Cosmic Life' (1916) which states that there is 'communion with God through earth'. This new orientation affects 'all the living branches of modern religions'; it will transform traditional Christianity just as much as 'the new forms of Islam and Buddhism'.[16] The impact of the modern world is so universal that it will effect a transformation of the traditional religious outlook which will, in fact, bring the different religions more closely together.

New forms of asceticism and mysticism are developing today, due to a new historical situation wherein man's consciousness of his own becoming in time has been tremendously expanded and revolutionized. In an entirely *new* way, spirituality is being closely related to the development of the tangible world, and needs to be even more so related. In the past, religious teachings were primarily linked to individual needs and hopes, or to national and racial movements. Today, mankind is experiencing itself as one in a sense previously unknown. However, the oneness of the human community and the necessary action to bring about world unity require a common focus; they need to be inspired by the vision of a single soul. This point was not only made by Teilhard but it was equally stressed by the Indian thinkers Sri Aurobindo and Radhakrishnan.

The new 'road of the West' encourages a dynamic attitude towards a world deeply affected by vast social changes and complex developments in science and technology. But why does Teilhard link the characteristics of this new 'road' specifically to the West? One can list two reasons for this. On one hand, modern science and technology, however much influenced by earlier ideas from both East and West, historically emerged in the West. On the other hand, Christianity, due to its central Incarnation-event, has frequently encouraged a positive attitude to matter and the world. Therefore, Teilhard saw the 'road of the West' as especially growing out of the central stem of the Christian religious tradition. Unfortunately he did not recognize that Eastern religions, particularly Taoism, but also certain aspects of Hinduism and Buddhism, possess their own world-affirming orientations.

It is also apparent that Christianity has not always actively promoted a dynamic attitude towards the world. Many negative aspects can be found in the history of Christian spirituality. In the past, the two 'roads' of world-negation and world-affirmation were often held in tension. Originally, Western mysticism was influenced by the East as can be seen, for example, in the ideal of renunciation and perfection which inspired the desert fathers. Teilhard looked upon the entire history of Western mysticism as a long-drawn-out effort to separate these two spiritualities: the Oriental way which suppresses matter, and the Occidental way which sublimates it. These are not simply two components which can be harmonized into one spirituality, as is sometimes thought; for him, they are basically 'two incompatible attitudes' – but they are attitudes which, on closer examination, can be found in both East and West.

For Teilhard, these two incompatible attitudes are at present to some extent still intermingled in Christianity. Yet there is an increasing need for distinguishing between these two 'roads'. Mankind has now arrived at an important bifurcation in its development: the path divides between the old 'road of the East' and the new 'road of the West' where, taking all earthly values into account, ultimate unity is found through the unification of the world rather than its abandonment.

By recommending this new 'road', Teilhard was far from encouraging any form of 'naturalism', 'hedonism', or 'pantheism'.

On the contrary, he wished to lead Christianity back to the central essence of its own tradition:

> If Christianity is to remain true to itself . . ., only one condition, and that is an essential one, must be fulfilled: to the maintenance of the primacy of the *spirit* over matter (which . . . brings with it the renunciation of possession), must be added the primacy in the spiritual of the *personal*, which brings together at the same time the maximum differentiation of the elements and their maximum union . . . In short, . . . if Christianity is to remain itself, it must come to the rescue of Western mysticism, and in so doing take it to itself.[17]

This passage shows clearly that Teilhard considered mysticism to be of major importance for contemporary spirituality. The two forms of mysticism – the 'road of the East' and the 'road of the West' – were not only two alternative orientations which he had personally experienced, but they represented two possible options for mankind at the crossroads: '. . . mankind has now reached such a degree of concentration and moral tension that it can no longer postpone taking the spiritual step which will give it a soul. Agnosticism and pluralism are either dead or impotent. It is only a renewed faith in some unity to be born of the world that can preserve our zest for life. And at this precise point we come to the parting of the ways . . .'[18] This parting of the ways is between the ancient 'road of the East' and the new 'road of the West', each of which leads to a different goal: an ultimate unity of 'impoverishment' or 'simplicity' is contrasted with a unity of 'richness' or 'complexity'. For Teilhard, there could be no hesitation about which 'road' to take. Indeed, he thought that the choice had already 'to all intents and purposes, been made' for both history and experience seem to indicate that life is advancing on the 'road of the West'.

II

Teilhard's essay 'The Road of the West' was not without its critics. But in spite of early criticisms of his two types of mysticism, he defended and continued to use the idea of the two 'roads'. This is significant for it shows that, however inadequate, this dichotomy expresses a very fundamental orientation of his thought.

Shortly after writing 'The Road of the West' (1932), he stated its main ideas again in a lecture in Paris of which only the notes taken down by two listeners have survived.[19] These reflect certain nuances in Teilhard's position which may be a response to early criticisms. The notes include statements such as 'The opposition between a contemplative Orient and an Occident immersed in life is a questionable one; we are attributing our own qualities to the Orient'. And also : 'This opposition is not right, not distinct enough; one must show that we carry the virtues of the East within us and we may try to bring them to light'. With reference to the Buddhist teaching on emptiness, Teilhard is reported to have said :

> Perhaps this *Void* is nothing other but what we call the *Ineffable*, perhaps this is a question of words. But what we can say is that their mysticism does not authorize them towards a positive attitude which makes them seek modern science and Western ideas. This gesture by which they try to catch up with us, seems to be condemned by Eastern mysticism. Given the conditions of the present world, it is the Western conception which tends to become universal.[20]

The term 'road of the West' is only used once, emphasizing again the *newness* of this 'road'. This newness presents perhaps less of a difficulty for most readers than Teilhard's all too summary treatment of the 'road of the East'. It was soon severely criticized by two of Teilhard's friends who were both particularly interested in Eastern religions.

One was the fellow Jesuit Father Henri de Lubac who, from 1931 onwards, taught a course in the history of religions at the Faculty of Theology in Lyons and later developed a special interest in Buddhism.[21] He immediately criticized 'The Road of the West', and possibly wrote to Teilhard something like 'Is there not a Christian detachment, and can it be maintained that Buddhistic renunciation is void of all moral validity?'[22] In a letter to de Lubac, Teilhard replied:

> I was most interested in your friendly criticisms of 'The Road of the West'. But if I am not mistaken, they prove precisely the importance of what I tried to show (not clearly enough, no doubt). I fully admit the alternation of detachment and attachment (cf. *Milieu Divin*). But I believe that it is in the particular, *specific* nature of Buddhist detachment that there lies the weakness and the (at least logical) danger of Eastern religions. The Buddhist *denies* himself in order to kill desire (he *does not believe* in the value of *being*). The authentic Christian also denies himself but *by excess* of desire and of faith in the value of being. This is one of those cases where the same appearances cover contrary realities. It seems to me highly important to unmask the ambiguity here. – This is not to say, of course, that, vitally speaking, Buddhist renunciation has no moral validity. But it is expressed in a false theory (as in the case of so many other pantheisms).[23]

Another criticism came from Abbé Jules Monchanin, an authority on Eastern religions. Deeply attracted by Indian spirituality, Monchanin later founded a Christian Ashram in South India which became a centre for the encounter of Christians and Hindus.[24] Transmitted through their mutual friend, Father de Lubac, Monchanin received 'The Road of the West' and criticized it at length. Well versed in Indian mystical thought, Monchanin found in Teilhard's views 'a certain pragmatist emphasis and a too exclusively western presentation'.[25] Were the religions of India in fact as negative as Teilhard believed? In a long letter to Father de Lubac, Teilhard took up several of Monchanin's points and a substantial part may be quoted here:

I was very touched by the trouble taken by M. Monchanin over reading and criticizing me. His observations lead me to make the following counter-observations:

. . . if the religions of India are less negative than I said, that fact does not essentially affect my thesis, the purpose of which is above all to distinguish 'two essential types' of possible mysticisms. It would be quite extraordinary, I admit, for either of these types to be met anywhere in the *pure state*. I therefore took Eastern mysticism as an example, as close as possible, of negativism. Given these reservations . . ., I still believe that, *logically*, Eastern religions and contemplation kill action . . .

. . . . . .

. . . It is impossible for me to admit the formula that mysticism 'is ultimately not meant to perfect the world but to allow the *praise of God*'. For years, my entire effort has precisely been to criticize these juridical and vague terms, and to find an organic and ontological meaning for them. What does it mean 'to praise God'? . . .

Nothing is, in my view, *more spiritual* than the consummation of the universe. Any spirituality pursued at the periphery of this effort is verbalism, attenuation, abstraction – the dreary piety of churches and convents. I fear that M. Monchanin has not really 'caught' anything of what I try to express – or that we are at antipodes of each other. In any case, he does not seem to have 'understood the world'.[26]

This passage expresses more clearly than any other that the 'road of the East' and the 'road of the West' are essentially *two distinct types*. They represent a theoretical distinction and are, so to speak, a heuristic device to investigate and interpret fundamental orientations to reality. This does not imply that either of these two types exists as such in practice in an individual adherent of a particular religion. The 'roads' are perhaps best likened to signposts which send people mainly into one direction or the other.

The harshness of expression characteristic of 'The Road of

the West' (1932) was somewhat modified by the more sympathetic and detailed treatment of Eastern religions found in the later essay 'The Spiritual Contribution of the Far East' (1947).[27] There, the term 'road of the East' is abandoned in favour of a more differentiated discussion of Asian spirituality to which we shall return later. The interrelationship and difference of the two 'roads' is also discussed in 'My Fundamental Vision' (1948).[28] Quoting Aldous Huxley's *Perennial Philosophy*, Teilhard refers to the apparently complete agreement of the mystics of all religions and times regarding their search for spiritual perfection. Their perennial quest seems to be characterized by 'an effort to escape spiritually, through universalization, into the Ineffable'. Yet contrary to Aldous Huxley and many others, Teilhard was convinced that this is only a 'superficial unanimity', disguising 'a serious opposition (or even fundamental incompatibility) which originates in a confusion between two symmetrical but "antipodal" approaches to the understanding, and hence to the pursuit, of the unity of the spirit'.

The two different approaches – either initial identification or ultimate differentiation and convergence – are equated with the two 'roads'. The first 'road' conceives spiritual unification to be a 'return to a common "divine" basis *underlying* and *more real than*, all the sensibly perceptible determinants of the universe'. Teilhard calls this 'road' more or less conventionally, as he qualifies, the 'road of the East'. From the perspective of the 'road of the West', 'the "common basis" of the Eastern road is mere illusion'. Given contemporary physics and an adequate metaphysics related to modern science, 'the only homogeneous form of spiritualization, the only viable mysticism, must be . . . a positive act not of relaxation, but of active convergence and concentration'.[29] As will be apparent by now, a central part of Teilhard's argument concerns the possible differences in understanding the nature of the spirit itself, and the divergent ways in which man can find ultimate unity. The distinction between two essential types of mysticism is also expressed in two brief notes whose very title reflects Teilhard's attempt to clarify his insights for himself and others: 'A Clarification: Reflections on Two Converse Forms of the Spirit' (1950)[30] distinguishes between 'unity through relaxation, or the search for a common foundation' and 'unity through tension, or the road to the universal centre'. Ultimate unity may thus be found either at the base through the elimination of all opposites between things, or at the apex, through ultra-differentiation.

'Some Notes on the Mystical Sense: An Attempt at Clarification' (1951)[31] speaks of the 'two principal ways' tried by the mystics. The 'road of the East' and the 'road of the West' are here replaced by a more neutral terminology. The difference in mystical orientation is simply presented in terms of 'two ways' or rather 'two *components*, that have hitherto to all intents and purposes been merged into one'.[32] However, the distinguishing characteristic of the two paths is now mainly perceived to consist in the absence or presence of love, ultimately centred on an ultra-personal God, rather than an impersonal, common ground.

These examples show that the 'road of the East' and the 'road of the West' cannot be understood on their own. Teilhard also uses many other words to express the same contrast and dichotomy in the mystic quest for unity. Representative examples of such dichotomous classifications are best listed in a table. [See p. 138].

III

A look at the table shows clearly that the contrast between the 'road of the East' and the 'road of the West' forms part of a wider group of comparisons, present throughout many years. In one form or another, they all express two distinctive spiritual orientations in man's search for the Absolute or two possible forms of conceiving ultimate unity. They also relate to two basic types of mysticism. Thus, the dichotomy of two 'roads' continues and further accentuates the difference between the two types of 'pantheism' to which Teilhard mainly refers in his earlier writings.

The major problem in interpreting the meaning of the

Dichotomous classifications used by Teilhard

Year	Dichotomy		Source
1931	*Two solutions to the problem of the One and the many:*		LI, 223
	'Eastern' solution	'Western' solution	LZ, 108
1932	*Two roads to unity:*		
	'Road of the East'	'Road of the West'	TF, 42ff.
	Two roads of spiritualization:		
	Eastern: suppression	Western: sublimation	TF, 52
1937	*Two entirely opposite forms of union:*		
	Union of dissolution	Union by differentiation or union of concentration (the *only* true union)	HE, 103f.
1939	*Two kinds of pantheism:*		
	The unity of the whole is born from the fusion of the elements	The elements are *fulfilled by* entering a deeper centre	CE, 136
1945	*Two ways of mysticism (often confused, though opposed):*		
	The way of simplification ('road of the East')	The way of synthesis ('new road of the West')	
	Unity through fusion	Unity through unification	SC, 183f.
1948	*Two ineffables:*		
	Eastern 'ineffable of relaxation'	Christian 'ineffable of tension'	TF, 194
1950	*Two converse forms or 'isotopes' of the spirit:*		
	Spirit of identification or fusion	Spirit of unification or of 'amorization'	
	Pantheism of identification at the opposite pole from love	Pantheism of unification, beyond love	AE, 218 AE, 223
1951	*Two principal ways tried by the mystics (or two components hitherto merged into one):*		
	To become one with a common ground; this leads to an identification, an ineffable of de-differentiation & de-personalization. This is mysticism WITHOUT LOVE.	To become one with all by access to the centre-unification of the elements within a *common focus*, the specific effect of LOVE.	TF, 209f.

two 'roads' is Teilhard's changing vocabulary with its resulting lack of definition and clarity. It is perhaps less in terms of exact philosophical analysis than in terms of a basic intuition that they must be interpreted and understood. Seen from within a wider context, it would be quite wrong, for example, to equate the 'road of the East' with the great variety of religions existing in the East. But there is the difficulty that Teilhard's approach to Eastern religions is mainly expressed through this comparison of abstract types and rarely relates to more concrete historical detail.

He emphasized more than once that the two 'roads' resemble two spiritual 'currents'; they are basically 'two essential types'[33] and their characterization must not be taken too literally. The two 'roads' represent a schematized comparison which requires a typological interpretation relating to other aspects of Teilhard's thought rather than to ideas introduced from outside his work.

The choice of the word 'road' itself is indicative here. Its meaning implies the existence of a path, as well as a certain direction and goal. Different roads lead into different directions and crossroads in particular stand for definite alternatives among which men must choose. Teilhard not only emphasizes the existence of a choice between contrasting 'roads' in religion and mysticism but many aspects of contemporary society and culture imply the necessity of making a choice. The entire situation of humankind today is one of being at the crossroads. At present, the necessity to opt for one road rather than another is particularly urgent with regard to man's power of choosing and shaping his own future. In Teilhard's view, such a choice cannot really be made without an adequate religious perspective, without the animating and sustaining powers of a rightly understood faith. This is the 'heart of the problem': to choose the right 'road' in a situation where the future of man involves a 'grand option'.[34]

Teilhard has an overriding concern with the future and the dynamics of time. Time possesses a historical and evolutionary importance and its role is different from that in the past.[35] This applies also to the understanding of spirituality although one can point to the Christian idea of the *kairos* here which has always had a special significance: it is a God-given moment in time, separate and distinct from any other moment.

The time factor is certainly an essential element in the dichotomy between the two 'roads' or 'types' of spirituality. I would suggest that the 'road of the East' and the 'road of the West' are not simply opposites on the same plane, existing simultaneously in time. As Teilhard wrote at the beginning of his essay, the 'road of the West' exists 'in continuity with' and also 'in opposition to' the ancient 'road of the East'. One can understand this to mean that the 'road of the East' typifies a 'road' of the past; it stands for a stage of man's religious quest which once existed to a greater or lesser degree in all religions. It is associated with passivity, world-negation, asceticism, and an excessive other-worldliness. In other words, the mystic search for ultimate unity is predominantly associated with world rejection in one form or another, characteristic of all the great historical religions.

However, this ancient 'road', dominant for so long, represents an outdated spirituality now for it is based on an inadequate understanding of the nature of the spirit as well as the nature of an evolutionary world. Although distinct from the temporal, the spiritual is not sharply separated from it but grows out of and beyond it. The next stage to be gained or 'road' to be taken is a new 'road', linked to a clearer perception of the importance of temporal realities, of the growth of this world in the present and future. This is what Teilhard calls the 'road of the West' and, in his view, Christianity contains in its essence the most powerful potential to chart this new 'road'. Ultimately, however, this new 'road of the West' represents, at least in the formulation of his later years, 'a hitherto unknown form of religion'[36] which requires a new but as yet unformulated mysticism.

Thus, the 'road of the West' must not be identified with Christianity as we know it or as it exists at present, containing a mixture of both Eastern and Western elements. In fact, neither the 'road of the East' nor the 'road of the West' can be fully equated with any particular religious tradition; each indicates a major spiritual orientation present in both Eastern and Western religions. These two types of spirituality might be compared with Max Weber's distinction between 'world-rejecting asceticism' and 'inner-worldly asceticism' as two fundamental attitudes towards the world. Weber relates these different religious orientations to the contrast between Oriental and Occidental religiosity.[37] Yet it must be stressed that, in terms of their relation to time, Weber's 'ideal-types' are also past-oriented. They oppose two existing attitudes and typify what has been. One of Teilhard's ideal-types, however, the 'road of the West', attempts to express what is not yet. It points to what is emerging now, and anticipates what may develop in the future. The incorporation of the time-process introduces, therefore, a different dynamic into his typological distinction. Taking into account the progressive developments over time, one could say that the 'road of the East' is the road of the past, in some form or another present in all religious traditions, whereas the 'road of the West' is the road of the future.

The general, ideal-type function of the two 'roads', expressing two possible types of spirituality, must not be confused with specific, historical-empirical examples. However, such a confusion does occasionally occur. It is easily made when such basic types are linked to geographical associations. Although some commentators infer an attitude of superiority from the use of the 'road of the West', this seems to have been far from Teilhard's own intention. Cuénot has pointed out that the 'criticism of Eastern thought did not arise from any belief that radically the Westerner is superior to the Oriental'.[38] In a new historical situation, Teilhard wished to draw attention to an increasingly important distinction, implying the choice of a new 'road' not really given in the past. This choice has only arisen with the growing differentiation of man's world and consciousness in recent times. In a more neutral way, the two 'roads' may be seen as two different forms of unity, and their main characteristics can be outlined in a diagram which shows their contrast as well as their continuity.

Two forms of unity

'*Road of the East*'   '*Road of the West*'
(both continuity and partial opposition)*

'Road of the East'	'Road of the West'
Return to primordial unity	Progress to ultimate unity, achieved through convergence
Detachment	Alternation detachment-attachment
Simplification	Complexity
Identification	Unification and differentiation
Vertical orientation (man-Absolute)	Diagonal orientation [synthesis of vertical (man-Absolute) with horizontal (man-world) orientation = via tertia]
Exclusive stress on contemplation	Alternation action-contemplation
Dehumanizing spirituality	Progressive spiritual transformation of matter
Emptiness	Fulfilment
Mysticism of identification with a common ground	Mysticism of union with a higher centre

Time – Process

Past ⟶ Present ⟶ Future

'Road of the East'	'Road of the West'
Historically first	Slowly emerging now
Ancient	New
Now outdated	Still incomplete
Stage to be transcended	Stage to be gained

*The curved line indicates that the distinction between the two 'roads' is a fluid one: the two forms of unity are not clearly divided from each other.

The difference between the 'road of the East' and the 'road of the West' thus expresses a fundamental alternative in religious and mystical orientation. Theoretically, the two opposite 'roads' exist together; yet, at the empirical level, the two alternatives overlap and succeed each other in time. The complexity of the 'road of the West' is also linguistically apparent for it is usually characterized by more than one word. The 'road of the West' points to a synthesis which, in this form, is new but incorporates certain features of the 'road of the East'.

Thus, one can conclude that there exists a double dialectic in Teilhard's thought with regard to the two 'roads' towards ultimate unity. On one hand, the two 'roads' are historically somehow connected, and yet they are fundamentally opposed: the 'road of the East' is linked to forms of spirituality which may have been sufficient for the past but differ from those needed for the present and future. On the other hand, it must be pointed out that the characterizations of the two 'roads' rest on entirely different premises: Teilhard always remained an outsider to the 'road of the East' if one understands the latter literally. Unlike Monchanin and others since, he never acquired a deep personal knowledge of Eastern religions. Thus, his criticisms are those of an outsider and remain necessarily superficial whereas he could characterize and criticize Christianity with much greater subtlety and sophistication because he knew it closely from the inside.

The comparison between two different 'roads' is also held in tension by the fact that Teilhard often speaks of a coming together or convergence of 'roads'. That the 'road of the East' and the 'road of the West' should meet, he judged a distinct possibility; indeed, he considered it a necessity if a truly new mysticism is to emerge. We must now turn to his all too summary assessment of Eastern religions and ask how this relates to the much wider idea of a convergence of 'roads', and what such a movement of convergence implies for the understanding of spirituality.

7

The Convergence of Roads

The idea of convergence is central to Teilhard's vision of unity. Convergence is a movement or process observable in all areas of human activity today. The development of the modern world is related to a profound change of age and direction affecting all aspects of contemporary culture, including religion. As early as 1923, Teilhard wrote that 'we are standing, at the present moment, not only at a change of century and civilization, but at a *change of epoch*!'[1]

The contemporary world is marked by a striking paradox, however. On the one hand, it seems deeply torn apart, filled with cries of battle, suffering and injustice, racial hatred and bloodshed. But on the other hand, in spite of divergence and disunity, numerous movements have come into existence which are working for the greater economic, political, and cultural unity of mankind. In fact, the past offers no parallel to the way the contemporary world is coming to be centred upon the belief that mankind ultimately forms one community. Never before in human history have so many been aware of the oneness of humankind, a oneness pertaining to a common origin, a shared development, and a unity of purpose. However, this is not a oneness actually given but existing as an ideal, a deeply felt wish and desire, a dream which may come true one day.

This general movement of convergence in contemporary culture has far-reaching effects on the world religions. Teilhard asked the important question whether the active 'currents of faith'[2] or the truly 'living branches of modern religions'[3] can give meaning to this tremendous change of epoch. Will they be able to respond creatively to a historically new situation?

He believed that the living religions themselves are moving closer together and also, that they have a valuable contribution to make to human convergence in general. Indeed, a greater unity of the world religions is indispensable if the full convergence of mankind is to come about.

How does Teilhard describe the active currents of faith, the living branches of religion? It is important to remember that, by and large, his approach to mankind's religious heritage rarely included historical and factual descriptions. It remained primarily typological and evaluative, especially with regard to the critical situation facing mankind today, a situation which demands decisive commitment and requires a specific 'road'. Is such a 'road' open to us?

The idea of a 'convergence of roads' suggests a new path, a synthesis which will overcome the opposition of different spiritualities of the past, particularly that of East and West. Teilhard's conception of an ultimate unity of convergence is inspiring. It is extraordinary, however, if one considers his summary and frequently negative assessment of Eastern religions, due perhaps more to a lack of knowledge than an absence of sympathy. Although he obviously knew far more about Christianity than Eastern thought, he emphasized the importance of the central insights of all living religions, but judged their value mainly from the perspective of the modern world and its future development. Let us briefly look at some of his comments on Eastern religions.

I

The first non-Christian religion which Teilhard encountered during his early years in Egypt was Islam. However, the few direct references to this great religious tradition in his work are mainly critical. Most of his statements on Eastern religions relate to Hinduism and Buddhism, followed by Confucianism and Taoism. None of these religious traditions were ever assessed from within, on their own grounds. Yet it is fair to say that, by and large, Teilhard's comparisons were not made from a narrowly dogmatic point of view. His comments are based on a largely universalist perspective, concerned with seeking a richer, more adequate spirituality for mankind today. In fact, this universalist perspective is the very reason why he often judged the existing religions so negatively.

Certain descriptions of Hinduism and Buddhism have already been quoted. Here, brief mention may be made of Teilhard's few and rather harsh comments on Islam. He described Islam most inadequately as 'no more than a backward-looking revival of Judaism',[4] a 'residual Judaism' which 'in spite of the number of its adherents and its continual progress . . . contributes no special solution to the modern religious problem'.[5] Although only made in passing, these remarks are not based on total ignorance. One must remember that Teilhard lived for three years in a predominantly Islamic country, knew several scholars concerned with the study of Islam and during his travels occasionally had the opportunity to discuss religious questions with educated, devout Muslims. This makes the brevity of his remarks and the obvious lack of understanding even more disconcerting.

There are also a few references to Islam which are more positive. Among them is a curt acknowledgment of the insights of medieval Islamic philosophy into man's close interrelationship with nature. Also mentioned with approval is the recognition of the organic nature of society, found in some Islamic thinkers.[6] Several references to the mysticism of the Sufis can be found too. The cosmic sense of 'oneness' experienced by the Sufi is similar to that of the Hindu and Christian mystic,[7] and yet it belongs to a 'mysticism of the monist or pantheist type'.[8]

Writing from a comparative perspective in 1933, Teilhard thought that Islam, like other religious beliefs, faced serious difficulties in the modern world.

Islam has retained the idea of the existence and the greatness of God. That, it is true, is the seed from which everything may one day be born again; but at the same time Islam has achieved the extraordinary feat of making this God as ineffective and sterile as a non-being for all that concerns the knowledge and betterment of the world. After destroying a great deal and creating locally an ephemeral beauty, Islam offers itself today as a principle of fixation and stagnation.[9]

To some extent, however, Teilhard was aware that Islam is showing signs of renewal. He spoke of 'high-minded' Islamic thinkers who were 'alive to modern requirements'.[10] Thus, an Islamic 'renascence' may well be conceivable. Yet he also asked whether it is really the spirit of the Koran which fires the enthusiasm of young Muslims or rather, whether it is not some kind of 'new religion' which, he thought, has been influenced by Christian ideas.[11]

It is easier to witness the dynamic activity of the Islamic world today[12] than it was during the thirties. Teilhard's severe judgment of Islam is basically due to the fact that his evolutionary thought 'represents the exact opposite of Islam' with its immobilist position, based on the Koran.[13] Thus, it is mainly the ideas of Islamic modernists and reformers which appealed to him. It is not surprising, therefore, that his thought is sometimes compared with the universalist and evolutionary perspective of the Islamic reformer, Muhammed Iqbal,[14] nor that Teilhardian ideas are said to have found an extraordinary response 'in certain Islamic milieux of Morocco'.[15]

Besides Islam, the historical riches of Confucianism and Taoism were largely ignored too. To Teilhard, it appeared 'that no one who has been deeply influenced by modern culture and the knowledge that goes with it can sincerely be a Confucian, a Buddhist or Muslim (unless he is prepared to live a double interior life, or profoundly to modify for his own use the terms of his religion)'.[16]

Although Indian thought always had a particular fascination for Teilhard he encountered Hinduism only briefly and rather late. But he did not feel attracted to its varied forms. In the judgment of one who knew him well, he 'always seems to have sympathized more with certain aspects of Buddhism' rather than with Hinduism.[17] It was particularly the universalist and cosmic perspective of Buddhism which appealed to him, and not so much the contemplative one. During his first visit to the Far East, he expressed the hope that Christianity might become renewed through the contact with Buddhism.[18] Later, however, he judged Buddhism to be dead in China[19] although he was aware of the existence of forces of renewal. Yet the 'varieties of neo-Buddhism' which could be observed in China and elsewhere, were quite rightly seen by him as developments linked to Western influence.[20]

Teilhard's approach to Eastern religious thought must be criticized for its all too summary assessment and undifferentiated use of the term 'Eastern religions'. Not unlike certain earlier Western scholars, he often subsumed both Buddhism and Hinduism under this term without distinguishing their beliefs and practices. For example, when speaking about the great appeal of Eastern religions, he writes 'let us, to put a name to them, say Buddhism'. But then he goes on to talk about India and especially Indian monism which contrasts most sharply with his own understanding of the spirit:

> For the Hindu sage, spirit is the homogeneous unity in which the complete adept is lost to self, all individual features and values being suppressed. All quest for knowledge, all personalization, all earthly progress are so many diseases of the soul. *Matter is dead weight and illusion.* By contrast, spirit is for me . . . the unity by synthesis in which the saint realizes his full being, carrying to the furthest possible point what differentiates its nature, and the particular resources it possesses . . . *Matter is heavily loaded, throughout, with sublime possibilities.*[21]

The 'venerable cosmogonies of Asia' did not reveal to Teilhard a God who is 'a saviour of man's work'. In earlier years, he thought that he might be able to discern such a God in the East but, by the beginning of the thirties, he became firmly convinced that a new path to mysticism was being built on the 'road of the West'. Although this new way implies 'a contagious faith in an ideal to which man's life can be given',[22] it is far from being a clearly signposted road. In fact, at present it may be conceived as offering several directions between which we still have to choose. Teilhard was always looking for a faith which could take up, sustain and further animate the dynamism of the modern world. But where is there such a faith? A faith which can grow and expand rather than regress and simply reaffirm a distant, deadly past against a living present? This tension between the present and the past has caused a state of crisis affecting all religions, whether in East or West. The recognition of this crisis led Teilhard to a general critique of the state of religions in the modern world which is more comprehensive in scope than his assessment of Eastern religions, but equally brief in its formulation.

II

The experience of the long 'Yellow Expedition' to Inner Mongolia during the years 1931-2 made Teilhard particularly sensitive to the question of what meaning religion has for today. For almost a year, a group of men from widely different backgrounds lived and worked as a closely-knit team. Many of them had no religious faith at all. With the help of a newly developed technology they penetrated into remote and hostile areas of the globe, characterized by many ancient features, not the least the religious customs and practices of their inhabitants. The contrast between the old and the new was particularly apparent here. During this time, Teilhard became acutely aware of the need for a new approach in presenting religion to modern man. After returning from the expedition, he not only developed the idea of two different 'roads', but two subsequent essays, 'Christianity in the World' (1933)[23] and 'How I Believe' (1934),[24] include an explicit discussion of the contemporary situation of the world religions. This is described as one of trial, for today the great religions are being 'put to the test'.[25]

All religions are now facing a crisis which has arisen through the development of the modern world. This development implies not only scientific and technological advances accompanied by deep social and cultural changes; it means even more a change in the nature of knowledge itself which, in turn, has led to a profound alteration in man's vision of the world and in his own consciousness. The historical roots of this transformation have often been analysed by Teilhard.[26] The following passage briefly indicates the nature of this change:

Among the most disquieting aspects of the modern world is its general and growing dissatisfaction in religious matters . . . there is no present sign anywhere of Faith *in a state of expansion*: there are only, here and there, *creeds* that at the best are holding their own, where they are not positively retrogressing . . . Any effort to understand what is now taking place in human consciousness must of necessity proceed from the fundamental change of perspective which since the sixteenth century has shattered and rendered movable to our experience what, until then, had always seemed to be the ultimate in stability: the world itself. To our clearer vision the universe is no longer a State but a Process. The cosmos has become a Cosmogenesis . . .
. . . and now we find that man in his turn is identified with an anthropogenesis. This is a major event which must lead, as we shall see, to the profound modification of the whole structure not only of our Thought but of our Beliefs.[27]

Man's deepest beliefs, that is, his search for an Absolute and his experience of God, are in need of new forms of expression. For Teilhard man has 'become adult',[28] responsible for the making of his own future. Yet at the same time, he is facing ever greater problems. Thus, a situation of turmoil has arisen. Contemporary man experiences a loss of equilibrium and often lacks a sense of purpose. Reflecting on the search for a goal of life, Teilhard wrote a passage in 1933 which rings even truer today:

Lack of employment. This phrase defines . . . the crisis the world is passing through at this moment . . . There are many symptoms to indicate that it [mankind] is now without occupation, and that it may well continue to become increasingly so, now that the balance has finally been upset between material needs and powers of production, so that, in theory, all men have to do is to allow the machine that emancipated them to run on, and fold their arms. The present crisis is much more than a difficult interval accidentally encountered by a particular type of civilization . . . it expresses the inevitable result of the loss of equilibrium brought about in animal life by the appearance of thought. Men no longer know today how to occupy their physical powers: but what is more serious, they do not know towards what universal and final end they should direct the driving force of their souls. It has already been said, though without sufficiently deep appreciation of the words: the present crisis is a spiritual crisis . . . mankind today is undecided, and distressed, at the very peak of its power, because it has not defined its spiritual pole. It lacks religion.[29]

What particular conditions must be fulfilled for religions to point a way out of this situational crisis, to reveal a 'road' leading to meaning? In Teilhard's view, religions which merely uphold the ideal of an established order and are static in their approach to man and the world, cannot make sense of the newly discovered 'dimensions and forward momentum of the universe'. If religions *are to appeal to us, and save us, they must be dynamic*.[30] They must be able to inspire human action here and now, sustain man's zest to live and relate man's life to an ultimate goal.

These are, briefly stated, the premisses from which Teilhard examined the living religions. His intuitions can be inspiring and spark off further reflections. But the lack of concrete detail is most unsatisfactory and can be truly misleading. It was not his aim, however, to develop a comprehensive sociology or theology of religions but rather, to emphasize what is at the centre of all true religion. Behind all the intellectual constructions, the many new words, the groping attempts to express what he had seen, felt, and experienced, his thought most emphatically points to the fire of that living flame which alone ensures that men become truly alive.

The present religious crisis has two major aspects. On one hand, many people today are undergoing an almost permanent crisis of identity and meaning which requires a spiritual answer. But anyone sensitive to current spiritual needs also realizes the inadequacy of past religious answers to the difficult questions of the present. On the other hand, there is the critical situation of the world religions themselves, unable to supply such an answer in adequate form. For Teilhard, modern man is basically not 'a-religious' but revolts against the narrowness of certain religious teachings. It is not atheism but an 'unsatisfied theism' from which the world is suffering at present.[31] The existence of atheism and the whole process of secularization contain signs of a metamorphosis of man's religious sense pointing towards the development of new forms of religiousness.

The possibility of such new forms is hinted at when Teilhard speaks of 'the religion of tomorrow'[32] and 'the convergence of religions'.[33] The idea of convergence or the closer coming together of the world religions implies a movement from diversity towards greater unity. Such a movement of convergence is inconceivable without a contribution of the 'road of the East'. The importance of convergence led Teilhard to examine again his understanding of the 'road of the East'.

III

At present, a vigorous process of reinterpreting the traditional religious heritage is taking place in both East and West. A growing interest in the teachings of the great world religions, especially those of the East, can be observed in many quarters. This is far more obvious today than during Teilhard's lifetime. But even then there were a considerable number of people already interested in Eastern religions. One needs only to think of the adherents of theosophy, and the followers of Vedanta or similar movements from the East which have been active in Europe and America since the late nineteenth century.

Teilhard tended to disagree with Western contemporaries who were over-enthusiastic and uncritical admirers of the East. He felt that nothing could be more unjust than the judgment of those who 'designate Western civilization as materialist'.[34] In a time of tremendous turmoil, when mankind is in search of a soul, many turn for enlightenment towards the East. To them, 'the East stands for spirit, the West for matter'.[35] For Teilhard, this is not only an oversimplified dichotomy but spirit and matter cannot be opposed in this way. His own position was almost at the opposite pole : for him it is the West which 'has set in motion a powerful mysticism'.[36] But this must not be seen in isolation, for certain elements of Eastern spirituality are of great importance in the development of contemporary religious life.

This idea is especially discussed in 'The Spiritual Contribution of the Far East' (1947),[37] written after Teilhard's final return from the Far East. Although this essay was backed by detailed reading and discussions with Orientalists, Teilhard explicitly states that he writes without claiming any 'special competence in the history of Asiatic thought'. Yet based on considerable experience of the Far East, he wants to offer some personal reflections to those who, under the influence of popular writings, have formed a vague and rather uniform impression of Eastern spirituality.

Basically, he distinguishes three types of Eastern spirituality found in India, China and Japan. India mainly represents an extraordinary sense of the one and divine, expressed through both pantheistic and theistic attitudes. However, for the Indian, in contrast to the Westerner,

the world is in some way less clear than God : so much so, that it is the world and not God whose existence presents difficulty to the intelligence and needs to be justified. The invisible is more real than the visible : that is the fundamental religious experience – initially diffuse in the poetry of the Upanishads, and gradually condensed later in the commentaries of the Vedanta – which, right up to the present day, has continually sought embodiment in a complex series of monist philosophies : while at the same time, through an accompanying exaggeration of the feeling of the 'unreality of phenomena', Buddhism was being born, causing a large proportion of mystical energies to evaporate in 'the intoxication of emptiness'.[38]

China, by contrast, is fundamentally naturalistic and human-ist. Chinese thought was dominated throughout its history 'by an ever-present sense of the *primacy of the tangible* in relation to the invisible'. This predominant orientation is not only found in Taoism and Confucianism but Teilhard rightly points out that it also transformed Buddhism when it arrived in the Far East by substituting for Nirvana 'the attractive, compassionate, and so human figure of Amida'.[39]

Japan's particular form of humanism, in contrast to China's, is 'an heroic sense of the collective'. These three different types of Eastern spirituality are characterized by Teilhard as pre-dominantly expressing a 'mysticism of God', a 'mysticism of the individual confronted with the world' and a 'social mys-ticism'. They are seen to be mutually exclusive rather than complementary types, at least in their present form.

If India is characterized by 'an atmosphere of the trans-cendent and divine', China has always been 'a focus of material and human aspirations'. But it is perhaps more the *'apprecia-tion* of man' than what Teilhard calls the *'faith in man'* and his possibilities which belong to ancient China. To preserve the harmony of an established order, to seek equilibrium rather than conquest, such is Chinese wisdom which comes to terms with the world.[40]

Japanese spirituality lacks neither dynamic movement nor the spirit of conquest but there exists no adequate structure to utilize 'this magnificent source of energy'. The practical spirit of service and sacrifice found in Japan has remained within the narrow boundaries of a racial mentality, centred on a common origin, giving rise to 'an exclusive, closed mys-ticism'.[41]

'God and his transcendence; the world and its value; the individual and the importance of the person: mankind and social requirements' – each of these problems have found a particular solution in Eastern spirituality but no overall syn-thesis has been attempted. It is precisely the search for such an integrated approach which Teilhard saw as 'the problem of the spirit, taken in its complete totality'.[42] The East has not solved this problem yet; nor, one might add, has the West.

However, Teilhard thought that a basically *new* solution, never tried before, may ultimately be found on the new 'road of the West'. This is described as 'an advance, a general breakthrough' of the spirit, a drive of 'all reflective consciousness in the direction of an increasing unity', a convergence still to be achieved.[43] This new type of spirituality is a hitherto untried synthesis which places a supreme value on all human effort, including man's most material activities. Far from having found its clear expression, Teilhard saw this spirituality as the basic 'note' or orientation underlying the 'creative fever of the West'. Combined with it, 'there is a true mystical ferment . . . a young mysticism, original and powerful, still perhaps clumsily constructed and ill-expressed in its theory, but perfectly defined in its main lines . . .' This mysticism is animated by love as 'the supreme spiritual energy' and centred on 'the irreplaceable and incommunicable essence' of the human person.[44]

Whilst Europe is looking to Asia for wisdom, Asia is turning to the West for its science and technology. But Teilhard asked with some justification : are there not also signs that the East is joining up 'not only technologically but mystically too, with the road of the West'? If such a juncture between the two 'roads' is to occur in the future, what will be the contribution, the specific 'note' of the East? Against the naive conception of a unitary form of Eastern spirituality, easily assumed by many Westerners, Teilhard briefly pointed out that the East has developed several types of spirituality, incompatible in their present form. These different types have not yet found their common meeting-point. Nor has the West, after surging ahead in certain developments, been able to determine the possible and necessary 'confluence of East and West',[45] understood as the future meeting of Eastern and Western spiritualities and cultures. The Eastern 'currents' will contribute 'greater vigour' and provide a 'qualitative enrichment' to the new 'road of the West'. Taken together, these two 'roads' may lead to the development of a new spirituality for mankind.

However, Teilhard did not envisage this meeting of the two 'roads' to occur like the merging of 'two complementary blocs' or 'two conflicting principles' into one. Instead, he likened their confluence and convergence to the way several rivers come together to cut a breach through a barrier common to them all. The breakthrough is first achieved through using and widening out an opening initially cut by one of the rivers. For complex historical reasons the opening of such a road, connected with 'a new surge of human consciousness', occurred in the West. But ultimately both East and West will contribute to the shape this road is going to take. For example, Teilhard saw signs of a spiritual rapprochement in the influence Western thought has had on contemporary Indian thinkers such as Tagore, and on recent developments in China and Japan.[46]

With human consciousness at the threshold of a new stage of development, the real battle for the spirit is only beginning now. All available forces, whether from East or West, have to be brought into action to win this battle:

For a long time now, the Eastern soul (Hindu, Chinese, or Japanese), each following its own specially favoured line and its own special way, has had the answer to the religious aspirations whose pole of convergence and whose laws we, in the West, are now engaged in determining more exactly: that answer is no doubt less clear than ours and less of a synthesis, but it has, possibly, a deeper innate foundation, and greater vigour. And what results may we not expect when the confluence is at last effected? In the first place, there will be the quantitative influx of a vast human flood now waiting to be used; but what is even more valuable, there will be the qualitative enrichment produced by the coming together of different psychic essences and different temperaments.[47]

In the religious as in the scientific domain, it is only in union with all other men 'that each individual man can hope to reach what is most ultimate and profound in his own being.' The spiritual contribution of the Far East does not so much lie in 'a higher form of spirit' which, some mistakenly think, it may give to the West but, rather, the new 'mystical note rising from the West' will be enlarged and enriched by the deepest insights of the East.

IV

What is meant by this? Why does Teilhard believe in a new 'mystical note' rising from the West? He thought that the new mysticism of the 'road of the West' is not only rooted in the Western religious tradition; it is also closely linked with new forms of humanism and the entire experience of modernity first encountered in the West, but now becoming universal.

In some way, this can be compared with the development of modern science as universal and global. It is well known that Western antique and medieval science absorbed many ideas of inventions from the East but the breakthrough to modern science first occurred in the West. Joseph Needham speaks about the 'fusion point' of Eastern and Western scientific ideas which has occurred in most sciences but not in all, and has brought about what he calls the 'oecumenogenesis' of modern science: 'The more "biological" the science, the more organic its subject-matter, the longer the process seems to take; and in the most difficult field of all, the study of the human and animal body in health and disease, the process is as yet far from accomplished'.[48] Leading on from this, one can say that a 'fusion point' of Eastern and Western ideas in the more abstract areas of philosophy and religion is even further away. Yet such a 'confluence' of thought is necessary if a truly universal civilization and a new realm of religious and mystical experience are to emerge.

Thus, as with the emergence of modern science, Teilhard thought that the creative religious effort required for the present will initially come from the West. In other words, it will develop in the direction which the West has begun to take already, but it is a process far from complete. It not only implies the transformation of the West's own religious heritage but an ultimate 'confluence' or 'convergence' of religions. It was a new type of spirituality he was thinking of when he referred, rather misleadingly, to the 'road of the West' as if it existed already and were complete. At other times, however, he described this new spirituality much more suitably as a 'new mysticism of convergence'.

Interreligious encounter and dialogue as we know it in the present, more open climate of thought, was less practised during Teilhard's days. Yet many of his ideas are favourable to a meeting of religions in a convergent perspective. For him this implied the search for a differentiated unity still to be achieved rather than the claim that an essential, reductionist unity already exists. The meeting of religions is not to be found in 'the sterile and conservative ecumenism of a "common ground" but [in] the creative ecumenism of a "convergence" ... on a common ideal'.[49]

But this is not to be understood as syncretism. Teilhard clearly perceived both the diversity and complementarity of the 'active currents of faith'. Religious diversity is here to stay just as social, cultural and racial diversity have to be recognized and lived with. Rightly understood, they offer tremendous resources for mutual enrichment. Besides, underneath the outward diversity, convergent lines of development can be perceived. One may wonder how far the different religious traditions today are not in the process of developing a unitary-and-differentiated, though not uniform, belief system which is becoming increasingly similar?

R. E. Whitson has fruitfully explored the potential of a convergent perspective for the encounter of religions. In his book *The Coming Convergence of World Religions*[50] he writes:

As with general cultural convergence, religious convergence is unitive yet diversified. It excludes reduction and substitution as emerging from the unitive process, expecting, rather, some form of unitive pluralism. Religious convergence is not syncretism ... [nor does it] consist in the emergence of one tradition as simply dominant and absorbing the others.

. . . . . .

. . . the religious traditions have developed separately and now will continue their development together. They have a *further meaning together* which we had not even suspected. It is not that we will discover that all along they really were all the same. On the contrary, we must expect to find that their differences . . . are actually meaningful together, contribute to each other and constitute the new unity out of their diversity.[51]

In Teilhardian terms, convergent lines towards a creative religious effort are appearing on the horizon. They hold the promise for a future of religion, but a religion unlike that of the past. It is a religion which sees the world as one and, through a continuous and dynamic development, seeks a new synthesis beyond the past dichotomies of the religious and secular, sacred and profane, spiritual and material, heavenly and worldly. It is in this sense that Teilhard wrote that the era not of religions 'but of *religion* has by no means been left behind: it is quite certainly only beginning'.[52]

Religions will converge through a concurrent process of differentiation and unification, and not through reduction and syncretism. It is not in terms of institutional forms and power but, rather, in the essential, activating force of what is traditionally called 'spirituality' that Teilhard saw the increasing influence of religion and, even more, of a rightly understood mysticism. From 1933 onwards he referred to the 'convergence of religions'. But it was only in later years that he expressed more clearly what this might imply. He then saw the tension between religious 'alternatives' less in terms of East and West than between opposing types of belief. What is most urgently required is the integration of the perennial insights of the world religions with the new insights of the modern world in evolution.

For him the convergence of 'roads' had to occur around a 'religion of action',[53] a premiss not necessarily accepted by all religious thinkers today. The image of different rivers using a breach first cut by one of them as well as the concept of convergence implies a predominant orientation, not an indiscriminate fusion. Convergence occurs around a principal 'axis'. The essential insights of the Christian tradition, together with certain developments of the modern world, are seen as such an 'axis' whose positive characteristics lie in its world-affirming and world-transforming capacity, and its potential for a mysticism of action.

Christianity itself was less and less understood as a particular set of doctrines by Teilhard than as a specific *axis of* development, important for the future of religion, acting as some sort of catalyst for the development of modern spirituality. The *new* 'road' of spirituality which he envisaged is 'amplified by a long living tradition' of what is most essential to Christianity.[54] Many past rituals and beliefs may well be irrelevant at present and one can ask what will remain of Christianity many years after now?[55] A merely backward-looking revival would be inadequate for any religious tradition; it would indicate the absence of true religious creativity. Christianity may have served as 'the matrix of western civilization' and 'everyone is prepared to admit the importance of Christianity *in the past*; but what about the present? and still more about the future?'[56]

Teilhard's writings include a detailed critique of certain Christian beliefs and suggest new lines of interpretation. This reinterpretation of Christianity for the modern world must be recognized as the major purpose of Teilhard's work but it can only be briefly touched upon here. In 1927, when speaking of the possibility of a spiritual collaboration between East and West, he wrote:

Look: we just can't breathe in our different compartments, our closed categories. Without destroying our more limited organisms, we must fuse them together, synthesise them ... The fact is, one sometimes gets the impression that our little churches hide the earth from us. I've just remembered a thought I first had over ten years ago. There are some who want to identify Christian orthodoxy with 'integrism', that is to say with respect for the tiniest wheels of a little microcosm constructed centuries ago. In reality, the true Christian ideal is 'integralism', namely the extension of the Christian directives to all the resources contained in the world. Integralism or integrism, dogma-as-axis or dogma-as-framework, there we have the struggle that has been going on in the Church for more than a century. Integrism is simple and convenient, both for the faithful and the authorities. But it implicitly excludes from God's Kingdom (or denies on principle) the huge potentialities whirling around us in social and moral questions, in philosophy, science, etc . . .[57]

Later, he stated in the important essay 'How I Believe' (1934), written as 'a personal confession',[58] what he considered this 'dogma-as-axis' to be. Whilst Christianity 'is eminently the religion of the imperishable and the personal', whose God 'thinks, loves, speaks, punishes, rewards, in the same way as *a person* does', much of the Christian 'road' has been too other-worldly in the past: 'Christianity gives the impression of not believing in human progress. It has never developed *the sense of the earth*, or it has allowed that sense to lie dormant in it'. It is precisely the encounter between Christianity and the development of the modern world – the sense of the earth in all its aspects – which make a new synthesis, a convergent road, possible and necessary.

However, the axis and centre of the Christian tradition relates to the figure of Christ, reinterpreted by Teilhard on a cosmic scale as the universal Christ who combines the personal with the universal. This mystery of the Divine incarnate in matter and flesh answers both monistic and theistic aspirations. Its powerful vision was for Teilhard the fulfilment of 'the very hopes which neither the pantheisms of the East nor those of the West could satisfy'. As a synthesis of Christ and the universe in evolution, the universal Christ represents a figure which can give 'meaning and direction to the world'.[59] The 'essence of Christianity is neither more nor less than a belief in the unification of the world in God by the Incarnation'.[60] Without the reality of the Incarnation, Christianity loses all its splendour and power of attraction, its distinctive dynamic. Abandoning this mystery would mean to lose sight of the true heart of reality. Thus, Teilhard could have had little sympathy with some of the arguments advanced in the book *The Myth of God Incarnate*. He emphasized, by contrast, the central role of the Incarnation and referred to the 'infinite possibilities which the "universalization" of Christ opens up for religious thought'.[61]

It was in this context that he first spoke of 'a general convergence of religions upon a universal Christ who fundamentally satisfies them all : that seems to me the only possible conversion of the world, and the only form in which a religion of the future can be conceived'.[62] However, it would be wrong to conclude from this that Christianity is the fulfilment of the world religions. Teilhard's symbol of the 'universal Christ' is by no means identical with Christianity but far transcends its limits. The central axis around which a convergence of religions might occur is not identical with Christianity as we know it but, rather, with *'Christianity faithfully extended to its utmost limit'.*[63] First expressed in 1933, this view was later further modified and itself 'universalized' when he recognized more clearly the implications of convergence for the contemporary situation of world religions. What Teilhard meant by the convergence of 'roads' can now be summarized.

V

Teilhard compared the different religions with 'living branches' which are developing on a central stem. He also likened them to 'rivers' joining a stream or 'currents' within the one great river of mankind. At present, these 'currents' are still at cross-purposes but they can be seen as 'coming to run together'.[64] Thus expressed, one might think of a simple fusion of all religions. This impression is also gained when he refers to 'confluence' which merely means the flowing together of various rivers, without any indication of the direction of the flow. Thus, he speaks about the 'confluence' as well as the 'convergence' of religions but one has to point out that there exists a subtle but very important difference between these two terms.

Teilhard applied the idea of 'confluence' to a number of inter-related phenomena. In subtitles, he referred to 'The Confluence of Religions' (1934),[65] 'The Confluence of Human Branches' (1939),[66] 'The Confluence of Thought' (1940),[67] and 'The Confluence of East and West' (1947).[68] They all express the idea that there is a movement towards greater unification at work in human life and thought, a movement also affecting the world religions. Nothing, however, is implied about the direction of this movement.

That there is such a direction and selection, rather than an indiscriminate random gathering, is definitely expressed by the term 'convergence'. It connotes a certain definite orientation, indicated by three aspects: convergence occurs around a central 'axis'; the movement of convergence leads towards a 'summit' where the different currents truly converge; and the term convergence also implies a certain irreversibility of movement. The most frequent similes used by Teilhard to describe this movement are either the spiral which, unlike the simple coil, is truly centred, or the cone with its apex.[69]

Like 'confluence', the term 'convergence' is applied to mankind itself and to human thought and civilization in general. In fact, the convergence of religions is a special case of the more general convergence of mankind which can be observed today. Through external conditions, mankind is being drawn closer together to form one world and ultimately one civilization. However, external forces alone are unable to bring about real unity. They can only produce what has been called 'a mechanistic unity';[70] they do not create a truly organic unity between men. To bring about unanimity and transform the disparate fragments of humankind into a new humanity, the spiritual energies of inner bonds of love and fellowship are required. For this reason, Teilhard particularly stressed the importance of the convergence of religions for the development of such unity.

'Confluence' and 'convergence' are sometimes used interchangeably but where this occurs, the first term tends to imply the directedness of the second. An exception is the explicit distinction between the two, found in a letter of 1953: 'I insist on the possible difference ... between human "confluence" and "convergence": the first would come to an end with the formation of a "pool" ...., – the second leaves open the possibility (or even the probability) of a critical point of Reflection ... ahead.'[71]

Convergence always occurs around a specific axis which

denotes the overall direction of future developments. In the evolutionary framework of Teilhard's thought, the 'stability of essences', characteristic of the static philosophies of being, has been replaced by the 'permanence of axes'. However, Teilhard's dynamic vision is not a philosophy of pure becoming in the Heraclitean sense where everything is simply in flux; nor, one might add, is it like the Buddhist view of impermanence and change. Instead of being an undifferentiated movement and constant flux, change occurs as 'convergent genesis', bringing about the birth of some new mutation or synthesis, both at a higher level, and in the forward move of time.[72]

To bring out this idea even more, Teilhard uses another concept from the life sciences and applies it to the development of religion. This is the concept of 'phylum'. The phyla are the major lines or branches of the evolutionary series of living forms, the 'natural units' of the world. In *The Phenomenon of Man*, Teilhard describes the phylum in the context of the expansion of life.[73] It is a living 'bundle' which develops on its own, autonomously; it is also a collective reality of many forms, bound together through a specific structure, and characterized by a dynamic nature which can only be seen properly in movement. By analogy, the term is used for religion. Christianity is said to be a 'phylum' in the development of religions, but so is 'the religion of tomorrow':

Religion, like science or civilization, has (if I may use the term) an 'onto-genesis' co-extensive with the history of mankind. Thus, true religion (by which I mean the form of religion at which the general groping of reflective action on earth will one day arrive), like every other reality of the 'planetary' order, partakes of the nature of a 'phylum'.[74]

The use of such terms as 'axis' and 'phylum' indicates that when Teilhard sees the different religions as branches, he does not mean this at all in the sense in which, for example, Ramakrishna and Gandhi speak about all religions being branches of the same tree. The latter imply by this image the undifferentiated unity of all religions, what one might call their 'common ground'. Their idea proceeds from the assumption of an 'essential unity' of all religions and points to the relative nature of all formulated creeds. In this sense, unity is there as a basis or essence; it is not a summit still to be achieved. A unity of convergence by contrast represents a synthesis which integrates and transcends rather than reduces the multiplicity of existing religions. Seen in this perspective, Hindu universalism towards other religions is comparable to its monistic pattern in mysticism. Thus, two incompatible attitudes are apparent in the notion of the 'convergence of religions' so long as it is not decided whether such convergence 'must be effected between lines of equal value (syncretism) or along a privileged central axis'.[75]

For Teilhard unity is not pregiven, not reducible to something already there. Like all living things it has to grow and take shape over time. The different branches of a tree are not all alike but differ in form and importance. The growth of a tree advances mainly through a central stem, a trunk, and individual branches have their points of growth too. There is both differentiation and unity, and there are major lines of development. In this perspective, the convergence of 'roads' is not a simple coming together, a mere random 'confluence'. It implies neither a reduction in what is essential nor an artificial syncretism. Particular elements of growth in the religious traditions of East and West favour convergence around a specific axis. But such an axis must nevertheless integrate several components from different sources.

The idea of convergence is a very fruitful and powerful one. It first took shape in Teilhard's mind through the convergent nature of his own experiences in West and East, in science and religion. But the idea of convergence has a great potential for further development,[76] going well beyond the use Teilhard himself made of this concept. It is without doubt that the distinctions between the 'road of the East' and the 'road of the West' recede into the background before his far more compelling and attractive vision of a 'convergence of roads'. But more than the 'convergence of roads' or the 'confluence of East and West' it is the emphasis on the 'convergence of religions' which presents a thought of seminal importance today. At least this is true for all who are longing for greater unity in the world and prefer planetary to ethnocentric thinking.

A convergent encounter of the world religions has vital consequences for the understanding and practice of spirituality today. More and more signs point to spirituality as of utmost importance. For more than any institution, ritual, or creed, it is the realm of the spiritual which is coming to be seen as the essential area of religion. The exploration of this field is gaining increasing interest, and more people than ever before are attracted to venture on hitherto uncharted roads into a territory of great promise.

However, the idea of a new spirituality born from the experience of convergent encounter belongs on to a wider context, namely, that of the close relationship between religion and the general dynamic of human, cultural and social evolution. The interdependence of evolution and religion is as decisive for understanding Teilhard's approach to Eastern religions as it is for his reinterpretation of Christianity. Only when considering this crucial aspect of his thought, can one understand why it is important to distinguish different types of spirituality and mysticism and why, in spite of the existing diversity of religions in the world, a unity of convergence can be conceived.

8

Religion and Evolution

The word evolution is often simply understood to mean bio-logical evolution or the development and growth of living forms as first outlined by Charles Darwin. But let us not forget that the word itself evolved and that Darwin was not the first to use it. Social and historical thinkers before him had already applied the concept to the development of the human mind and different societies, and only subsequently was the idea introduced into biology. It was in fact the suggestions of his predecessors which inspired Darwin to adopt the view of evolution to explain the observations made during his famous voyage to South America on HMS *Beagle*.

Since Darwin's days the scientific understanding of the working of evolution has been greatly expanded and modified. Several scientists have also proposed interpretations of the wider meaning of evolution, for it is without doubt that the social importance of evolution is enormous, not only for understanding the past but for providing insights or even guidelines for the future. The fact of organic evolution is one of the basic characteristics of the world in which we live. But how does this basic fact relate to the way we think and act? So far, the consciousness of many individuals has been little affected by the discovery of evolution. The life of their inner world has taken little cognizance of the dynamics of the outer world. However, the recognition of evolution as a unifying perspective and process affecting all aspects of the modern world has revolutionary consequences. Few religious thinkers have taken the trouble of wrestling with this challenging issue; few have reflected on the crucial importance of evolution for religious thought and practice.

Teilhard is one of the few modern thinkers on religion for whom evolution provided the dominant note of his entire work. As he wrote in his best-known book, *The Phenomenon of Man*, evolution was to him much more than 'a theory, a system or a hypothesis'. On the contrary, he considered it to be 'a general condition to which all theories, all hypotheses, all systems must bow . . . Evolution is a light illuminating all facts, a curve that all lines must follow'.[1] From early on, he was conscious of the importance of evolution for contemporary religion and much of his search for a new spirituality commensurate with the modern world revolves around the attempt at bringing together mystic-religious insights and evolutionary understanding.

The basic structure of an evolutionary perspective underlies all his thought on religion; it shaped his critical comments on particular religions and provoked certain general reflections on the place of religion in the modern world. Already in 1916 he wrote: 'Religion and evolution should neither be confused nor divorced. They are destined to form one single continuous organism, in which their respective lives prolong, are dependent on, and complete one another, without being identified or lost . . . Since it is in our age that the duality has become so markedly apparent, it is for us to effect the synthesis.[2]

This synthesis he saw as his life-long task and, in one way or another, all his essays touch upon religion and evolution. But three main themes can be singled out in particular: the recognition of the historical evolution of religion in the past; the evolutionary role of religion for mankind's present and future development; and the further evolution of religion itself.

I

In the past, religions developed for the most part independently of each other. Like the great civilizations they grew 'in patches', in separate geographical and historical contexts. When they came into contact at all, it was frequently in a situation of contrast and opposition where one religion tended to dominate, supplant, or conquer the other. Today, in a politically post-colonial world, all societies are economically, technically and scientifically closely interdependent and need to co-operate if they want to survive. With more direct communications and many more sources of information, we are also gaining a growing acquaintance with each other's religious heritage. This new situation calls for a new understanding of religion which will make more people comprehend each other's religious differences by referring to them in a mutually meaningful way rather than in terms of exclusive opposition.

Reflecting on religion today from a historical and evolutionary perspective, Teilhard was convinced that the historical evolution of the great religions cannot provide the full answer as to the nature and meaning of religion itself. The quest for the origin of religion in the past history and prehistory of mankind has proved as elusive as the search for the absolute origin of man himself. Nineteenth-century scholars committed a 'genetic fallacy' when they assumed that the beginning or genesis of religion could be fully traced and analysed or, alternatively, that the beginnings would provide the ultimate touchstone by which existing religions could be assessed. Teilhard often expressed the view that the meaning of a particular religion cannot be exhaustively expressed at its moment of origin.

Thus, he did not share the views of those who nostalgically preach an eternal return to the origins of religion, to a golden age when man was supposedly at unity with nature and himself. Nor did he side with progressive thinkers who take religion to be an outdated stage of man's earlier development, now surpassed. The knowledge of evolution may have led some to think

that nothing of our past beliefs remained. Indeed there have been a great number of systems in which the fact of religion was interpreted as a psychological phenomenon linked with the childhood of humanity. At its greatest, at the origins of civilization, it had gradually to decline and give place to more positive theories from which God (a personal and transcendent God above all) must be excluded. This was a pure illusion.[3]

It is necessary most of all to combat a narrow understanding of religion which is based on the assumption that 'science has made God and religions superfluous'. In the past, religions encompassed a complex variety of beliefs and practical skills from which, through increasing differentiation over a long period of time, separate disciplines with their own methods and results emerged. However, this does not mean that 'the need for an Absolute' on which, according to Teilhard, all religions are based, disappeared in the course of that differentiation. In fact, this need is becoming more apparent in the modern world than ever before. It is precisely the function of religion to provide a 'dominating principle of order, and an axis of movement'. More than anything else, it is religion which gives men 'something of supreme value, to create, to hold in awe, or to love'.

In certain cases, religion may well be an 'opium' or simply a wish-fulfilment, providing man with solace and escape; yet this is not the true role of religion. At the critical stage of man's present development, the nature of religion, too, is coming into sharper focus and may be more clearly recognized. For Teilhard, 'the phenomenon of religion cannot be regarded as the manifestation of a transitory stage, which is destined to grow weaker and disappear with the growth of mankind'. Rather, religion 'must of itself grow greater and more clearly defined' to the same extent that man becomes more adult.[4] Teilhard was fond of quoting Julian Huxley's idea that in man evolution has now become conscious of itself, 'dangerously and critically so – conscious and perfected to the point of being able to control its own driving forces and to rebound upon itself'.[5]

But despite or, in fact, because of a tremendous drive towards human unity, 'we are passing through a critical phase of individualism' where a 'kind of rebellious independence becomes the ideal moral attitude. Intellectually, this dispersion of past efforts and thoughts takes the form of agnosticism'.[6] Teilhard thinks it possible and likely that mankind is at the threshold of higher forms of consciousness at both a personal and social level. The responsibility for further self-evolution lies now with man himself rather than with external factors. Rightly understood, a higher social integration of mankind, so necessary for human survival, is linked to a fuller development of the inner resources of the human person. The development of both individual and community are, therefore, not seen as mutually exclusive but as interdependent.[7] Thus, Teilhard emphasizes both the personal and social dimension of religious teachings and this has practical implications for both religion and politics.

The immense evolutionary process is seen as progressing towards a summit. This summit is understood as both spiritual and personal. Because of the importance assigned to the personal, Teilhard considered theistic forms of belief as the highest expression of religious consciousness so far developed. However, it is precisely this form of belief which is currently experiencing its acutest crisis. The awakening of 'the sense of man' and 'the spirit of the earth', rather than the spirit of God, has led to the emergence of a faith in man and the world unknown before. Religious consciousness itself is undergoing a radical transformation, not comparable to the previous emergence and development of any particular religion: 'The present event is much more massive than the coming of Buddhism or Islam . . .' Modern man is beginning to understand that in the future the only religion possible 'is the religion which will teach him, *in the very first place*, to recognize, love, and serve with passion the universe of which he forms a part'.[8]

At the moment, Christian monotheism is more explicitly affected by this metamorphosis than any other religious tradition. However, the increasing impact of the modern world, or what others would call the growing forces of secularization, will eventually come to be felt by all religions.[9] Speaking about the growing indifference to Christianity, Teilhard wrote:

Faith in the world is irresistibly establishing itself at the heart of a civilization which is still dominated by, or which at any rate was formed by, faith in Christ. Inevitably, an extremely grave organic conflict is being produced between these two principles. If we appreciate the depth of this dramatic struggle, we have a perfectly clear explanation of the troubles which, for the last century, have been disturbing the world of established religions in the West.[10]

It was especially the image of God which Teilhard saw in need of urgent redefinition. Modern man has not yet found the God he can adore, a God commensurate to the newly discovered dimensions of the universe. In 1950, he noted in his diary: 'God is not dead — but HE CHANGES'.[11] In a letter to a friend, he referred to 'the transformation . . . of the "God of the Gospel" into the "God of Evolution" — a transformation without deformation'. This dynamic approach to the concept of God and his relation to the world forms in fact the central theme of modern process theology.[12]

However, a new religious vision cannot develop in cultural isolation. In Teilhard's view it requires the coming together of experiences drawn from different religious traditions. This is nowhere more apparent than in his emphasis on the evolutionary role and function of religious insights in the general development of mankind.

II

For some people the process of evolution appears to be so multi-directional that no clear pattern is discernible. Others believe evolution to occur either at random or to develop towards greater divergence. Teilhard, however, considers the evolutionary process to be of a convergent rather than divergent nature, pointing to the possibility of an increasingly greater unity. As expressed in a brief 'profession of faith',[13] drafted in 1933, Teilhard also saw this unity as gradually being built up through the work going on in the world. Ultimately, it is a unity of a spiritual kind with 'spirit being understood, not as an exclusion, but as the transformation or a sublimation, or a climax of matter'. Seen from this perspective, 'the substantial joy of life is found in the consciousness or feeling, that by *everything* we enjoy, create, overcome, discover, or suffer, in ourselves or in the others, in any possible line of life or death (organic, biological, social, artistic, scientific, etc.) we are gradually increasing (and we are gradually incorporated into) the growing Soul or Spirit of the world'.

This passage expresses clearly that evolution is not taken to be an impersonal, automatic process occurring outside man. On the contrary, man's work has a decisive role to play in influencing the direction of evolution. To further a spiritually transforming evolutionary process towards something 'supremely conscious and personal' is, to Teilhard, man's most noble task, a task in which he is helped, sustained and guided by religion.

From his earliest days, Teilhard regarded religion as the most important source of the psychic, mental and spiritual energy required for human action. He wrote in 1915 that 'one of the surest marks of the truth of religion, in itself and in an individual soul, is to note to what extent it brings into action, that is, causes to rise up from sources deep within each one of us a certain maxim of energy and effort. Action and sanctification go hand in hand, each supporting the other'.[14]

If religion is here presented as a source of energy for the individual, the dynamic and 'energizing' aspects of religion were later predominantly expressed with reference to the human group. For example, in the essay 'The Phenomenon of Man' (1930) the achievement of greater human unity is seen as closely interlinked with morality and religion which assume 'a strictly energizing and structural value' and are 'both closely concerned with the true conservation and progress of the universe'.[15]

In 'The Spirit of the Earth' (1931) the true function of religion, not always clearly perceived in the past, is 'to sustain and spur on the progress of life'. Thus, the 'religious function' increases in the same direction and to the same extent as 'hominization'. Religion grows 'continuously with man himself' by taking on a new and more closely determined form with each new phase of mankind.[16] As stated elsewhere, religion is biologically 'the necessary counterpart to the release of the earth's spiritual energy'. It was 'born to animate and control this overflow of spirit' and 'must itself grow greater and more clearly defined in step with it and in the same degree'.[17]

The 'phenomenon of the spirit' consists of 'interiorization' or 'concentration'.[18] It is the 'biological role' of religion not only to lead to such inner concentration but to be an 'animator' of human action in the widest sense by giving 'a form to the free psychic energy of the world'[19] and sustaining man's zest for life.

This theme is more fully developed in 'The Zest for Living' (1950),[20] originally a lecture given to the French branch of the *World Congress of Faiths*. There Teilhard explains that the mainspring for mankind's further self-evolution lies in the maintenance of a vigorous 'taste for life' and action. Contemporary man's greatest enemy is a *'taedium vitae'*, that is to say, a sense of inner boredom and indifference, a lack of meaning and ultimate value. In his view, the most essential requirement in furthering evolution consists in the provision of the necessary spiritual energy. This is *'entrusted* to the expert knowledge and skill of *religions'*. Religions have an 'evolutionary role' in animating man; they alone can give him what is most vitally necessary: 'a faith – and a great faith – and ever more faith'. Yet in the present situation this role of maintaining the zest for living is dependent on 'the combined effort of religions'.[21]

Teilhard enquires into the spiritual energy resources available to the world and points to a striking contrast which applies even more forcefully to our own energy-conscious days:

. . . all over the earth the attention of thousands of engineers and economists is concentrated on the problem of world resources of coal, oil or uranium – and yet nobody, on the other hand, bothers to carry out a survey of the zest for life: to take its 'temperature', to feed it, to look after it, and (why not, indeed?) to increase it.[22]

For him all energy is 'psychic in nature', defined as 'a capacity for action or, more exactly, for interaction'.[23] Scientists are rightly concerned with the material energy resources of mankind; it is equally necessary, however, to take stock of our inner resources which continually feed and shape fundamental attitudes to life and action.

Evolution in the sense of continuing development and growth will also affect the 'reserves of faith'. For Teilhard, the quantity and quality of the religious sense available in our world must continually increase. This view is very much dependent on his overall perspective of evolution. Others might argue with equal persuasion that the forces of religion are decreasing rather than growing at present, that religion is on the retreat. However, Teilhard did not share this position; he saw the growth of religion linked to the development of increasing convergence which includes a specific direction: 'A sifting and general convergence of religions, governed by and based on their value as evolutionary stimulus' for the whole of mankind.[24]

Arguing for an interdependent development of evolution and religion. Teilhard contended that in the past religions were largely concerned with individual salvation, but in the present they must also be able to provide an ideal for the human community. Yet up to now, the various creeds have not fulfilled this function: 'However universal their promises and visions of the beyond might be, they did not explicitly . . . allow any room to a global and controlled transformation of the whole of life and thought' on earth here and now. The different religions grew up at a time when a truly universal perspective did not really exist and the need for a greater human unity was not yet realized. What is needed today is:

No longer simply a religion of individuals and of heaven, but a religion of mankind and of the earth . . .
In these circumstances, we are forced to recognize that nothing can subsist tomorrow . . . except those mystical currents which are able, through a synthesis of the traditional faith in the above and our generation's newborn faith in some issue towards the ahead, to make ready and to provide a complete pabulum for our 'need to be'.[25]

As expressed elsewhere, over the last century mankind has seen 'the birth and establishment of a new faith: the religion of evolution'. This 'youthful form of religion', represented by various neo-humanist and Marxist movements, is a 'contagious faith in an ideal to which a man's life can be given'. Contemporary collective and social movements embody a powerful vision whose force of inspiration Teilhard often admired. Such movements possess a vivid 'sense of the earth', a dynamic vigour and deep commitment to the development of the world which the older religions often lack. Contemporary social and political movements are based on a concern for social action and justice, and their sense of urgency contrasts sharply with the dreary piety of many religious bodies. However, ultimately, neo-humanism and Marxism leave us with a 'feeling of insecurity' and 'incompleteness' through their inability to point towards a transcendence beyond man. Although vitally concerned with the raising of consciousness, many contemporary movements do not understand the true nature of the spirit as 'endowed with immortality and personality'.[26]

But if the developments of modern society are really so truly novel, one might well ask why not 'regroup the whole of the earth's religious power directly and *a novo* upon some "evolutionary sense" or "sense of man" – and pay no attention to the ancient creeds'? Why not, in fact, have 'a completely fresh faith, rather than a rejuvenation and confluence' of the old religions?[27]

Teilhard posed this question very deliberately. It may have been especially asked with reference to Julian Huxley's attempt to create a new religion under the name of 'evolutionary humanism'. It is known that he greatly admired Huxley's work and recognized the similarity of its direction and intent to his own.[28] Although in sympathy with Huxley's aim to construct a suitable 'ideology' for evolution by creating a faith which relates to man's contemporary situation, he considered this 'human faith', religiously speaking, a 'little elementary'. Thus, he judged it to be a 'hazy and inefficient *Weltanschauung*'. Huxley's endeavour 'to establish a new religion' cannot be successful because it lacks a divine pole and does not include the expectation of some Ultra-human.[29]

In a personal letter to Julian Huxley, Teilhard stated his conviction that evolution cannot continue without a 'faith' to maintain its élan, and that 'such a faith (in some Ultra-human) is from now on a necessary ingredient for any form of religion (and for Christianity in particular)'. Evolution has grown conscious of itself. This, as well as the phenomenon of human convergence, requires an irreversible centre, both 'lovable and loving'. Christianity discovered this empirically and this gives it an irreplaceable hold 'as long as one has not found anything better in the same direction'.[30]

In the subsequent essay 'The Christic' (1955) he doubted, however, whether human consciousness left to itself could, even in an effort of planetary co-reflection, ever found a new religion, 'the sort of religion that has been foretold with such warmth and brilliance by my friend Julian Huxley: to which he has given the name of "evolutionary humanism" '.[31] Neo-humanism may be a dynamic and even spiritualizing force but it cannot provide man with the transcendent focus disclosed by divine revelation. In fact, it is over this issue of revealed transcendence and the central message of the traditional religions that Teilhard differed most markedly from Huxley's understanding of the relationship between religion and evolution.

III

In 'The Zest for Living' (1950), Teilhard listed two reasons why the existing religions are of vital importance for man's further evolution and cannot be replaced by a completely new faith:

First of all, there can be no doubt that, in each of the great religious branches that cover the world at this moment, a certain spiritual attitude and vision which have been produced by centuries of experience are preserved and continued; these are as indispensable and irreplaceable for the integrity of a total terrestrial religious consciousness as the various 'racial' components . . . may well be for the looked-for perfecting of a final human zoological type.

But it is not only the 'irreplaceable elements of a certain complete image of the universe' which the various currents of faith, 'still active on earth, working in their incommunicable core', are handing down:

> Very much more even than *fragments of vision*, it is *experiences of contact* with a supreme Inexpressible which they preserve and pass on. It is as though, from the final issue which evolution demands and towards which it hastens, a certain influx came down to illuminate and give warmth to our lives . . .
> To preserve and increase on earth the 'pressure of evolution' it is vitally important . . . that through the mutual buttressing provided by the reflection of religious ideas a progressively more real and more magnetic God be seen by us to stand out at the higher pole of hominization.[32]

The great religions all point to the revelation of a transcendent level and focus somehow related to the realms of human experience. But through the encounter and closer coming together of the different religious traditions man's religious discovery and experience will be greatly enhanced. For Teilhard, it is in a higher divine focus and centre that man will find the deepest source of energy and action, a centre which animates all evolution and provides its final culmination too. We can best contribute to the world's development if 'sustained and guided by the tradition of the great human mystical systems along the road of contemplation and prayer, we succeed in entering directly into receptive communication with the very source of all inner élan'.[33]

It is from this source that man, in the depth of his being, can receive love 'as an effect of "grace" and "revelation"'. Thus, man's 'taste for life'[34] does not only relate to a sense of survival but beyond that includes an aspiration towards a higher form of life, a life of the spirit animated by the great insights of the religious traditions. The closer contact between the world religions today may perhaps initiate a new level of reflection, a higher form of consciousness among men.

Such contacts may help to create closer bonds of love which can provide a more compelling focus for human unity than merely external forces of unification.[35] Indeed, it was Teilhard's firm conviction that the further evolution of mankind towards greater unity 'will never materialize unless we fully develop within ourselves the exceptionally strong unifying powers exerted by inter-human sympathy and religious forces'.[36] He saw the encounter of religions as full of promise for the future of religion and was anxious to encourage efforts towards unity.

Today we can perceive the beginning convergence of the world religions but this development has not yet gained its full momentum. In fact, a further convergence of the historically diverse religious traditions appeared to Teilhard a structurally necessary requirement for the higher evolution of mankind itself. However, such convergence is not an individual but a collective phenomenon. Religion is not 'a strictly personal matter' as some might think. Teilhard condemned any individualist claim of this kind and stated from his 'spiritual-evolutionary point of view' that

> the religious phenomenon, taken as a whole, is simply the reaction of the Universe as such, of collective consciousness and human action in process of development . . .
> Religion, born of the earth's need for the disclosing of a god, is related to and co-extensive with, not the individual man but the whole of mankind. In religion, as in science, is accumulated . . . an infinity of human enquiries. How could I fail to associate myself with that accumulation . . .? I would not be so foolish as to seek to build up science by my own unaided efforts. Similarly, my own effort to reach faith can succeed only when contained within a total human experience and prolonged by it. I must therefore plunge resolutely into the great river of religions into which the rivulet of my own private enquiries has just flowed. Yet when I look around me, I see the waters are disturbed; the eddies are whirling in so many different directions. From so many quarters I can hear the summons of this or

that divine revelation. To which of these apparently opposed currents am I to surrender myself, if the stream is to carry me to the ocean?[37]

In later years, these 'opposed currents' were not so much seen in terms of Eastern and Western religions than in those of 'rival mysticisms', cutting across the existing religions rather than opposing one group of religions to another. There exists a general tension between modern science and traditional religions; more specifically, many people experience a polarization between a 'faith in God' and 'faith in the world'.[38] Mankind today is divided into two profoundly separated categories of 'believers':

a) Those whose hopes are directed towards a spiritual state or an absolute finality situated beyond and outside this world;

b) Those who hope for the perfection of the tangible Universe within itself.[39]

For Teilhard, each of these hopes provides man with 'a source of a magnificent spiritual impulse' but they must be brought together; they also must give equal room to both personality and transcendence. To combine in a unified gesture of worship man's passionate desire to conquer the world and his passionate longing to transcend it and be united with God is the required vital religious act, 'specifically new, corresponding to a new age in the history of the Earth'.[40]

These thoughts were further elaborated in the important address 'Faith in Man' (1947),[41] given at the inauguration of the French branch of the *World Congress of Faiths*. It stresses the possibility that men of different religious backgrounds can initially come together and co-operate through a commonly shared 'faith in man', defined as 'the more or less active and fervent conviction that Mankind as an organic and organized whole possesses a future' which, beyond mere survival, implies some form of higher life. Such a faith in the possibilities of man and the future of humanity is the necessary foundation for a 'basic ecumenism'. Without it an ultimate ecumenical encounter of the world religions 'at the summit' is impossible.[42] This 'faith in man' can be a 'uniting force' in the contemporary world :

> Present-day Mankind, as it becomes increasingly aware of its unity – not only past unity in the blood, but future unity in progress – is experiencing a vital need to close in upon itself. A tendency towards unification is everywhere manifest, and especially in the different branches of religion. We are looking for something that will draw us together, below or above the level of that which divides.[43]

But this 'faith in man' has to be combined with both a 'sense of the earth' and a sense of the transcendent. To achieve unity, it is necessary to share a common view of humanity and divinity. What is needed for the evolution of religion and a mutually enriching encounter of religions is

> the clear perception of a sharply defined (and real) 'type' of God, and an equally sharply defined 'type' of humanity. – If each group retains *its own* type of God and *its own* type of humanity (and if those types are heterogeneous) then no agreement can have serious value : it will be based only on ambiguities or pure sentimentality.[44]

For Teilhard, a more sharply defined 'type' of God is found in the 'universal Christ', a figure 'incommensurable with any prophet or any Buddha'. This particular concept of God is seen as 'a privileged central axis' around which a convergence of religions might occur. Yet he also says that man's image of God is not complete; the human discovery of the Divine is an ongoing process. In this sense he speaks of a 'Christic nucleus'[45] or what he calls in his diary 'Christ – the "spearhead" of monotheism'.[46] On the margin of the same diary entry one can read the addition 'Christ-Shiva'. I have mentioned before that some months earlier he had noted down that our understanding of Christ must somehow integrate those aspects of the Divine expressed by the Indian god Shiva.[47]

These ideas were never fully developed. They indicate a

search for a richer understanding of the concept of God and suggest the need for a cross-fertilization of different theological systems. Teilhard was aware that the necessary reinterpretation of Christianity could not take place without certain insights from other religious traditions. The most important reorientation, however, has to occur with regard to evolution itself. In the past all great religions have 'succeeded in determining certain definite axes of justice and holiness' but at present, 'a disturbing gap is constantly widening between our moral life and the new conditions created by the progress of the world'. One can maintain, therefore, that 'however admirable and progressive these codes of interior perfection may be, they generally have the defect of having been developed, and of being kept alive, outside the perspectives of a universe in evolution'.[48]

Faced with contemporary problems, 'it would be useless and even wrong-headed to look to the saints of the past for explicit approval or condemnation of the new attitudes suggested — since the problem of human progress (as we understand it today) *did not arise* for them'.[49] Teilhard's view of the inter-relationship between religion and evolution is linked to the fundamental conviction that 'from the depths of Matter to the highest peak of the Spirit there is only *one evolution*'.[50] Religions have an indispensable role to play in furthering man's evolutionary advance towards the spirit. But there is the difficulty that no past religious teachings can fully cope with the newness of mankind's present development. What is most needed is a creative religious effort. What is urgently required is 'a whole new philosophy of life, a whole new ethical system, and a whole new mysticism'.[51]

It is of crucial importance today whether religions can, in fact, animate and further human progress. Teilhard always maintained that the convergence of religions will occur around those elements in each religious tradition which are most suitable for activating human energy and effort. Not all religious teachings are equivalent in this respect nor do all religions have the same inner strength to animate man's forward search and his effort of building the earth. Teilhard associated 'true religion' with the 'main axis of spiritualization', closely related to the understanding of personality and transcendence.[52] Although the different religious traditions are to some extent complementary, it is important to discern a central 'axis' which can provide maximum activation for man's evolution towards the spirit. In this sense, the evolutionary value of different religions, their dynamic qualities to activate and further man's taste towards a progressive spiritualization, differ considerably.

Teilhard thought that contemporary man has to choose between three possible attitudes towards religion and evolution. Firstly, the evolutionary perspective may be so completely embraced that all traditional religions are rejected. Secondly, traditional religious teachings may be upheld in their entirety so that all evolutionary insights are excluded. Thirdly, religion may be reinterpreted in the light of evolutionary understanding so that some religious teachings are maintained and others have to be reformulated. It is in this latter sense that Teilhard foresaw a further evolution of religion as necessary, leading to a new breakthrough in spirituality. However, only the future can tell whether such a creative religious breakthrough will in fact occur. His critique of Eastern religions closely relates to particular religious values which he thought were incompatible with a modern evolutionary understanding of man and the world. That evolution is such a decisive criterion is apparent from the following remark made to a friend in Peking: 'There are *two* general attitudes with regard to evolution: either one denies or admits it. Those *who admit* it can serve it (that is the humanitarian movement) and love it (that is Christianity); those *who deny it*, condemn the process. I mean Hinduism and Buddhism'.[53]

IV

This statement can be taken as yet another expression of his frequently negative attitude to Indian religions. Yet it is perhaps in no other religious tradition that the issue of evolution has been so much debated, especially in modern times. Several Hindu reformers see the ultimate meaning of man and the cosmos in terms of a spiritual evolution. Teilhard primarily understood Indian thought to contain a certain antithesis to his own ideas through its particular understanding of unity in terms of monism. But it is equally clear that he saw yet another important difference in the respective approach to evolution.

On closer comparison, it can be maintained 'that there are many points of similarity between Teilhard's thought and the structure developed over the centuries by Hindu religious thinkers'[54] but it certainly does not apply to the understanding of evolution, as he was the first to admit. The recognition of evolution is for him part of the difference between Christianity and Hinduism although elsewhere he was apt to point out that Christianity has not sufficiently taken evolution into account either. He wrote in his *carnet de lecture* : 'Real critical dividing line between

Hinduism 1. Unity of synthesis in God.
Christianity = 2. Cosmos in evolution.'[55]

The same difference is brought out in his critical comments on the teachings of the great Hindu theologians of the Middle Ages, Shankara and Ramanuja. It would be as anachronistic, of course, to expect modern evolutionary insights from these thinkers as from medieval Christian theologians. However elevating their thought is in some respects, to Teilhard it was inadequate when looked at from the contemporary perspective of an ongoing evolution.

He stressed in particular that the Hindu understanding of evolution is primarily one of prior involution or emanation of the Divine, not unlike the emanationist philosophy of Plotinus. The process of evolution is here only a 'self-analysis of God' in the cosmos and not a true synthesis which implies that the development of man and the world really achieves something of ultimate value and significance.[56] Teilhard's idea of the process of 'evolutionary creation' is not the self-making of an always pre-existing divinity. He objected to the semi-pantheistic theories' of India which assume 'the evolution of man out of God'; this, in fact, is 'involution'. However, in spite of these differences, he also expressed the view that if the modern Vedanta were to incorporate new evolutionary insights it might coincide much more closely with a reinterpreted form of Christianity.[57]

Some may think that a modern synthesis of Indian and evolutionary ideas has been realized in the important work of Sri Aurobindo. His 'integral yoga' presents itself as a reinterpretation of Advaita Vedanta in the light of modern evolution. Although Teilhard was unfamiliar with Sri Aurobindo's writings, he may have recognized at the end of his life that *The Life Divine* is marked by a similar thrust and orientation as his own work. Yet there are fundamental differences, too, not only with regard to their understanding of the ultimate goal of evolution, and the role of individual and collective in the process of further spiritualization, as was early pointed out by Father Monchanin,[58] but also in their respective concepts of evolution and involution.

Teilhard uses the term involution but it describes a different reality from what it means in Aurobindo's thought. For both thinkers involution is the fundamental law of evolution but in an almost opposite sense.[59] When Teilhard speaks of a universe in process of involution, he refers to its increase in both external and internal complexity. The turning-in upon itself or involution of the evolutionary process is what he calls 'the great *Law of complexity and consciousness*'.[60] Stated briefly, it indicates that at all levels of life a direct correlation exists between an increased complexity of matter and a corresponding growth of interiority and consciousness.

Thus, for Teilhard, involution is part of the very process of evolution itself. For Aurobindo, however, evolution always presupposes prior involution; the latter is a condition of the former. Involution in the Aurobindian sense means 'that the Absolute, *before* evolving out of matter, first involved itself into it'.[61] Evolution is, therefore, understood as the gradual manifestation of what existed already – the divine life. There is nothing really new, no new being and no real growth.

For Teilhard 'evolution is a discovery which does not generate its term' whereas for Aurobindo the same process is 'a rediscovery of itself by the original term'. Consequently, the Absolute 'literally re-generates itself through evolution out of involution'.[62] If this is so, then Teilhard's objection that Hindu thought does not recognize newness and progressive growth as part of evolution but merely equates evolutionary development with the involution of spirit in matter, applies also to Aurobindo's reinterpretation of Hinduism. We cannot discuss this difficult issue further here but it is certain that Teilhard clearly distinguished between his own understanding of the evolutionary process and the Indian approach to evolution in terms of involution.[63] He also related this difference to a fundamentally different religious orientation towards man and the world. The interpretation given to the process of evolution is of paramount importance for, beyond explaining the organic evolution of the past, it has an even greater bearing on the present world and the shape of man's future.

V

Scientists, of course, greatly vary in their interpretation of evolution. They disagree as to its overall direction and precise mechanism and even more, its meaning for us. Some mock, ridicule, and criticize what they consider Teilhard's grand evolutionary speculations. However, this is not unlike the late eighteenth and early nineteenth century when the idea of evolution itself was first laughed at and mocked by the scientists of the day. What Teilhard glimpsed and hinted at when he spoke of the further evolution of mankind, and of religion and mysticism, may still prove to possess more substance than many dare to dream.

Already Darwin in his diary on the *Beagle* noted with wonder the stupendous dimensions of one world. Since then many scientists have both experienced and commented upon the exhilarating sense of discovery and enrichment accompanying their venture of research. Today the number of those who wish to free science from its narrow presuppositions is growing. Although the company would not be numerous, Teilhard would not be alone in seeing the insights of science as closely related to those of mysticism.

What meaning has the development of religions throughout human history? Scholars of religion have asked this question and so have sociologists. One of them has even proposed a detailed scheme of 'religious evolution', correlating different types of religious symbols with religious action, organization and social meanings.[64] Teilhard's ideas were never systematized in this manner; his reflections remain fluid, his vocabulary changing. He spoke of the evolution of religion not simply in terms of recurring religious experience but in the sense of a growing religious awareness. Several types of religious and mystical experience developed in the past but the religious sense in man is still growing. It is becoming more unified and intensive as time advances.

In spite of its past and present diversity, religion is ultimately a unitary phenomenon. Like science it is one, universal and global but embracing many different aspects. Like man himself and human culture in general, religion is subject to further evolution; it will undergo mutation and transformation. This perspective of a further evolution of religion is an integral part of Teilhard's attempt to combine the insights of religion and science and he may have pointed towards a way for their eventual reconciliation which, in the words of Julian Huxley, 'will come when the religiously minded understand that theology needs a scientific foundation, and grasp the fact that religion itself evolves, and when the scientifically minded accept the equally basic fact that religion is part of the evolutionary process and an important element in its psychological phase, of human history'.[65]

The complex developments of the contemporary world, affecting both individual and social life, have a critical effect on man's religious awareness. Modern man experiences an acute tension between the developments of secular life and the call of traditional religious precepts. Not only does the individual search for ultimate meaning and value but the whole of mankind is in need of a goal of life. Teilhard's critical attitude towards Eastern religions may be related to the fact that, during his lifetime, there existed less awareness about the necessary transformation of religion in the East than in the West. In the East, religions were more closely identified with the dominant culture and were difficult to distinguish from the traditional way of life. However, at present major social changes are taking place on a revolutionary scale, particularly in China, but also in Japan and, more recently, in Cambodia and Vietnam. Many political movements and events now challenge traditional beliefs and are vehemently anti-religious. This trenchant critique of established religions whose values were taken for granted rather than deliberately chosen in the past will necessitate a reflection on what is essential to a particular religion and what is not.

In some notes written in 1953, Teilhard indicated 'two general conditions for the future evolution of "the religious" ' :

1 If man is to reach the natural term of his development, it is essential that the religious 'temperature' rise higher and higher in mankind as it proceeds towards greater unification.
2 Of all the forms of faith tried out as possibilities in the course of time by the rising forces of religion, only that form is destined to survive which will prove capable of stimulating or 'activating' to their maximum the forces of self-evolution in man.[66]

The importance of religions is here again related to their dynamic capacity of providing man with energy for individual and social action. In the last years of his life, Teilhard was particularly concerned with reflecting on the 'ethic-mystical consequences of evolution',[67] and with developing a 'science of human energetics'.[68] He understood this as a systematic study of the energy required for the further self-evolution of man. Teilhard's emphasis on the place of energy in evolution has been recognized[69] but the central role of religion and mysticism for this 'energetics' has so far been little explored. He referred to the necessary encounter of 'physics' and 'mysticism' within 'the area of (evolutionary) energetics'. Such a new 'energetics' alone is capable of defining the necessary conditions of culture, morality and religion. However, he was aware of the difficulty of such a project when he asked the rhetorical question : 'But how to speak of all this . . . without being repudiated by both scientists and theologians?'[70]

To Teilhard, as to some other contemporary scientists and

thinkers, it had become clear 'that human progress cannot go further on without developing a Mystic of its own, a Mystic based on a *faith* in the value and "infallibility" of Evolution'.[71] Whereas he presented Christianity in his earlier years as 'the very religion of evolution',[72] he later increasingly stressed the need for a deep transformation of his own religious tradition : 'Christianity has only a chance to survive . . . if it shows itself capable . . . to activate to a maximum in man "the energy of self-evolution", i.e. if it is successful . . . not only in "amorizing" the world but in valuing it more highly than any other form of religion'.[73]

What is needed is no longer simply a 'Christianity faithfully extended to its utmost limit',[74] but a 'Christianity which surpasses itself',[75] the emergence of something 'trans-Christian' in theology and mysticism.[76] It was in this sense that he talked about 'the urgent need for the formulation of a mysticism of the West', a 'new mysticism, at once fully human and fully Christian' which could be the source of a new energy for which 'we have as yet *no name*'.[77] These formulations express suggestions, they point to possible explorations in need of further development. Approached in a spirit of encounter and convergence, they leave room for important insights from Eastern religions although Teilhard himself did not think that the major breakthrough in the future evolution of religion would occur in the East. But however critical his remarks, his letters and diaries show that his thought on Eastern religions was characterized by what Paul Tillich has called 'a dialectical union of acceptance and rejection'.[78] Speaking from an evolutionary perspective, Teilhard emphasized the need to take full cognizance of the rich and diverse religious experience of mankind so that a truly global religious consciousness can be developed.

Elsewhere he referred to the possibility of a 'mystical evolution'[79] for he did not regard mysticism as something of merely historical interest but, on the contrary, of the greatest contemporary importance, and decisive for the continuity of religion in both East and West. This emphasis on a new understanding of mysticism is closely linked to Teilhard's attempt at seeking an integration of the worldviews of both science and religion which he considers to be part of the same deep quest for ultimate unity. In this sense, science itself becomes tinged with mysticism.

This does not mean that Teilhard suggested a naive concordance between science and religion. All his endeavour was devoted to seeking an ultimate coherence of man's manifold experience, to convey a convergent vision greater than what either traditional religion or science offer on their own. Religion and mysticism are seen as man's search for ultimate union and communion with God *via* the process of the unification of the world. All human efforts, whether religious or scientific, whether action or contemplation, must finally lead to worship, adoration and ecstasy.

One can argue that he underestimated the capacity of Eastern religions to adapt themselves to an evolutionary and scientific understanding of the world. Also, the difficulty about evolution is less great perhaps with regard to the compatability of religion with the scientific teaching about the organic evolution of life in the past than with the attitudes regarding evolution now, and the decisions required to shape the direction of evolutionary developments in the present and future. However, traditional religious teachings of the East may contain more 'mystical reserves' for animating man's action than Teilhard as an outsider was able to perceive. The growing convergence of world religions is particularly important in this respect. Without being tied to the traditional boundaries of religious institutions, the mutually enriching encounter of men from different faiths may itself be a decisive influence on the further evolution of religion.

A more recent discussion of the mutual interaction of religion and evolution is found in the work of the geneticist Theodosius Dobzhansky. In his book *The Biology of Ultimate Concern*[80] he, like Teilhard, points out that mankind's evolution has left its earlier stage of

happy spiritual childhood far in the past. Modern man must raise his sights above the simple biological joys of survival and procreation. He needs nothing less than a religious synthesis. This synthesis cannot be simply a revival of any one of the existing religions, and it need not be a new religion. The synthesis may be grounded in one of the world's great religions, or in all of them together.

By education and upbringing he favours, again like Teilhard, Christianity as the framework for this synthesis. But he admits that the possibility of other frameworks cannot be excluded. He is equally adamant in stating, however, that it must be a true synthesis which integrates the rational and evolutionary views of science as much as those of religion.[81]

There is no going back in time to the religion of the past, only a going forward within the dynamic of an evolutionary perspective. Thus, traditional spirituality has arrived at important crossroads: either a new religious vision will emerge or religion will stagnate and die if we cannot separate the ossified from the living tradition. For Teilhard, the direction to take, the path to follow, is the road of a 'new mysticism' for it is the realm of the mystical which represents the most living element in religion. The phenomenon of mysticism is still growing, and the intensity of its flame can best feed our common endeavour.

9

A New Mysticism

What is the nature of mysticism? Which major features characterize the mysticisms of the past? And how far are these still relevant or perhaps redundant for contemporary spiritual practice? These are some of the questions underlying Teilhard's enquiry into mysticism. They also provide the dominant perspective for his approach to Eastern religions. He frequently used the words 'mystical' and 'mysticism' but, from early on, he objected to their narrow definition. For example, he wrote with reference to Christian theology that it has the tendency 'to give the word "mystical" (in mystical body, mystical union) a minimum of organic or physical meaning'. This is due to 'the very common mistake of regarding the spiritual as an attenuation of the material, whereas it is in fact the material carried beyond itself: it is super-material'.[1]

Besides numerous references to mysticism throughout his work, some major essays are entirely devoted to this theme.[2] Written over a lifetime and often presented in autobiographical form, apparent even from their titles, they confirm the view that his understanding of mysticism is closely related to his own experience. Given the need to interpret this to himself and others, he enquired at random into the presence of mysticism inside and outside Christianity. Thus, his comparisons were initially personally motivated and undertaken to illuminate his own experience. This helps to explain their particular orientation and also accounts for some inherent limitations of his views on Eastern and Western mysticism.

Although all his writings have a mystical matrix, they do not primarily provide descriptive reports of individual experiences, as the works of most other mystics, but include reflections on the role of mysticism in contemporary society and culture which far transcend the concerns of personal mystical experience.

The mystical quest of Teilhard's life has found a moving expression and climax in his final essays 'The Heart of Matter' and 'The Christic'. Many commentators have recognized the importance of mysticism in his work[3] but most have examined his Christ-centred mysticism and its place in contemporary Christian theology. His comparisons with Eastern religions, his distinction of different paths and goals in mysticism, as well as the central role of mysticism in the future evolution of religion, have received comparatively little attention so far.

The study of the history of mysticism with its rich store of mystical literature has increasingly come to the fore over the last few decades. Every religion possesses its great mystics, and the accounts of their different experiences have been examined from many points of view. Recent studies on mysticism are mostly concerned with rigorous analysis and classification in an attempt to account more systematically for the diversity of mystical experience in the religious history of mankind.[4]

It is easy to see that Teilhard's reflections are not of this kind: he was not an academic writing *about* mysticism; on the contrary, his prime interest was *practice* rather than theory, the practice of spirituality in the modern world. Yet reference to Teilhard's thought in contemporary works on mysticism are practically non-existent. But his reflections supply important data which ought to be taken into account when scholars construct their classifications and theories about mysticism.

As with the experience of other mystics, Teilhard's vision entails claims about the nature of reality which require close examination. What is more, his emphasis on the need to go beyond merely historical studies and strive towards a new form of mysticism deserves serious consideration. At present, this is perhaps more recognized by people in the natural sciences than by those working in the area of religion.

From the beginning of his reflections, Teilhard claimed an element of newness in his understanding of mysticism, distinct from that of earlier mystics.[5] What is this new mysticism of which he spoke so much in his last years? He groped for a new approach, a mysticism of convergence, which he described as a new road in spirituality. He thought that this road had begun to open up in the West but could not develop in a truly convergent manner without Eastern religions. What is the meaning of this mysticism, what is its newness, and what is its importance for religion today?

I

All his comparisons between Western and Eastern mysticism are undertaken from the premiss that man's spiritual quest is not perennially the same. A change in human consciousness and self-understanding, linked to new historical and social developments, has brought about a situation where man's spiritual needs have come into sharper focus. The protagonists of an essential unity of all religions, of a common mystical core, are upholding an eternal timelessness of spirituality which leaves no room for further development.[6] Teilhard disagrees with this most emphatically. He does not think that all mysticism is and always has been the same, nor that it always will be. What is ultimately at issue is the question of what pertains to spirituality today, and the answer may well lead to a parting of ways.

New developments in contemporary culture also require a new approach to the understanding and practice of spirituality. It is this need, born from a historically new situation, which Teilhard saw and felt with extraordinary depth and intensity like few others. Based on formative mystical experiences and a lifelong reflection on the meaning of mysticism in the modern world, he put forward a particular interpretation which diverges from that of other writers in several respects.

Usually, mysticism is taken to refer to extraordinary states of contemplation, inner visions, trances, stages of illumination, and so on. In this sense, it means an experience of inwardness without correlating it to outwardness, to man's external world and the multiple concerns of society. Thus, traditional mysticism is, par excellence, an individual quest which has often been in tension with official religious institutions. Teilhard, however, does not restrict mysticism to contemplative states or extraordinary experiences of the individual alone, but gives it a more comprehensive meaning. Even when talking about mysticism primarily in relation to the individual, he links it to a continuum of progressively more centred experiences, ranging from pantheistic and monistic to theistic forms. But mysticism stands also for the goal of *all* spiritual life. It then refers to the most powerful and activating centre of human spirituality which can only be achieved through correlating and integrating man's outer activities with his inner life.

If an exclusively introvertive and individual quest for contemplation and spiritual union was the predominant ideal of the past, it is no longer adequate for the present and future. The time-vector is essential here for, in Teilhard's view, the integration and perfection of man's inner life, as well as his search for an Absolute, do not occur independently from time. The acceptance of an extended meaning of evolution implies development and growth, the existence of different, organically related levels of development, and the directionality of time and history. The evolutionary process has not only shaped the history of the cosmos, world and men; it also affects man's thought, religion and the understanding of the spirit itself. Not all writers on mysticism would admit these premises; although mainly Western in origin, they are not without parallels in certain Eastern forms of thought.

Given modern developments, an adequate religious worldview for the present and future cannot be entirely modelled on the patterns of the past. To seek ultimate unity implies at the same time a changed relationship between man and all other phenomena in the world; thus, it must be accompanied by a process of unification. Consequently, the interpretation of mysticism is closely linked to a new emphasis on the importance of man's action. It is, in fact, in and through action that the spirit unfolds, and that man's spirituality grows. Spirituality is no longer simply a problem of inwardness as in the past. On the contrary, the problem of human action, together with the choice of the right values and beliefs on which to base such action, is the major problem of the spirit today.

Ultimately, Teilhard sees the vast process of evolution as one of expanding interiorization and spiritualization through integration and unification. Thus, mysticism is not only of individual, but great social importance. It acquires a significance for humanity as a whole, and for the future of religion itself. Seen from this perspective, it is neither a nature-, soul-, or God-mysticism which characterizes Teilhard's thought; it is rather, if such a formulation be permitted, a personal-universal world-in-evolution mysticism, implying a dynamic process of convergence.[7]

II

Although not himself a specialist in these matters, Teilhard was always aware of 'the vast and polymorphous domain of mysticism',[8] that is to say, the great variety of experiences designated by the word mysticism at different times and places. However, unlike Zaehner, he did not argue for a sharp break between natural pantheism and religious mysticism of a monistic or theistic kind at the experiential level. He saw these different experiences as continuous and organically related although each also possesses a distinctive element of its own. Structurally and ontologically, he always distinguished two basic types of mysticism as fundamental alternatives or even opposites but this does not imply that the individual experiences them as such psychologically.

Different types of mysticism are often distinguished on the basis of whether fundamentally unitive experiences of the soul are described in terms of man's absorption into or union with God. Teilhard hinges his distinction of two basic types on the process of *unification*. The very choice of this word indicates that mysticism does not simply imply the union of two given terms, i.e. man and God, but it means an ongoing process of successive 'centring'. It then involves the inner unification of man's self as well as the outer unification of what surrounds man, that is to say, other men as well as man's work and nature. This process of unification has such a central importance in Teilhard's worldview that it is sharply set off from any mysticism of *identification* which, in his opinion, was traditionally mainly prevalent in the East, and is summarily and quite wrongly referred to as the 'road of the East'. However, on closer examination, it is clear that the characterization of this 'road' is primarily dependent on what he knew of the various monistic trends in Indian thought. His typological method misled him into thinking of Eastern religions as far too unitary without sufficiently taking into account the historical diversity and pluralism of the great religions of the East. This may be partly due to the fact that he neither possessed the close contacts nor pursued the necessary study to gain a deep insight into Eastern mystical thought whereas his background, training and personal commitment gave him much fuller access to the wide range of Christian mysticism.

Many essays express the fundamental distinction between two basic types of mysticism without reference to either Eastern or Western religions. We shall use one of the latest, 'Some Notes on the Mystical Sense: An Attempt at Clarification' (1951).[9] On one hand, it describes man's mystical sense as a presentiment of ultimate unity of which man somehow becomes part or, alternatively, as a cosmic sense of 'oneness'. Yet, on the other hand, it emphasizes that there are two different ways in which this oneness is experienced or realized. In other texts, these two ways are referred to as 'roads', or, better, 'components'. In 1951, Teilhard even wondered whether there may be more than two ways in realizing oneness. This may have been a rhetorical question, yet it is also acknowledgment of the diversity of mystical experience at the empirical level, not to be confused with the theoretical distinction between two basic or pure types.

The first basic type is called *mysticism of identification*. This implies an identification of man, 'of each and all' with an undifferentiated common ground. It means the fusion or dissolution of man's specificity, represented by his personal consciousness, with an Ineffable 'of de-differentiation and de-personalization'. Because of the negation of the central core of personhood, both in the Absolute, and in man's experience of It and of himself, this is 'both by definition and by structure' a 'mysticism WITHOUT LOVE'.

The second basic type, by contrast, is called *mysticism of unification*. Instead of dissolution and fusion, it is the concentration and unification of each and all 'through a peak of intensity arrived at by what is most incommunicable in each element'. Although not specifically mentioned, personhood and its ultimate fulfilment in a higher personal centre are central to this second type, as the context clearly shows. This type of mysticism represents 'an ultra-personalizing, ultra-determining, and ultra-differentiating UNIFICATION of the elements within a *common focus*; the specific effect of LOVE'.

The first type of experience describes an impersonal 'God', if that is not a contradiction in terms, as *all*. By contrast, the second type of experience sees God as 'all in all', to use St Paul's phrase. This is 'an ultra-personal', a 'centric' God – expressions which emphasize that God must not be thought of as a person in an anthropomorphic manner.

The main difference, then, between a mysticism of identification and unification is the absence or presence of personal love, itself dependent on a particular understanding of the personal nature of man and ultimate Reality. This basic typology must not be understood to reiterate the common distinction between a monistic and theistic type of mysticism. The presence of personal love here does not only mean a loving relationship between man and God. It implies more than a simple coming together and union, for it is linked to a complex and increasingly convergent process of unification. Thus, the meaning of love itself is being transformed and understood in a much more dynamic sense. Even when Teilhard refers elsewhere simply to 'union' or 'unity', he still associates the idea of unification with these terms.

The second type of mysticism, that of unification, is not strictly identical with theistic forms of mysticism either. Instead, it is 'a road not yet described in any "book" (?!) . . .

the true path "towards and for" oneness'. It is said to be the new 'road of the West', a path of unification only become possible through the contact of Christianity with the modern world. There is no reference to the 'road of the East' here. On the whole, this short text favours the more neutral terminology of the two basic 'ways' of mysticism, distinguished by the absence or presence of love in an *ultra-personal* God. The first type, then, is an essentially monistic mysticism; the second a *trans-theistic* mysticism towards which Christianity tends but which has not been fully worked out yet. Structurally through its theology, and practically through the emphasis given to charity, Christianity belongs to this second type. Yet its mysticism showed a certain 'lack of richness' in the past: it was 'not sufficiently universalist and cosmic' because oneness was too exclusively sought '*in singleness*, rather than in God's *synthetic power*'. God was loved '*above* all things' rather than '*in* and *through* all things'.

This passage, like so many others, emphasizes again the difference between mysticism in the past and what is required for the present. Teilhard's typology, here and elsewhere, is only an 'attempt at clarification',[10] and not a fully worked out scheme of classification and interpretation. This is also evident from his changing terminology for, in another context, he speaks of two types of pantheism rather than mysticism: 'Pantheism of identification, at the opposite pole from love: "God is all". And pantheism of unification, beyond love: "God all in all".'[11] In each case, the same emphasis is placed on the difference between the process of identification and that of unification. R. C. Zaehner has understood the text just quoted as a confirmation of his own views on mysticism put forward in his book *Mysticism Sacred and Profane*.[12] He considered Teilhard as 'one of the very few who draw clear distinctions between different types of mysticism'.[13] However, their typologies do not completely coincide. Zaehner overlooks both the time-factor and the dynamic complexity in Teilhard's mysticism of unification; similarly, he insists on too sharp a separation between the different types. The fact that Teilhard referred to the types as both 'pantheism' and 'mysticism' is an indication that he saw the two phenomena as interrelated, as part of a continuum. This is also borne out by his insistence on the possibility of a true, Christian pantheism: the experience of the oneness and unity of the cosmos must become an integral part of the Christian faith.

III

One can gain yet another view of Teilhard's interpretation of mysticism. Certain of his texts do not oppose the process of unification to that of identification but express the basic polarity by a predominantly forward or upward orientation. Their inherent tension is transcended through a third direction which represents a new synthesis. Diagrammatically this can be shown in the following way: [14]

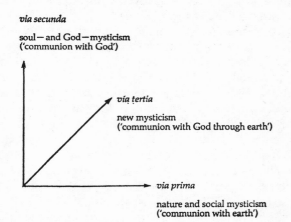

via secunda

soul— and God—mysticism
('communion with God')

via tertia

new mysticism
('communion with God through earth')

via prima

nature and social mysticism
('communion with earth')

The horizontal line stands for pantheistic nature mysticism and a social mysticism of the collective, represented by various forms of neo-humanism. This mysticism of the world is the *via prima*, opposed to the vertical line of the *via secunda*, the way of all traditional mysticism which seeks to link man directly with the Absolute to the exclusion of the world (i.e. all forms of either soul- or God-mysticism). The diagonal *via tertia* indicates the emergence of a new kind of mysticism whereby man is united with the Absolute *via the unification of the world*. Each of these three lines can in turn be identified with parts of the early maxim of 'Cosmic Life' (1916).

At other times, these three lines are described as three 'currents'. The upward direction is thought of as a predominantly 'Eastern current' but subsumes under it the other-worldliness of past Christian spirituality. The forward direction is mainly found in the neo-humanist and Marxist 'world-current', and the diagonal represents a 'neo-Christian current', a new synthesis between the essential 'axes' of Christian belief and a new-born faith in the world. This example shows once again that Teilhard's thought on mysticism is not confined to a systematically elaborated typology. Rather, it is expressed by different schemata which cut across each other, and are also open to varying interpretations.

Teilhard understood the search for unification via the tangible as primarily a Western preoccupation. The concern for the value of the material world is closely linked to the Christian understanding of the Incarnation. Yet the full implications of an incarnational approach, i.e. the transformation and sanctification of all human and earthly realities, take on an altogether different dimension with the relatively modern discovery and analysis of what these realities in themselves are. With advancing knowledge, the limits of the real are for ever pushed back further; the world surrounding man is expanding its parameter. For Teilhard, the search for a systematically unifying knowledge in the area of science is akin to man's mystic search in the area of religion. This interrelated quest for oneness made him seek a new mysticism where unity is achieved through ultra-differentiation.

However, in spite of his insistence on man's unitary quest for oneness and his conviction that the general awareness for mysticism is growing today, one can say that nobody has ever become a mystic through his own choice. The very gratuitousness of the mystical phenomenon seems to indicate that the initiative for it comes from outside man. For this reason, a receptive state of passivity has traditionally been associated with the mystic. Teilhard does not overlook this. In his essay on the interior life, *Le Milieu Divin*, he treats of both activity and passivity, attachment and detachment. However, as he frequently emphasizes man's activity and choice in a world-affirming manner, in contrast to a traditionally passive and world-negating attitude, some misinterpret his thought as too activist. They forget that although *Le Milieu Divin* begins with 'the divinization of our activities', it is followed by 'the divinization of our passivities'.[15] Whether this is meant to be an alternative rhythm or an advance by progression, may be open to debate.

One commentator, Father Ravier, is of the opinion that in spite of Teilhard's occasionally severe words against pure contemplatives, he nevertheless acknowledged the path of the mystic to be a particular vocation he himself did not possess. According to Ravier, a true mystic must ultimately pass from the *via tertia* to the *via secunda*, to an intimate soul – God relationship to the exclusion of the world. As the *via secunda* was not given to Teilhard, the *via tertia*, the integration of the love of God with the love of the world, was the only option open to him.[16]

If one accepts this interpretation, then the *via tertia* is merely a compromise, unworthy of being pursued by the genuine mystic. Ravier reaffirms the utter passivity and withdrawal of the mystic state without leaving room for any new development. However, this seems to do injustice to Teilhard's own position. His frequent references to a new 'road', a new mysticism, definitely indicate the search for a synthesis which is more than a compromise. Many passages could be quoted in support, especially from the unpublished diaries of the last years. Teilhard writes there for example:

Via tertia – distinguish syncretism and synthesis.

. . . . . .

My line: to synthesize mysticism and evolution (cosmic effort: detachment and synthesis). Union implies unification, that is to say, an evolutionary mystical union.

. . . . . .

THE MYSTICAL ILLUSION = pretends to Union and Presence *independently of Time* and Evolution . . . as if the contact with God could be achieved without the Evolution of Consciousness – from the beginning . . .[17]

The idea of a new 'mysticism of evolution' and a 'mysticism of action' suggests a new vision related to the development of a new world. This understanding of mysticism cannot solely be assessed by reference to the mystics of the past[18] for Teilhard's interpretation of mysticism is strongly future-orientated, and it is also basically evaluative. The mysticism of identification and that of unification are not simple equivalents but one type is seen as more developed, fuller, richer, truer.

Many passages indicate this evaluative perspective which, in spite of his emphasis on convergence, still remained too Western-orientated. For example, Teilhard is reported to have said at a 1948 meeting of the French branch of the *World Congress of Faiths* in Paris:

I believe the mystical is less different, less separated from the rational than one says, but I also believe that the whole problem which the world, and we in particular, are presently facing, is a problem of faith . . .

I have the weakness to believe that the West has a very strong latent mysticism, underlying, not made explicit yet, but at least as strong as Eastern mysticism.

If the Western group were really able to express in a new manner, or to renew that mysticism of the West of which I once spoke, I think that would be something much more powerful than even dialogue, for it would make a faith appear within mankind, a mysticism which exists not yet . . .[19]

Perhaps it is Teilhard's main achievement to have sought a new formulation for a mysticism of the West, that is to say, a mysticism rooted in the Christian doctrines of Creation and Incarnation, but expressed in a new manner. However, the use of the term *via tertia*, the references to a new 'road', to a not yet existing mysticism, all point towards a synthesis going beyond the past distinctions of West and East. The element of newness and the process of convergence associated with the new 'road' indicate that the new mysticism of unification or union must ultimately transcend the traditional religious heritage of the West.

Weighing up different texts, particularly those of Teilhard's later years, one realizes the necessary, in fact essential, contribution of Eastern religious insights to a newly emerging mysticism. In 1951, Teilhard wrote:

> . . . as time goes by, I have a curious impression of liberation and simplification . . . the moment one realizes that the Universe flows (and always has flowed) in the direction of 'ever greater order and consciousness', a whole group of values is introduced into things which . . . give everything an extraordinary savor, warmth, and limpidity: a superior and synthetic form of 'mysticism' in which the strengths and seductions of Oriental 'pantheism' and Christian personalism converge and culminate! Impossible for me not to pursue this vision in a series of essays that keeps getting longer without my yet having managed to grasp exactly and fully what I feel . . .[20]

This passage brings out the suggestive and exploratory nature of Teilhard's ideas about a new mysticism. They are in need of a great deal of further development. The most fruitful approach would be a comparison between the understanding of love and personhood in different religious traditions, for he maintains that a specific form of love is what most separates and distinguishes the two main types of mysticism. It is impossible to explore this here in full but the emphasis on love has a special bearing on Teilhard's remarks about Indian religions.

IV

The emphasis on mutual love between man and God is often seen as the most significant characteristic dividing theistic from monistic forms of mysticism. Examples for this can be found in Hindu, Muslim and Christian religious thought. For

Teilhard, too, the presence of love is the most distinctive feature which separates the mysticism of unification from that of identification, and it is for him intimately bound up with certain Christian teachings. However, from a comparative perspective one must ask whether the loving devotion of Hindu *bhakti*, for example, is not the same as Christian love? Teilhard raised this question several times and referred to it even in one of his last essays, 'The Christic'.[21] But whilst admitting a close similarity between the two, he nevertheless maintained a distinctive difference, mainly due to a more complex understanding of the nature of love.

He often speaks of love in a traditional manner, but sometimes he also understands it in a new way. For example, he refers to a 'neo-love', that is, a new integration of the love of God with that of a world in evolution. Love then is not only an eminently personal attraction between two partners, leading them to union and communion. More than that, love is a unifying energy, in fact it is 'the supreme spiritual energy' linking all elements and persons in their 'irreplaceable and incommunicable essence' in a universal process of unification.[22] Love has a central, irreplaceable part in a general 'energetics' for it possesses a personal and cosmic dimension, and is a creative force in the evolutionary process itself. At the cosmic level, it is an animating energy pulsating through the universe, almost like the *shakti* of Hindu Tantra which Teilhard does not seem to have known.[23]

The comparability of Teilhard's ideas with certain Tantra teachings is also evident from the fact that, in his view, one of the ways in which man partakes of this great cosmic force is sexual energy. This is part of the cosmic dynamic and constitutive of man's being-in-the-world. There are numerous references in his writings which describe human sexuality as a fundamental force providing the basis for any other human love, including the love of God and that form of love which finds expression in charity. It is not the repression of sexuality but, on the contrary, its acceptance and transformation which are necessary for a full flowering of mysticism. The mystical quest for unification has its natural roots in the powers of attraction linked to human sexuality. Thus, the dynamic of sexuality and mysticism are closely interrelated. In 1916, he wrote in his diary that 'the transformation of love – with sexual roots – into a *cosmic* passion is a *natural* evolution. This rather vague stage gives birth to *all mysticisms* . . .'[24] Many years later, he criticized a contemporary book on the mystical life by saying that it possessed 'no original element. The mystical phenomenon regarded as rather an exception . . . – almost historical'. The author 'does not see that it is a universal phenomenon . . ., linked to the axis of reflective life: sense of the One, cosmic sense, sense of Evolution; – nor does he discern the physico-psychological relation between sexuality and mysticism. In short, he does not see . . . the *evolutionary* value of the mystical phenomenon'.[25]

Beside the cosmic and sexual dimension, Teilhard emphasizes the personalizing aspect of love as particularly important for mysticism. A human being becomes a person through a process of personalization, that is to say, through a gradual movement of inner centring and unification, made possible through being linked to others by love. He distinguishes three phases in this process: 'If man is to be fully himself and fully living, he must, (1) be centred upon himself; (2) be "de-centred" upon "the other"; (3) be supercentred upon a being greater than himself'. He calls this also 'the happiness of growing greater – of loving – of worshipping'.[26] The unifying force of personal love, its power of centring and integration, is so important that Teilhard speaks of 'a mysticism of centration'.[27] This mysticism is closely associated with the understanding of personhood as the essence of the human being. More than anything else, it is through his personal centre that man relates to God who is a person in a much more eminent sense. The philosophy of personhood has a long history in Christianity and operates with concepts largely alien to Eastern traditions. Many misunderstandings arise from this fundamental difference in approach. People often confuse 'person' with the empirical ego or with a psychological 'personality' which true mysticism strives to abandon. Because of the limitation of this empirical personality and the possible anthropomorphic connotations of the personal, Indian writers often place the impersonal above the personal and define the

Absolute as impersonal, in contrast to any theistic conception. In the Indian Advaita context in particular the personal is seen as limiting because it is understood to imply duality and circumscribed individuality which are transcended in the realization of a universal *Atman*.

Teilhard argued so much against Indian monism because he saw it overwhelmingly as a mystical experience of man's identification with the One alone, implying the loss of personal consciousness.[28] Similarly, he criticized Aldous Huxley's *Perennial Philosophy* for confusing the impersonal with the universal, and the personal with the anthropomorphic. In Teilhard's view, it is essential to distinguish clearly between the universal and the personal, but also, to relate them to each other and see them both in an evolutionary perspective. Only in the Christian understanding of love are all these elements brought together for no other religious faith has ever released in history 'a higher degree of warmth, a more intense dynamism of unification' than Christianity, especially the Christianity of our own day.[29] It is the essential elements of Christian love which find themselves prolonged in what he called 'a new mystical orientation', linked to the 'love of evolution'.[30] In the past, Christian love has not always found its full expression as it has often been too 'other-worldly'. Instead, a truly dynamic form of Christian love must be concerned with the effort of developing man beyond himself. Therefore, he referred to 'a radical reinterpretation' and 'recasting' of the notion of Christian charity.[31]

Teilhard obviously seemed to think that Eastern religions did not understand love in its highest, personal form, nor as love of evolution. In his diary, he briefly acknowledged the presence of an 'affective theism' in Indian Vaishnavite and Shaivite *bhakti* and also in Japanese Amida Buddhism. Yet although psychologically very similar, to him this was not the same as a fully dynamic, person-centred love. The importance of this difference appears from some other remarks too :

. . . the *mystic* (and most fundamental) current which has kept running and developing in Christianity . . . a current of love (love of God and love of Mankind) – *not* the buddhistic 'piété', but a personalistic form of love. This is important, because . . . such 'love' (of the World in its elements and as a whole) is probably the very axis of future human progress and evolution.[32]

He judged Hinduism to be 'less unitary, less amorized than Christianity', lacking a homogeneous point of convergence. It appeared to him to be 'doubly without *true love* : 1. because the Absolute is without a real "nucleus"; 2. because love is supposed to pass over into *identity* . . .'[33] From these and other passages, it is clear that Teilhard was obviously unfamiliar with the details of the rich *bhakti* tradition of Indian theism with its wide-ranging theological reflections on the nature of love between man and God. It is not so much personal love which is absent here but, rather, the love of evolution with its accompanying dynamic approach.

It is certain that the emphasis on a new kind of mysticism is closely dependent on a particular understanding of love, as well as on the nature of the human person and the role of theism, all of which are reinterpreted from an evolutionary perspective. However, one can again point to a certain dialectical tension in Teilhard's thought here: on one hand, he assigns a central place to the Christian 'personalistic form of love' in his interpretation of mysticism but, on the other, he stresses that this love, identified as the 'Christian mystical act' par excellence, has not found its fullest expression yet but must grow further and become more universalized.[34]

V

If one compares Teilhard's understanding of mysticism with that of others, what similarities and differences emerge? More than once it has been pointed out that significant parallels to his thought exist in the traditional mysticism of both Western and Eastern Christianity. This is not surprising as he prolongs all that is most authentic in the Christian mystical tradition. Yet there is also an additional and quite new element present, for Teilhard's emphasis on the role of mysticism far transcends the concerns of those who seek a simple reawakening of past Christian mysticism.

Francis Kelly Nemeck, superior of a Canadian contemplative prayer house, has undertaken a comparative study of the mysticism of Teilhard and St John of the Cross[35] in which he shows that they have more in common than might be at first assumed. He considers the two mystics to some extent complementary but judges Teilhard's mysticism 'as on the whole better balanced with regard to the convergence and complementarity of transcendence and immanence' whereas St John penetrates more into the darkness of faith and the 'night' of the senses and the spirit.[36]

The comparison between St John of the Cross and Teilhard is of particular interest when taking into account that the Hindu Swami Siddheswarananda considers St John's understanding of mysticism as akin to Indian teaching on *jnana-yoga*, *bhakti-yoga* and *raja-yoga*.[37] As is to be expected from a Ramakrishna-Mission monk, Swami Siddheswarananda specifically affirms the unity of mystical experience underlying different religions. At the same time, he emphasizes that mysticism can, strictly speaking, only be pursued by monks. Even the teachings of Christ are interpreted by him as being essentially monastic. To follow the path of mysticism requires a single-minded pursuit of the spiritual life to the exclusion of everything else. There can be no realization in and through the world if one uses Teilhardian terms; the orientation of the mystic is strongly vertical and individualistic.

Teilhard met Swami Siddheswarananda through their mutual work for the French branch of the *World Congress of Faiths* and discussed certain questions regarding the interpretation of mystical experience with him.[38] However, he disagreed with the Swami's comparison between the mysticism of Vedanta and St John of the Cross. In 1948, when speaking about the two basic types of mysticism, Teilhard wrote in 'My Fundamental Vision':

Surprisingly, it would not appear that a clear distinction has yet been drawn between these two diametrically contrasted attitudes: and this accounts for the confusion which muddles together or identifies the ineffable of the Vedanta and that of, for example, St John of the Cross – and so not only allows any number of excellent souls to become helpless victims of the most pernicious illusions produced in the East, but also (what is more serious) delays a task that is daily becoming more urgent – the individualization and the full flowering of a valid and powerful modern mysticism.

The difference between these two perspectives is further enhanced through an additional note which says :

When approached by the road of the East (identification) the ineffable is not such that it can be loved. By the road of the West (union) it is attained through a continuation of the direction of love. This very simple criterion makes it possible to distinguish and keep separate, as being antithetical, verbal expressions that are almost identical when used by Christian or Hindu.[39]

Here again Teilhard equates the Hindu position with monism, which gives Indian thought much of its characteristic flavour without being universal in Hinduism. There are closer parallels than he realized. In particular his understanding of spirituality as a 'detachment by super-attachment'[40] as well as his unifying vision of convergence possess a remarkable affinity with certain teachings of the *Bhagavad-Gita*, especially as understood in modern Hinduism. Although Teilhard must have encountered a discussion of this Hindu scripture in his reading, he never refers to it all. The *Bhagavad-Gita* culminates in a tremendous theophany, disclosing the vision of a supreme personal God who unites all beings within himself. This is a close union of love which is not identity, and it represents a vision of convergence not unlike the ultimate unity of Teilhard's mysticism. At least, this is the view taken by Zaehner.[41] But one must not forget that the *Bhagavad-Gita* has been subject to widely divergent interpretations, and not everyone sees in it the same vision of convergent union which Zaehner does. Another objection relates to the fact that an evolutionary perspective introduces a new complexity and dynamic which requires a much more subtle notion of convergence than could have been originally intended by the *Bhagavad-Gita* But admittedly this scripture lends itself particularly well to reinterpretations in the light of modern understanding and provides a strong basis for a theistic mysticism.

The most surprising and in many ways closest contemporary parallel to Teilhard's understanding of mysticism exists in Sri Aurobindo's work. His reinterpretation of Hinduism, however, is deeply influenced by ideas of Western origin. In Zaehner's view, both Aurobindo and Teilhard, in their separate traditions, 'represent something totally new in mystical religion'.[42] Yet it is of little help in furthering understanding or comparative assessment when some of Aurobindo's disciples maintain that Teilhard has written little which Aurobindo has not expressed much better, or claim that the latter has in fact achieved the mystical realization the former only talked about.

In one respect, however, Teilhard and Aurobindo are curiously alike: despite their efforts to find a synthesis of thought between East and West, both remain locked in their own religious and cultural perspective. Aurobindo emphatically claims that the future development of religion is linked to his reinterpretation of Indian mysticism in the form of 'integral yoga' whereas Teilhard conceives of it mainly in terms of a new 'road of the West' or a Western-based 'mysticism of evolution'. These positions are opposed to each other. To achieve true synthesis and convergence, both need to be transcended. That such a movement of convergence requires a further development of Teilhard's ideas, he himself would have been the first to admit. A thinker who repeatedly emphasized that evolution is an all-comprehensive, generalized social and cultural phenomenon, could hardly expect that the process of religious evolution would come to a halt with himself, as Aurobindo seems to have done.

VI

On comparison, the newness of Teilhard's mystical experience and interpretation is a relative one, due mainly to a change in emphasis, perspective and scale. Independent parallels exist in Christian mysticism, both ancient and modern[43] but, unknown to him, examples of a unifying cosmic vision and of world-affirming attitudes can also be found in Eastern religions. This is not only true of Hinduism and Buddhism but even more so of traditional Chinese thought.[44] However, there is a real danger of making too facile and even anachronistic comparisons which may completely misrepresent Teilhard's intentions. It is always necessary to investigate closely whether particular aspects of different religions and cultures are truly comparable at different times in history, and on what assumptions such comparisons are based.

Teilhard's interpretation of mysticism combines in a unique manner the appeal of the transcendent with that of a dynamic, tangible and evolving world, transformed from within through the immanence and presence of the Divine. Although many mystics before him have seen this wonderful 'Diaphany',[45] he was aware that their understanding of mysticism in relation to the world has often been very different indeed. This is largely due to the fact that the problem of the modern world and its progress did not arise for them in the way we experience it now.

The problem is assuming increasing urgency today. It is related to the development of science and technology, the expansion of knowledge into ever new fields and the increasing differentiation of modern society. Frequently, however, this is misunderstood as a development which is merely external to man whereas it is, in fact, closely linked to a fundamental change in human consciousness and self-reflection, individual as well as social.

The negativity which Teilhard often associates with the 'road of the East' is linked to the recognition that the underlying structure of Eastern spiritualities frequently implies, at least theoretically, a negation of the world. This is especially true of certain aspects of Indian religions: matter is illusory, the world and its phenomena are ultimately unreal. Consequently, there can be no real evolution, no real growth and progress in the world or in the work of man. Ultimately, renunciation is the highest ideal and all action has to be abandoned for man to achieve true realization in complete inwardness.

However, this ideal is, in practice, little different from the asceticism, contemplation and otherworldliness found in much of the Western monastic and spiritual tradition. Teilhard argues against any kind of one-sided asceticism and seeks a harmonious balance between man's inwardness and outwardness. The experience of mysticism, of spirituality at the deepest level, becomes centrally linked to the importance of the experimental universe, the world surrounding man. Thus, the mystic is not a dreamer who escapes the world and its problems but, on the contrary, he is the supreme realist. Instead of seeking separate, inner contemplation apart from the world, he is the one who alone can chart a new road *in* and *into* the realities of this world. Here, too, the superiority of praxis over theory is emphasized.

The way of mysticism must be integrated with the many-sided aspects of social and practical life here and now. It must provide mankind with a viable spirituality to cope with the problems, responsibilities, and choices of the contemporary world rather than invite individuals to an inward escape from it. Teilhard's emphasis, however, lies not so much on stressing a 'this-worldly' as against an 'other-worldly' attitude but on making a fervent plea to develop what has been called a 'changeful orientation to the world'.[46] In other words, his approach to spirituality is closely concerned with man's capacity for world-transforming action and decisive moral choices. A new spirituality must combine in an entirely new way a commitment to the rich diversity of the world and human experience with man's search for absolute oneness, transcendence and divine union.

He foresees the rise of a new 'mysticism of evolution' which is different from and opposed to an earlier 'mysticism of evasion'.[47] This 'neo-mysticism' implies not only a 'love of evolution' but refers also to the possibility of a further 'evolution of mysticism' whereby man's mystical sense, his search for ultimate oneness, is assuming planetary dimensions. He thought that the experience of mysticism, instead of being an isolated phenomenon found in a few outstanding individuals, will become more widespread than has been the case so far. The 'mystical temperature' of mankind is rising to the same extent as human consciousness and self-reflection are growing.

Teilhard's two basic types of mystical orientation may easily be mistaken by some to repeat simply the well-known distinction of monistic and theistic forms of mysticism. Yet there is a subtle and very important difference here: a new element is introduced through the emphasis on a *dynamic typology*. The two different types of mysticism are separated from each other through a process of either identification or unification. This dynamic and processual character is closely related to a critical awareness about the different place of time in modern consciousness as well as the importance of matter, world and cosmos for man's spiritual development.

The fundamental stress on the newness of the present time ultimately overcomes and transcends mankind's past divisions in space, linked to separate religious developments in East and West. What can the religious teachings of the past, whether Eastern or Western, contribute to the 'building of the earth', to the shaping of the future? Moved by this question, Teilhard looked for the active and animating elements in different religious traditions, for pointers towards a new religious breakthrough, and for a yet unformulated new mysticism. He conceived of this as a synthesis which would integrate in a new way two traditionally exclusive concerns of man: the search for God and the development of this world.

Mysticism in Teilhard's thought does not refer, therefore, to the traditional, individualistic, exclusively soul- or God-centred spirituality so often associated with the mystical quest. If mysticism is the very heart of religious life, it must provide human beings today with the deepest springs of energy for both action and interaction with others.[48] It cannot be a mere *spirit*-uality but must stand for a spirit-in-and-through-matter mentality, for spirit and matter are not seen as separate and opposed, but interdependent.

Man's spiritual development and his religious experience are thus understood as closely interwoven with and inseparable from his human experience in general. One might say that, ultimately, Teilhard looked for unity, homogeneity, and a final coherence of man's mystical vision in the light of modern science. Although science itself can neither determine man's image of the Divine nor the nature of his religion, it nevertheless rules out certain representations of God and certain forms of worship 'as *not being homogeneous* with the dimensions of the universe known to our experience. This notion of homogeneity is, without doubt, of central importance in intellectual, moral and mystical life'.[49] The mystic 'seer' who can perceive the intimate union of God with all the elements of the world has overcome the twofold danger of seeking either monistic fusion with the world or spiritualist escape from it into a 'beyond'. Instead, he realizes that ultimate unity with God can be found on a third and completely new road in and through the world.[50]

Seen from this perspective, much in the mystical spirituality of the past was criticized by Teilhard, both in East and West. The search for a harmonious balance between the unification of the world and man's inner life introduces an element of newness into the understanding of mysticism, widening it out to include aspects usually thought of as separate. Closely connected with man's attitudes to the natural and social world, and made dynamic through a stress on convergence and unifying action, this 'mysticism of action' becomes an experience potentially open to all men. In his comparative study of mysticism, F. C. Happold has described Teilhard's mysticism as 'springing from the inspiration of a universe seen as moved and compenetrated by God in the totality of its evolution . . . This is essentially a new type of mysticism, the result of a profound, life-long, reconciling meditation on religious and scientific truth; and it is thus of immense relevance and significance for a scientific age such as ours'.[51]

Teilhard's mystical vision was truly that of a 'scientist and seer', to quote the subtitle of Charles Raven's biography; it embraced 'physics', 'metaphysics', and 'mysticism',[52] with the meaning of each extended in an unusual way. However, his approach to mysticism, although including a particular interpretation, was not primarily intellectual but experiential, existential and action-orientated. Both his life and thought bear witness to the dynamic centre of all religious life : the ardour of a mystic vision. Here lies the real centre of gravity for his entire work and without seeing this, no interpretation can do it full justice.

To conclude then, one can say that Teilhard looked at religion and mysticism from a universal rather than a particular perspective. With varying degrees of clarity, he affirmed throughout his work that in man's reflection on himself the presence of religion is an essential datum, a basic fact, to be taken into account in any systematic study of man, historically as well as theoretically. Religion is an integral part of the phenomenon of man, and at the very heart of religion lies the phenomenon of mysticism, culminating in a radiant centre of energy and love linked to a dynamic mysticism of action. Instead of being an exceptional occurrence mysticism, in particular a dynamic mysticism of action, represents a major axis of man's development. Mysticism, rightly understood and practised, is of the greatest evolutionary importance in furthering human self-understanding and future development.

This interpretation can be presented in the form of a diagram :

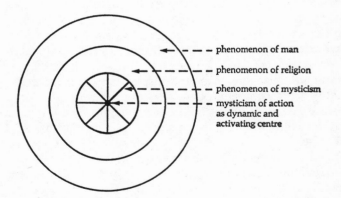

Although this mysticism of action is deeply grounded in Christian incarnational theology, the full flowering of an active and activating spirituality can only emerge in the contemporary world if the different religious traditions meet each other and work more closely together in convergent encounter.

To solve the problem of the spirit, the combined effort of the world faiths is needed. Eastern religions have an essential place in man's religious quest, as Teilhard rightly recognized, although he himself failed to explore all that this might entail.

However, this mysticism of action is growing and much debated at present, as can be seen from William Johnston's penetrating study *The Inner Eye of Love* (1978). Like Teilhard, he emphasizes the universal call to mysticism as well as the central role and unifying force of love, an existential love which is not purely spiritual but has its roots in matter. With great compassion he writes that 'modern people are looking for a new spirituality and a new asceticism which will enable them to benefit from the good points of scientific progress while at the same time developing and training those mystical faculties which lead to enlightenment. This is quite a challenge'.[53]

After living in Japan for many years, Johnston is exploring the enriching insights of Eastern mysticisms, especially of Zen Buddhism, in a way Teilhard never did nor could have done during his lifetime. By now, several religious thinkers have gone far beyond him in discovering a deep complementarity and convergence between East and West. But this is what he expected. His vision of ultimate unity and coherence lacks the necessary detail; indeed, this is its most serious defect. Yet his reflections on Eastern religions and a new mysticism can provide a stimulating challenge and act as a catalyst. They can be creatively applied both in the contemporary study of religion and in a situation of interreligious encounter.

Teilhard's emphasis on a new mysticism for a new world stems from the burning desire to develop an adequate spirituality for today, a spirituality which can give meaning to human lives in a fast changing world by pointing to a direction and definite goal. He insists on the existence of fundamentally different spiritual orientations and, most of all, argues against a mere revival of the mysticisms of the past. The spirituality of the past is simply not enough for today; the development of a rich contemporary spirituality requires a crucial choice. What kind of spirituality is chosen will not only affect the shape of our future but also be decisive for the place of religion in the modern world. Teilhard's choice lies with a new mysticism, a mysticism of action and convergence which to him alone holds the promise of a future for religion. Such a new mysticism can only become a reality insofar as others go beyond him in exploring this new path.

Epilogue

Contemporary Spirituality
at the Crossroads

Today, Eastern religions are better known and appreciated in the West than was the case in the past. Encounters between people of different faiths are coming to be increasingly valued and accepted. Will these new developments help or hinder the growth of a mysticism of action, of a truly integral spirituality for the modern world?

Only the future can answer this. At present, we need discernment to know which road to explore, which direction to take in order to find an active and life-giving, rather than a life-negating spirituality. In religion, as in many other areas, humankind is truly at the crossroads. The choice is not simply one between the acceptance or rejection of religion; it is rather between two fundamentally different directions, a past-oriented revival or a forward-looking new religious synthesis.

Rival spiritualities and mysticisms now cut *across* the different religions, for past- and forward-looking movements exist everywhere side by side. To achieve a new religious breakthrough it is not enough to return to the insights of the past, whether of East or West. All living religions possess a great spiritual heritage; however, this has been developed, handed down, and kept alive outside the perspectives of a fast evolving world. It is now essential to relate these insights in a creative way to our contemporary situation.

Teilhard de Chardin recognized the need for a dynamic and creative approach to mankind's global religious heritage earlier than most. From the 1930s onwards, he perceived and pursued a definite path towards a new mysticism. It is apparent, however, that this exciting new path is far from clearly signposted; he also misjudged it as too narrow. For someone wishing to gain a deeper insight into the experiential and spiritual dimension of Eastern religions Teilhard's works are obviously inadequate. His life and travels in the East brought him into contact with many aspects of Eastern religions, yet none the less he remained a 'chance passer-by' as he first described himself on arriving in China. He never acquired a detailed knowledge of Eastern religious beliefs and practices although his general acquaintance with the peoples and cultures of the East was greater than is usually acknowledged. Moreover, his reading on Indian religions and different forms of mysticism was more extensive than has previously been assumed.

From the contemporary perspective of interreligious encounter and the growing attempt to understand cultural and religious differences in the world, his comments on Eastern religions make difficult reading. Understood literally rather than typologically, they are often inaccurate, harsh and unjust. His views about the value of Eastern religions in the modern world remain in an oppositional mode of thought instead of being genuinely inclusive and universal. In many ways, his perspective regarding the East is closely akin to that of Carl Gustav Jung who spoke of the 'assiduously cultivated credulity of the West in regard to Eastern thought' and affirmed with similar emphasis that 'the West will produce its own yoga, and it will be on the basis laid down by Christianity'.[1]

Teilhard remained convinced that a new breakthrough in spirituality and mysticism would originate from the West. There are other writers today who maintain with equal fervour and conviction that a spiritual renewal can only come from the East, and from nowhere else. Such a possibility cannot be ruled out *a priori* although, given present religious interaction, this seems perhaps less likely. Eastern religions are becomingly increasingly important for the reorientation of religion in the West yet, at the same time, Western religious ideas also help to create a new focus for religious self-understanding in the East. Thus, there is a growing movement of complementary interchange and convergence, at least among those in West and East most alive to the spiritual needs of the contemporary world.

The growing importance of the convergence of world religions was seen with extraordinary clarity by Teilhard although he remained almost blind to the great spiritual treasures of Eastern religions. What are some of the reasons for this lack in perception and judgment?

Most important of all, the major focus of his thought on religion was always contemporary rather than historical. He was mainly concerned with the relevance of religion for humankind in the present, confronted with the task of building the future. Thus, many details relating to traditional religious life in the East were of no interest to his world- and action-oriented approach.

Equally important is the fact that his contacts with Eastern religions were restricted by the milieu in which he lived. The foreign concessions in Tientsin and the international diplomatic and scholarly community in Peking were an effective barrier, separating Westerners from the indigenous population. This applied perhaps less to Teilhard than to many others; he had the opportunity to travel in China and elsewhere and also to work in close collaboration with the Chinese. However, he primarily came into contact with Western-educated Chinese or at least with members of a Western-oriented, scientific elite, often alienated from their own religious and cultural tradition. The opportunities to see Eastern religious life in an active and dynamic situation were relatively rare. For this reason, he may well have underestimated the dynamic qualities of Eastern religions and their intrinsic strength in meeting the problems of the modern world. Judging from contemporary accounts, Chinese religious life was at a very low ebb during Teilhard's stay, and one wonders whether his views would have been significantly different had he spent a major part of his life in India or Japan rather than in China.

Like an explorer, he lived much of his life in the open air. Whether on field-trips or in the laboratory, his scientific research consisted of teamwork with other people, drawn from widely different backgrounds. Given this experience, his approach to religion and mysticism was necessarily very different from that of religious specialists and theologians whose thought develops within the confines of their own study. It is possible, in fact, that Teilhard's views on Eastern religions were so critical because he lived in the East for so long. Unlike other Westerners who, well removed from the East, emphasize rather selective features of Eastern spirituality, he personally experienced the religions of the East in their wider social and cultural context and, therefore, did not make the mistake of seeing Eastern spirituality in isolation from social reality.

But his understanding of religion and mysticism was also due to a particular religious temperament. The blending of mystical experience with scientific thought and practice produced a unique personal-existential synthesis which is not matched by an equally satisfactory synthesis at the intellectual-philosophical level. One can ask whether his interpretation of mysticism, for example, is not too exclusively based on a unitary model of consciousness, leaving little room for wide psychological and cultural differences or for the immense historical diversity of the world religions.

It is true to say, however, that the fundamental vision he wanted to communicate to others stems less from the desire to construct a philosophy than from the vivid experience of the living God, and from the need to affirm and praise his presence in the world today.

Teilhard's personal synthesis cannot be repeated in the way it was lived but many aspects of his thought can be taken up and developed further. His understanding of the role of religion in the modern world can inspire others to study and experience the contribution which world religions can make to the building of a world society. Teilhard's importance, like that of the sociologist Max Weber, may ultimately lie more in having first explored a particular perspective and asked important questions than in the provision of specific answers.

From the vantage point of a traveller between different worlds – that of East and West, as well as from the recesses of the past to the threshold of the future – Teilhard realized earlier than most the revolutionary impact of contemporary scientific, social and cultural changes on the traditional teachings of the world religions. During his travels he could observe that, in many respects, mankind already possesses a common global culture in a material sense. With rare acuity he pointed to the urgent need for sharing supreme spiritual values which could provide mankind with a coherent view of reality and give meaning and direction to the dynamic developments of contemporary life. He was also one of the first to emphasize that the major issue in the 'battle of the spirit' today concerns the confrontation between a religious and a humanistic-atheistic worldview. In other words, beyond the need for interreligious encounter there is the pressing task for world religions to engage in dialogue with contemporary culture.

Religiously speaking, Teilhard thought, mankind is still living in the far-away past, in the neolithic age, as it were. Certain religious beliefs and practices of the West, for example, can be described as a form of 'palaeo-Christianity' which he wished to see replaced by a dynamic 'neo-Christianity'. Yet no religion is free from fossilized forms. What he rather inadequately described as the 'road of the East' appears, on closer examination, to refer to all past forms of religious 'other-worldliness', to any outdated spirituality, whether Eastern or Western. The need for a new 'road' exists at present in all religious traditions. Nowadays, major changes are taking place in the world religions in terms of a new 'this-worldly' orientation. This shift accounts for the emergence of new forms of Buddhism, Hinduism and Islam, as well as for new interpretations of Christianity.

What matters most today is the necessary transformation of our own religious heritage. This must bring out its central insights and distinctive contribution but must also point to a vision of universal truth and ultimate unity which can be shared by people from different faiths. When a friend once discussed the possibility of religious conversion with Teilhard, he is said to have replied: ' "One should never, or almost never, change the religion of one's forefathers . . . One must always try to carry the past with one, but carry it with greater understanding and deeper revelation . . ." Perhaps foolishly I said: "Do you mean if you are a Buddhist or a Hindu you should not become a Christian?" He hesitated. "Well, I really meant if you are a Christian", he said. "But even so, if you were of another religion altogether, it would be better to try to carry its truth with you and transform it if you could, though of course sometimes this might not be possible." '2

Teilhard travelled to the East both physically and mentally but in a sense he did not travel far enough. By now, others have travelled farther and journeyed more deeply into the religious heritage of the East. Some can relate this new experience of discovery and enrichment in a significantly new way to our own Western heritage. This experience marks a new beginning for we are in need of a global, worldwide ecumenism which goes beyond the ecumenism of the Christian churches by being truly universal.

As Eastern countries have achieved political independence, greater self-determination, and a new awareness of their own cultural and religious traditions, a genuine interreligious dialogue can now come into its own. Frequently, however, such dialogue is still taking place at too superficial a level. Instead of leading to an existential commitment and a new religious experience, it remains for many a purely intellectual and verbal exercise. Up to now, personal participation in dialogue-in-depth is still relatively rare but this experience must grow for a new spiritual dynamic to emerge.

When Teilhard first learnt about Tibetan Buddhism, he thought that the insights of Tibetan monks may be reserved for 'a new season'. Perhaps this season has come now with monks from Tibet teaching in the West and with Western monks, such as Thomas Merton and Aelred Graham, learning from Tibetan masters in India. An active exchange of ideas and a sharing of experience is now taking place between certain Buddhists and Christians, to name just one example of interreligious dialogue. Western people are perhaps more drawn to Buddhism than to any other Eastern religion; the mutual attraction is strongest here and the encounter most enriching for both sides. However, many inspiring examples of in-depth dialogue between Hindus and Christians exist too. If man's understanding and experience of God provides an important unifying focus for believers from different faiths, then the rich Indian heritage of *bhakti* theology and the Hindu vision of the Divine have much to contribute towards the development of a more differentiated, richer image of God among men.

It is interesting to know that Teilhard's own thought, characterized by the synthesis of a modern scientific worldview with religious and mystical insights, has aroused considerable interest in the East, especially in India, Sri Lanka and Japan. In the opinion of Father Heinrich Dumoulin, the historian of Zen Buddhism, Teilhard's ideas provide a particularly suitable preparation for the intellectual and religious dialogue of the West with Asia.[3]

This mutual dialogue has to grow, for a new religious vision cannot develop in cultural isolation. At present, however, too many people in the West still inhabit ethnocentric, cultural and religious ghettos of the past. It is essential to learn what John Dunne has imaginatively called the 'passing over' into other people's lives and cultures. Writing about his encounter with Eastern religions, he says : 'When you pass over to other lives, and by way of other lives to other cultures and other religions, you come back again with new insight into your own life, and by way of your own life to your own culture and religion'.[4]

Western people can learn a great deal from Eastern religions; for example, the non-dogmatic, experimental approach to the search for truth; the emphasis on finding the true self, a search which requires a recentring of one's inner being, a withdrawal of the senses from overactivity and distraction and, at its best, the exploring of a dimension of consciousness beyond ordinary consciousness; regular meditation, as practised in Hinduism and Buddhism, represents an enriching activity of 'cultivated non-activity' which can achieve inner integration and wisdom and, in certain instances, lead to union and communion with one's fellow-beings and with God.

These aspects are initially beneficial to the individual to arrive at peace with himself. In addition, however, they can provide inner resources for developing peaceful relationships with others and thus be beneficial to man's social life. To live in harmony with nature and society is a theme found in Indian and, even more, Chinese religions, and it is precisely this inner and outer harmony we are so much in need of.

We are living in the midst of an information explosion: a welter of ideas, images and sounds constantly confront and assault us. A growing number of people realize that we require not only an outer, but also an 'inner ecology', a restoration of true inwardness, which implies a deliberate restraint in thought, speech and action, a special kind of asceticism to disentangle and reduce the complexity of our needs. Without such a restraint, we will cut ourselves off from the inner springs of spiritual energy and creativity.

It is little surprising that, in the current experience of widespread disorientation and alienation, there has been a fast growing interest in the mysticism of all religions in the West. The Western enquiry into the varieties of religious experience and different types of mysticism is a comparatively recent phenomenon which points to the awareness of the presence of mystical elements in most, if not all, religious traditions.

Comparisons in this field are very difficult, however, and can be misleadingly simplistic. Non-Western languages often possess no word which exactly corresponds to the meaning of 'mysticism' in Western religion. Instead, Eastern religions speak of *samadhi*, *nirvana*, and *satori* – words which possess quite different semantic traditions and may have other connotations than 'mysticism'. Here again, more study, encounter and dialogue will help to evolve a new understanding and possibly bring about a more commonly shared focus of vision.

Besides the current Western interest in the mystical heritage of the world religions there exists another, quite different area of dynamic growth where religious insights are applied to the transformation of the social order. The message of spiritual freedom is related to the liberation of man from external structures of oppression, whether expressed in the liberation theology of South America or in socialist reinterpretations of Buddhism in South Asia. In a way, the greatest religious problem today is how to be both a mystic and a militant, as Adam Curle has expressed it;[5] in other words, how to combine the search for an expansion of inner awareness with effective social action, and how to find one's true identity in the synthesis of both.

The necessary return to the centre cannot only be a journey

inwards but must meaningfully relate to the outer world. Therefore, interreligious dialogue which remains a monologue among monks, contemplatives and a few individual seekers is not enough. The need for a new spirituality, a new mysticism of action, is much greater and more universal. The search for an adequate contemporary spirituality is in many ways a lay movement; it relates to the concerns of all rather than only to those of a social and spiritual elite. The new religious vision for today cannot be found in an eclectic spiritual syncretism nor in a return to simpler states of inwardness and withdrawal, based exclusively on Eastern forms of meditation. Teilhard saw this clearly and, like Jung, he warned Westerners not to seek in the East what they cannot find there : an integral spirituality for the modern world. Spirituality is not meant to be an alternative life-style, a road of retreat and escape, but must be an active leaven for life.

The development of religion and society is always closely interrelated. This applies not only to religious institutions but also to the religious self-understanding and spiritual practice of the individual. With the increasing expansion of knowledge we are also gaining a growing acquaintance with each other's religious heritage. This is more than a merely quantitative development; one should not underestimate the possible qualitative effect of a greater knowledge *about* world religions on religious awareness itself. Taking full cognizance of the religious experience of mankind may produce what has been called a 'global religious consciousness'. It may bring with it a profound transformation, a mutation in religious awareness and a new awakening to what is most central to all faith and genuine spirituality, on a scale unknown in the past. Perhaps this is what Teilhard meant when he said that the era not of religions but of religion, far from being bygone, is only beginning.

Many signs are already pointing to such a change in man's religious awareness. However, this transformation is taking place outside or at the margin of the great religions, and it is also largely beyond institutional control. It represents a genuinely open religious quest, cutting across major religious and denominational differences. These are changes on a revolutionary scale which seem to pass almost unnoticed in some quarters.

The experience of an emerging global society has brought with it the idea that we must develop a new consciousness and identity as world citizens. Similarly, we perhaps need a new kind of 'world believer' who can meaningfully relate to the perspectives of more than one religious tradition and thereby find a deep enrichment. This requires the intersection of both a particular and universal dimension: rooted in his own religious traditions, the individual also needs to be open to the faith of others. He can thus deepen and widen his religious understanding to a vision of universality.

The creative tension between the particular and universal was perhaps best expressed by Gandhi who wanted the windows of his house wide open to the winds from all corners of the earth without wishing to be swept off his feet. Gandhi tried to learn from all religions and yet, fundamentally, he remained a Hindu. Similarly, we can think of many a Christian who has been enriched and transformed by the experience of either Hinduism or Buddhism, or by that of Judaism or Islam, without giving up his own faith.

To relate Eastern religions creatively to our own religious background it is imperative to provide more education about world religions in homes, schools, colleges, universities and churches. This is not only important for spirituality. A well-informed and balanced study of the world religions can help towards a better understanding of other races and cultures; it can lead to a deep appreciation of the central values which have shaped other civilizations than our own. What is more, if in the future we will be increasingly free from the necessity of physical labour and possess more abundant leisure, time for reflection on fundamental questions of meaning will become available to a greater number of people. It will no longer be just an elite who can cultivate inwardness and the life of the spirit but a new road of spirituality will become a genuine option for a much greater number. Thus, one might envisage the practice of religion as less institution- and culture-bound whilst the activating and dynamic elements of spirituality are more universally shared.

Contrary to what some may think, it is no longer possible to return to the original monism of early mankind in order to find a unitary form of consciousness. The great historical religions were originally linked to a dualistic worldview which is now fast breaking up. Today, new modes of thinking, feeling and being are sought, leading to the experience of new forms of unity and community, both more complex and more differentiated. Such a unitive approach may eventually overcome the separations and oppositions of the past, not least the division between religion and science.

The adventure of discovery and knowledge associated with the modern scientific quest has been one of the most powerful developments in human history. However, many people today are experiencing a disenchantment with science because of the reductionist and pragmatic narrowness frequently associated with scientific practice. Some want to exchange the realm of science with that of the mystical, magical, and occult but this would mean regressing rather than advancing. Again, others are masters at praising the insight and understanding reached by modern science without having any room for religion and mysticism. For Teilhard and other scientists, however, the way to the future lies in a new synthesis of the rational and mystical, in a truly integral vision which can animate all areas of human endeavour.

The contemporary quest for a new spirituality transcends the needs of individual seekers. Today, more than ever before, spirituality must be understood and practised in relation to the central concerns of society. The Russian philosopher Berdyaev already perceived this when he pointed out that an altogether new spirituality is required to come to terms with one of the most basic problems of human societies, that of work and labour. In other words, spirituality cannot be pursued in isolation from social action, without concern for the vital areas of economics and politics.

Thus, spirituality is now seen in a new way as closely related to the development of the world and the dynamics of society. In this situation we also need a truly creative exercise of the religious imagination in our approach to the religious heritage of mankind. We require a new breakthrough in our understanding of faith as a core element in being human. This does not mean a narrow and dogmatic faith but one which is truly alive and more universal than in the past. It also implies a quality of trust and openness without which neither human life nor science can progress.

The living religions are already drawing more closely together in their understanding of such central themes as the importance of the human person, the value of the world and society, and the place of transcendence in man's life. The possibility of a new mysticism provides a powerful focus of attraction: it leads man into the world rather than out of it. A mysticism of action can inspire the spiritualization of man in and through the unification of the world in all areas of becoming. The ascent of man is more than an ascent to knowledge. Humankind is called to the height of the spirit but no one can reach this summit on their own, in separation from others. The present generation will only follow the call to such an ascent if a dynamic and action-oriented spirituality becomes the true driving force of contemporary society.

Appendix

I

Teilhard's Years in The East

Country	Date	Place of residence (in italics), visits or expeditions
EGYPT	*1905–08*	*Cairo*, Alexandria, Nile Valley, Memphis, Luxor, Karnak, Upper Egypt.
CHINA	*1923–46*	
	1923–24	Via Suez, Colombo, Penang, Malacca, Saigon, Hong Kong, Shanghai to *Tientsin*. Expeditions to Ordos Desert and eastern Mongolia.
	1926–27	Via Saigon, Annam, Hanoi to *Tientsin*. Expeditions to eastern Mongolia and Yellow River area (Shensi and Shansi provinces).
	1928–30	After two months in Ethiopia and French Somaliland, via Ceylon to *Tientsin*. Expeditions to Manchuria, Yellow River area, Chou-Kou-Tien, and Gobi Desert.
	1931–32	Via Hawaii and Japan to *Peking*. 'Yellow Expedition': Gobi Desert, Black Gobi, Hami, Urumchi (Sinkiang), Aksu, Bäzäklik, Liangchow, Pei Ling Miao, Shara Muren, Kalgan, Peking.
	1933–35	Via Ceylon, Penang, Singapore, Port Said, Saigon, Shanghai to *Peking*. Expeditions along Yangtze River and in South China.
	1936–37	After four months in India and Indonesia (1935/36), via Hong Kong and Shanghai to *Peking*.
	1937–38	After four months in Burma and Indonesia, return to *Peking*
	1939–46	*Peking*, Shanghai.
INDIA	*1935*	October-December: Via Bombay to Rawalpindi, Kashmir, Punjab: Salt Range, Mohenjo-Daro, Lahore; Sind and Baluchistan; central India: Narbada Valley; Calcutta. Via Rangoon and Singapore to Indonesia.
INDONESIA	*1936*	One month (January). Djakarta. Expeditions to the centre and south of Java.
	1938	Fortnight (April). Island of Java: Bandung, Surakarta, Trinil, La Solo.
BURMA	*1935*	Visit to Rangoon over Christmas.
	1937–38	December–March: Rangoon, Pagan, Upper Burma, Irrawaddy Valley
JAPAN	*1931/37/38*	Three brief visits: Kobe, Kyoto, Nara.

II

Early Writings which include
a Discussion of Pantheism, Monism and Mysticism*

Year	Title	English edition	French edition
1916	'Cosmic Life'	WTW, pp. 13–71	vol. 12, pp. 17–82
1917	'The Mystical Milieu'	WTW, pp. 115–149	vol. 12, pp. 153–192
1917	'The Soul of the World'	WTW, pp. 177–190	vol. 12, pp. 243–259
1918	'My Universe'	HM, pp. 196–208	vol. 12, pp. 293–307
1918	'Note on the "Universal Element" of the World'	WTW, pp. 271–276	vol. 12, pp. 387–393
1919	'Note on the Presentation of the Gospel in a New Age'	HM, pp. 209–224	vol. 12, pp. 395–414
1919	'The Universal Element'	WTW, pp. 289–302	vol. 12, pp. 429–445
1923	'Pantheism and Christianity'	CE, pp. 56–75	vol. 10, pp. 71–91
1923	'The Mass on the World'	HM, pp. 119–134	vol. 13, pp. 139–56
1924	'My Universe'	SC, pp. 37–85	vol. 9, pp. 63–114

*See the list of ABBREVIATIONS (under NOTES) for the English titles and the BIBLIOGRAPHY for the volumes of the French edition.

III

Later Writings which include
Specific Comparisons with Eastern Religions*

Year	Title	English edition	French edition
1932	'The Road of the West'	TF, pp. 40–59	vol. 11, pp. 45–64
1933	'Christianity in the World'	SC, pp. 98–112	vol. 9, pp. 129–145
1934	'How I Believe'	CE, pp. 96–132	vol. 10, pp. 115–159
1939	'The Grand Option'	FM, pp. 37–60	vol. 5, pp. 57–81
1940	*The Phenomenon of Man*	PM, pp. 209–212	vol. 1, pp. 231–235
1944	'Introduction to the Christian Life'	CE, pp. 151–172	vol. 10, pp. 177–203
1945	'Action and Activation'	SC, pp. 174–186	vol. 9, pp. 219–233
1946	'Ecumenism'	SC, pp. 197–198	vol. 9, pp. 251–255
1947	'The Spiritual Contribution of the Far East'	TF, pp. 134–147	vol. 11, pp. 147–160
1948	'My Fundamental Vision'	TF, pp. 163–208	vol. 11, pp. 177–233
1950	'A Clarification: Reflections on Two Converse Forms of the Spirit'	AE, pp. 215–227	vol. 7, pp. 223–236
1950	'The Heart of Matter'	HM, pp. 14–79	vol. 13, pp. 19–74
1951	'Some Notes on the Mystical Sense: An Attempt at Clarification'	TF, pp. 209–211	vol. 11, pp. 225–229
1955	'The Christic'	HM, pp. 80–102	vol. 13, pp. 94–117

*See the list of ABBREVIATIONS for the English titles and the BIBLIOGRAPHY for the volumes of the French edition. Only book titles are printed in italics, all essay titles are set in quotation marks.

IV

Teilhard's Reading

It has been mentioned that Teilhard kept a *carnet de lecture* in which he listed and commented on the books he had read. Unfortunately, it is impossible to reconstruct a comprehensive list of his reading as only three *carnets* have survived, two dating from 1945 and one from 1950. However incomplete and fragmentary, these notes and comments on particular books provide a valuable insight into the working of Teilhard's mind and his reaction to other people's thought. So far, no full study of the unpublished *carnets de lecture* has been undertaken. Where extracts of particular books have been noted down, these can be compared with the original works from which they are taken. Teilhard's comments on his reading can frequently be supplemented by further evidence from the later diaries which at present also remain unpublished.

As far as I am aware, only Teilhard's comments on reading Karl Barth have received closer attention up to now.[1] Here, some extracts are commented upon which relate to two works on mysticism and Indian religions. They possess a note-like character and their content appeals perhaps more to people with a specialized interest in Indian religions. However, as it is little known that Teilhard read such books at all, and as the notes throw additional light on his attitude to Eastern religions, it is important to present this material and interpret its meaning in a wider context.

1   Comments on Maréchal's 'Studies in the Psychology of the Mystics'

Teilhard had known Joseph Maréchal and his work since 1910. At an early stage, he may have read Maréchal's essay 'On the Feeling of Presence in Mystics and Non-Mystics' (1908-9) but no conclusive evidence exists for this. Much later, however, in 1945, his *carnet de lecture I* gives several pages of extracts from Maréchal's *Etudes sur la Psychologie des Mystiques*.[2] These provide an interesting example of Teilhard's use of sources and document his continuing interest in mysticism. Maréchal's work includes, among others, a comparative discussion of Hindu and Muslim mysticism, an essay on mystical grace centring on Al Hallaj, and an extensive, annotated bibliography on mysticism.

Apart from a brief reference to Leuba's work in the psychology of religion, Teilhard's notes relate exclusively to one particular essay, entitled 'Réflexions sur l'étude comparée des mysticismes'.[3] It deals with doctrinal and psychological elements in the study of mysticism, and contains sections on Buddhism, Patanjali's Yoga, and the different psychological attitudes of Eastern and Western mystics. In addition, Muslim and Christian mysticism and asceticism are discussed.

Teilhard's notes are particularly concerned with doctrinal points. After a brief reference to Persian dualism, the Hindu teaching on the immanence of the Divine is described as a position which does not allow 'an increase in the mystical movement'. This is followed by Maréchal's characterization of Buddhism as 'neither a cosmological dualism nor a monism' but a practical agnosticism. The content of liberation ('i.e. Nirvana', Teilhard added) is undetermined ('logically apersonal') leaving room, however, for a hypothetical transcendence.[4] In brackets, Teilhard noted that it is necessary to explain 'the development of Buddhist mysticism (Great vehicle? Amida-Buddhism?)'.

Most of the notes are taken from subsection four of Maréchal's essay dealing with 'Le monisme panthéistique'.[5] They are primarily concerned with Indian, that is to say, Upanishadic monism and also with Western philosophical monism. Teilhard copied a long passage from La Vallé Poussin, used by Maréchal: The Upanishads are the perennial source of idealistic mysticism for both orthodox and unorthodox Indian thinkers, from Buddha to Shankara, from Ramanuja to Rammohun Roy.

Teilhard then summarized Maréchal's discussion of Shankara's Vedanta, dealing with the *Atman-Brahman* identification. The Absolute is absolute non-duality, and all multiple is equated with illusion or *maya*. One does not know Brahman, one simply is Brahman. Teilhard's only comment is *'No love!'*

Whereas Hindu monism seems to inspire a mysticism of exclusive inner withdrawal which abandons the evanescent world and its nothingness, Western pantheism, even in its most daring introvertive developments, never completely renounces the idea that an ascent towards the Divine can be achieved through the world. In Maréchal's words, copied by Teilhard, 'renunciation is superior integration rather than simple detachment'.⁶ This is followed by an emphatic 'No!!' For Teilhard, this is not the most fundamental difference between Western and Hindu monism; it consists much more in 'two antithetical notions of unity' and a 'profound difference in the subjective attitude'. Both forms of monism share a common aspiration towards the One but the movement to reach it is different. When Maréchal states that Western monism maintains, through analogy, a positive relationship between finite forms and the Absolute, Teilhard adds 'road of the West'.

One of the primary sources of Western philosophical monism is the *Enneads* of Plotinus. Teilhard noted details of Maréchal's discussion, especially on the possible influence of Plotinus on Vedanta, Muslim Sufism and, through Pseudo-Dionysius, Christian mysticism.

Modern philosophical monism is represented through Fichte, Schelling and Hegel. Maréchal draws a sharp distinction between 'natural' and 'supernatural' mysticism, still maintained by certain writers today. Teilhard does not accept this view; for him, the main difference lies in the possibility or impossibility of love.

Maréchal's subsequent section is entitled 'Le monothéisme et la possibilité d'une Mystique surnaturelle'.⁷ Teilhard simply copied this title and commented: 'The Christian mystical act has not yet found its metaphysics'. This sentence is underlined twice in red and black. With it, the notes on Maréchal's book in the *carnet de lecture* come to an end.

The meaning of this comment becomes clearer when read in conjunction with a contemporary diary entry, referring to Maréchal's book. In the diary, the 'Christian mystical act' is identified with 'love'. Its corresponding 'metaphysics' has not been adequately expressed yet. It would have to give maximum room to an ultimate unity as well as to the intrinsic value of the cosmos by which Teilhard means the world in its fullest sense, natural as well as human.⁸

The significance of these notes is twofold. Firstly, they show that in 1945 Teilhard was still interested in the different interpretations of pantheistic monism. Secondly, the few personal comments prove that, whilst he admitted an affinity and continuity between various forms of monism, he saw the different types of mysticism as distinguished through their divergent views about the relationship between the manifold and the Absolute. The fundamental question is whether or not the One is reached by man through a union of love, including a love for the realities of this world. Such love is not a simple attraction but it implies a dynamic movement which, through the ultimate convergence of all elements in the One, realizes the highest possible form of union. This particular interpretation led Teilhard to disagree with certain aspects of Maréchal's presentation of Christian mysticism, as he disagreed elsewhere with that of other writers.

The references of Maréchal's work in the *carnet de lecture* and diary show a dialectical tension in Teilhard's thought: considering the monistic and theistic interpretations of mysticism, he accepted certain aspects of each whilst rejecting other elements in both. It would seem, therefore, that he searched for a new synthesis in the understanding of mysticism which has not been developed so far.

II Comments on Johanns's 'To Christ through the Vedanta'

Soon after reading Maréchal's book, Teilhard turned to a more specialized work on Indian thought. The first ten pages of his *carnet de lecture II*, also dating from 1945, deal with a book by Pierre Johanns, *Vers le Christ par le Vedanta*.[9] These extracts are considerably longer and because of their importance, they deserve detailed comment.

First the background of the book may be briefly mentioned. In the early part of this century, Father Johanns[10] was well known among Roman Catholic missionaries for his attempt to bring about a closer encounter between Christianity and Hinduism. He studied Hindu religious thought in depth because he considered it to be an eminent 'praeparatio evangelica'. Thus Hinduism was seen as providing the natural foundations for the supernatural revelation of Christianity. Johanns's attitude may be regarded as a Roman Catholic variant of the Protestant 'fulfilment school' which dominated missionary circles at the beginning of this century.

In pursuit of his aim to show that the best of Eastern thought finds its completion in Christianity, Father Johanns edited a journal, called *The Light from the East*.[11] A series of articles, published in this journal between 1922-34, was entitled 'To Christ through the Vedanta'. Published in book form in French translation, this title became the best-known of Johanns's works on Indian religious thought.

The two volumes of *Vers le Christ par le Vedanta* represent a well-annotated scholarly study. In the introduction, Johanns states that there exists no important Catholic doctrine, as formulated by St Thomas of Aquinas, which cannot also be found in one or the other system of Vedanta philosophy. On one hand, he argues for the complementarity of the various branches of Vedanta philosophy and, on the other, for the affinity of this synthesis with Thomistic doctrine.

One third of Johanns's first volume is devoted to the great ninth century Hindu theologian Shankara, and two thirds to the eleventh-century theologian Ramanuja. Whereas Ramanuja has a well-developed doctrine of God, man, and the world, Shankara gives such an exalted position to the Absolute that the treatment of man and the world remain secondary in his work. Johanns emphasizes, however, that pantheism is not only foreign to Shankara's doctrine but has been clearly refuted by him. At the same time, Johanns was aware that Shankara's lofty doctrine ought to be supplemented by a fully positive philosophy of man and nature and an adequate philosophy of religion. As will be seen, Teilhard's comments are along similar lines but they go beyond Johanns's criticisms by questioning some of the latter's own presuppositions.

Volume two of Johanns's work is entirely devoted to the study of Vallabha, a Vedanta theologian of the sixteenth century. The introduction claims that this volume, published in 1933, is the first exposition of Vallabha's thought in any European language.[12]

Teilhard's extracts and comments on Johanns's two volumes are sufficiently copious to draw certain conclusions as to his interest in reading such a work, and his method in assimilating its content. The main body of the notes either summarizes certain ideas about Vedanta, as found in Johanns, or it quotes passages in full. However, these quotations do not always strictly follow the original; they may carry a different orthography, leave out words, or abbreviate them. Although not always literally correct, they always reproduce the correct meaning. In addition, the notes include critical comments from Teilhard, referring to either the Vedanta or Johanns. Through a close comparison of the extracts in the *carnet de lecture* with the original text, the personal comments can be clearly discerned from the copied notes. Teilhard's own remarks are mainly found on the margin of his notebook or sometimes they are inserted in brackets following the extracts.

The notes begin with the author and title of the book: *Vers le Christ par le Vedanta*. Above 'Vedanta', Teilhard added in brackets 'Late Neo-Vedanta, influenced by Christianity'. This may appear surprising if it were meant as an explanatory comment. However, it does not seem to relate directly to the title of Johanns's work but appears to be an afterthought. One can interpret this remark as intended to distinguish the classical Vedanta, dealt with by Johanns, from the modern Neo-Vedanta of the nineteenth and twentieth centuries. In the latter, a reinterpretation of classical Vedanta teaching occurred, initially influenced through the contact with Western, especially Christian, ideas.

The first page of notes is devoted to Shankara. The date of his death is mentioned, and also the fact that, through his defence of brahminical orthodoxy, he conquered Buddhist heterodoxy. His teaching predominates among educated Hindus but is not universally accepted in India. Shankara had some difficulty in interpreting certain Vedic texts which state that the universe is an evolution from God. Through his exclusive emphasis on the Absolute, the world and the individuality of the soul become pure illusion or *maya*. By concentrating solely on the true nature of *Brahman*, Shankara so exalts the nature of the Absolute that no internal relationship within it may exist.

Commenting on Johanns's remark that Shankara is led by his own logic to negate the existence of the world, Teilhard noted on the margin: 'Logic of the Absolute is exaggerated! Evolution equals zero!' Shankara leaves no room for the world and its development; he cannot explain the manifold in relation to the One.

Teilhard's notes do not reproduce any excerpts from Johanns's detailed chapters on Shankara's analysis of the Upanishadic statement *tat tvam asi*, understood as a strict identity between *Brahman* and *Atman*. Whether or not he read these chapters is difficult to say. It is evident that he could not accept an exclusively absolutist position. The relationship between an absolute One and a manifold world, as well as the understanding of evolution, always remained his major interest. This is borne out by the subsequent notes on Ramanuja and Vallabha. The last remark on Shankara mentions that his absolute position, which allows for no synthesis whatsoever, strikes objective as well as subjective pantheism at its roots.

Whereas just over one page of Teilhard's notes are devoted to Shankara, over two pages deal with Ramanuja, followed by more than three pages on the comparison of the two thinkers. This faithfully reflects the distribution of material in Johanns's first volume.

Teilhard, like most Christians, finds Ramanuja more attractive than Shankara's metaphysical monism. Following Johanns's exposition, he notes that for Ramanuja, God is personal and loves man. His concept of God may be philosophically less elevated than Shankara's but it corresponds more to our religious needs. Whilst Shankara evades any real explanation of the relationship between the world and God, Ramanuja wants to save the reality of the world by seeing it as absolutely within God.

Teilhard noted on the margin of his notebook that this may be identical to his own view of things except that it is 'static' and without 'centre-complexity'. However, this statement is preceded by both an exclamation and a question mark. For Teilhard, the great metaphysical discovery of modern times is the principle of evolution rather than *involution*. Hinduism, like Neo-Platonism, does not accept evolution in its true sense, but only emanation. Many of Teilhard's remarks bear on this distinction between evolutionary creation and involution or emanation. A consequence of the latter is the acceptance of matter as evil or illusory. He remarks: 'Even for the theist Ramanuja the cosmos equals involution, and matter is an obstacle!'

Other notes are concerned with the nature of the Indian concept of *karma* as an impersonal, objective law, leading to the involvement of the soul with matter. There is no answer to the question where *karma* comes from. One of the ways to gain liberation from the effects of *karma* is through *bhakti*, consisting of loving devotion linked to disinterested meditation and asceticism. For Ramanuja, the liberated soul is not annihilated in the fullness of God but becomes wholly conscious whilst matter falls away. Thus matter is always seen as the oppressive element. Teilhard added the comment: 'Always the road *of the East.*'

This is followed by a reference to Johanns's 'fortunate distinction' in saying that God is not the *self* of the soul, as Ramanuja maintains, but its '*Super-self*', perhaps better expressed as the higher Self which makes love possible. Teilhard mentions in addition that love requires God to be the higher Self of the cosmos.

The comparisons between Ramanuja and Shankara, found in the second half of Johanns's volume I, relate to the concept of God, the understanding of the universe, and the relationship between God and the world. Teilhard notes that for Shankara this is a relationship of identity whilst Ramanuja maintains the inherence of the world in God. After this, two different understandings of *Nirvana* are mentioned, Buddhist 'emptiness', and Shankara's 'positive indetermination' which may be 'plenitude'.

With reference to Ramanuja's treatment of God as personal, Teilhard wrote: 'NB. Christianity is thus not alone in maintaining a personal God'. It is important to know that he made such a comment. It shows that, at least when reading this book, if not before, he was aware that theism is an integral part of the Hindu religious tradition, and Christianity can claim no uniqueness in this respect. The same comment asks what, then, is specifically Christian? It is suggested that this may be a new form of love, linked to 'Christ-Omega' as incarnated.

In Teilhard's view, neither Ramanuja nor Shankara offer man an ideal which is in any way related to mankind or the world. Rather, they present a pure spirit in a real (Ramanuja) or illusory (Shankara), but nevertheless accidental, relationship to the world of matter. Thus, matter is rejected as either illusory, or it is simply juxtaposed to spirit. Such a position is, according to Teilhard, due to a complete disregard for the true nature of evolution which implies the interdependence of matter and spirit. Whilst for Christianity the idea of salvation involves the notion of progress, the Vedanta concept of self-realization really means a regress, a return to the One, arrived at negatively through silence and meditation.

Teilhard's comments on Johanns's text emphasize that the author does not see that Hindus, in spite of a personal God, fail to recognize an ultimate unity achieved by convergence, nor do they acknowledge the real implications of evolution. That is to say, whenever there is talk of evolution, what is really meant is the involution of spirit in matter.

Ramanuja's system is crowned by *bhakti* – the love of God as both the end and means of man's self-realization. Teilhard notes his difficulty here: love may be evasion or negation of the cosmos; alternatively, it may lead the devotee to a fusion, a drowning in God. Ramanuja's love, then, would be a 'pseudo-love'. Is the entire cosmos only a 'play' or, as noted earlier, a 'panorama' where the divine light is dimly diffused? Is it not also 'a plan to be realized' a 'serious work' to be achieved?

Johanns attributes much of the difference between Hinduism and Christianity to a different notion of creation. For him, the Christian doctrine of *creatio ex nihilo* implies the idea of the realization of the self in a way which complements the Indian view of its liberation. Teilhard, however, thinks that the difference between Hinduism and Christianity is less related to the doctrine of creation than to the concept of two different forms of unity. *Creatio ex nihilo* is simply a 'deus ex machina', a 'metaphysical monster', if not related to the idea of a 'maximum unity' achieved through the integration of the multiple into the One.

Johanns's second volume is exclusively concerned with Vallabha's teaching to which Teilhard's notebook devotes two and a half pages. Vallabha's date of death is stated and his system is characterized as some kind of qualified pantheism. His thought attempts a synthesis of the different positions of Shankara and Ramanuja. This is achieved through introducing the threefold distinction between an utterly transcendent God (*nirguna brahman*), a God accessible through his qualities (*saguna brahman*), and a God who appears in the world through Krishna.

For Vallabha, the personality of God is a supreme attribute of the Absolute. The phenomenal world owes its existence to a self-analysis of God. It consists of divine fragments which see themselves only from the outside, not recognizing their true nature. Vallabha's thought raises 'the great question' how to reconcile the idea of an unchangeable God with that of the cosmos, understood as God becomes explicit.

Where Shankara suppresses the cosmos, Ramanuja treats it as the body of the Lord, and Vallabha sees it as an explicit unfolding of what has always been. This means that creation and evolution never add anything really new. Teilhard concluded, therefore, that Hindus do not really have creation: it is *not* a process of *synthesis* but merely of *analysis*, of involution rather than evolution. This is a 'deforming projection' which remains in the realm of the static and identical.

Perhaps written at a later stage, these notes bear an additional comment as follows: 'True solution of the problem Hinduism/Christianity: to christianize/christify/evolution (satisfies the aspirations of Shankara, Ramanuja, Vallabha . . .)'. This is matched by a similar remark made subsequently: 'The entire Vedanta would coincide with Neo-Christianity if transposed into evolutionary-unifying matter' [*Matière évolutif-unitif*].

This proves that, for Teilhard, an adequate understanding of matter and evolution is a more decisive difference between Christianity and Hinduism than traditional theological doctrines. However, the full implications of a dynamic, evolutionary view also have to be further integrated into Christianity. This is the reason why he refers to 'Neo-Christianity'.

Teilhard's further notes include, among others, references to Vallabha's views on such matters as grace (*pushti*), detachment, and *rasa* as a search through suffering; the dance of Krishna which makes the universe vibrate in exultation, and the importance of the body and the world. Whilst Vallabha's view of detachment is judged as static, Teilhard compares his interpretation of *rasa* with St John's dark night of the soul. Then he goes on to emphasize once more the distinction between love in Vedanta and Christianity, dependent on whether unity is achieved by fusion or synthesis. This is followed by a short note on Vallabha's place in the 'philosophia perennis'.

For Johanns, not only the doctrine of creation, but also of

original sin, implies a basic difference between Christianity and Hinduism. Teilhard disagrees with this and, consequently, criticizes Johanns' for his 'palaeo-Christianity'. The whole concept of 'original sin' ought to be changed – and he states that this is said not 'out of a lack of humility, but out of love for God!'

In a final remark Teilhard points to what he considers the real dividing line between Hinduism and Christianity. It relates to two decisive issues, namely, whether there is a unity of synthesis or convergence in God and whether the cosmos is in process of evolution.

The ten pages of extracts and comments are important in several respects. First of all, they show that Teilhard studied two philosophically demanding works on Indian religious thought presenting ideas of the classical Vedanta in considerable detail. The extracts also provide evidence of his continued interest in monism which exercised a lasting fascination on his mind. The exaltation of the One always raises the inherent philosophical difficulty of how to account for the manifold realities of the world and their evolutionary development.

Furthermore, the notes clearly indicate that Teilhard knew of the theistic strands of Hinduism. He realized their difference from monistic teachings of which he learnt much earlier. This may be due to the fact that, historically, they were the first to become generally known in the West and, in many people's mind, Hinduism is still equated with monism.

Lastly, the comments also include several comparisons between Hinduism and Christianity, emphasizing what are, in Teilhard's view, deficiencies in the Hindu position. Yet at the same time, traditional Christian doctrines are criticized as 'palaeo-Christianity', in contrast to his own conception of a reinterpreted 'neo-Christianity'.

These comments underline once again that Teilhard favours a theistic and convergent, rather than a monistic approach to the Absolute, and sees the cosmos as an ongoing process of evolution towards a higher syntheis. From this perspective, he criticizes both Hinduism and Christianity. Yet he also points to the possibility of a much greater affinity between Vedanta and neo-Christianity, if the former were to incorporate a dynamic evolutionary perspective which sees evolution as more than involution. This is perhaps an indication that, in spite of his criticisms, Teilhard's attitude ultimately implies the complementarity and convergence of the two religious traditions.

NOTES

ABBREVIATIONS

Frequently quoted titles among Teilhard's works have been abbreviated. For a full list of his writings see the BIBLIOGRAPHY.

Collections of essays

AE   *Activation of Energy*, London, 1970.
CE   *Christianity and Evolution*, London, 1971.
FM   *The Future of Man*, London, 1964.
HE   *Human Energy*, London, 1969.
HM   *The Heart of Matter*, London, 1978.
HU   *Hymn of the Universe*, London, 1965.
MD   *Le Milieu Divin*, London, 1960.
OSc   *L'Oeuvre Scientifique*, 11 volumes, Olten, 1971.
PM   *The Phenomenon of Man*, London, 1959.
SC   *Science and Christ*, London, 1968.
TF   *Towards the Future*, London, 1975.
WTW   *Writings in Time of War*, London, 1968.

Letters

LF   *Lettres Familières de Pierre Teilhard de Chardin Mon Ami 1948-1955*, Paris, 1976.
LI   *Lettres Intimes à Auguste Valensin, Bruno de Solages, Henri de Lubac, André Ravier 1919-1955*, Paris, 1974.
LT   *Lettres from a Traveller*, London, 1966.
LTF   *Letters to Two Friends 1926-1952*, London, 1970.
LZ   *Letters to Léontine Zanta*, London, 1969.
MM   *The Making of a Mind. Letters from a Soldier-Priest 1914-1919*, London, 1965.
TB   *Pierre Teilhard de Chardin-Maurice Blondel Correspondence*, New York, 1967.

PREFACE

1 The three most significant comparative studies undertaken so far are R. C. Zaehner, *Evolution in Religion*. A Study in Sri Aurobindo and Pierre Teilhard de Chardin, Oxford, 1971; B. Bruteau, *Evolution toward Divinity*. Teilhard de Chardin and the Hindu Traditions, Wheaton, 1974; M.-I. Bergeron, *La Chine et Teilhard*, Paris, 1976. Two unpublished Ph.D theses are also concerned with an investigation of Teilhard's thought from the wider perspective of religious studies: M. V. Duvall, *Man's Concept of His Religious Fulfillment*: A Cross-Cultural Study of Major Perspectives in Teilhard de Chardin and Classical Hindu, Buddhist, and Confucian Thought, Fordham University, New York, 1966; T. Kramlinger, *The Sacred and Salvation*. A Study of Teilhard de Chardin's Religious Experiences in Evolutionary Being and Time and their Relation to Contemporary Religious Experiences, University of Tübingen, 1971. Mircea Eliade has suggested that the cultural significance of Teilhard's work, whose literary success has been far greater than that of the most popular philosopher of his generation, Jean-Paul Sartre, may well deserve the attention of the historian of religion (see his 'Cultural Fashions and the History of Religions' in J. M. Kitagawa ed., *The History of Religions*, Chicago, 1967, pp. 21-38).

2 CE, p. 122.

3 *Génèse d'une Pensée*, Paris, 1961, backcover; my translation.

CHAPTER 1

1 A. Speer, *Spandau: The Secret Diaries*, London, 1976, p. 121.

2 Both essays are found in P. Teilhard de Chardin, *The Heart of Matter*, London 1978, hereafter abbreviated as HM. The book represents the English translation of *Le Coeur de la Matière*, Paris, 1976, volume 13 of Teilhard's collected works in French, plus some additional material not translated before. For the essay 'The Heart of Matter' see HM, pp. 14-79, and for 'The Christic' HM, pp. 80-102. 'My Fundamental Vision' is found in TF, pp. 163-208.

3 TF, p. 164.

4 PM, p. 33.

5 PM, p. 35.

6 MD, p. 29.

7 MD, p. 122.

8 Originally published in P. Teilhard de Chardin, *Ecrits du Temps de la Guerre*, Paris, 1965, pp. 263-79, it remained untranslated until it was recently included in HM, pp. 196-208.

9 See P. Teilhard de Chardin, *Journal*, Paris, 1975, p. 223; my translation.

10 See *Journal*, p. 49.

11 HM, p. 25.

12 HM, p. 25 f.

13 Teilhard's vision of Christ is fully discussed in C. F. Mooney, *Teilhard de Chardin and the Mystery of Christ*, London, 1966. Besides the discovery of evolution, Newman's *Essay on the Development of Christian Doctrine* was of cardinal importance in influencing Teilhard's reinterpretation of his religious beliefs. The developmental process involved in the emergence of Teilhard's cosmic-christic vision has been analysed with great subtlety by H. C. Cairns, *The Identity and Originality of Teilhard de Chardin*, unpublished Ph.D thesis, University of Edinburgh, 1971.

14 See MM, p. 26.

15 Quoted in C. Rivière, *Teilhard, Claudel et Mauriac*, Paris, 1963, p. 52 f.

16 The essays 'Cosmic Life', 'The Mystical Milieu', 'The Soul of the World', and 'The Universal Element' are found in P. Teilhard de Chardin, *Writings in Time of War*, London, 1968, hereinafter abbreviated WTW. 'The Spiritual Power of Matter' was first included in the collection *Hymn of the Universe*, London, 1965; it can now also be found in *The Heart of Matter*, pp. 67-77. The English translation of 'The Great Monad' and 'My Universe' is now printed in *The Heart of Matter*.

17 WTW, p. 32.

18 WTW, p. 32.

19 MM, p. 155 f.

20 For a comprehensive account of the extraordinary difficulties which Teilhard's manuscripts faced, see the study by his former Jesuit Superior in Paris, R. d'Ouince, *Un prophète en procès. Teilhard de Chardin dans l'Eglise de son temps*, 2 vols, Paris, 1970. Further misunderstandings and criticisms of his work are discussed in the latest work of H. de Lubac, *Teilhard Posthume. Réflexions et souvenirs*, Paris, 1977.

21 HM, p. 47.
22 LT, p. 83.
23 See W. Grootaers, 'When and where was the "Mass on the World" written?', *The Teilhard Review*, vol. XII (1977), pp. 91-4.
24 HM, p. 132.
25 HM, p. 133.
26 HM, p. 125.
27 HM, p. 126.
28 LT, p. 105.
29 LT, p. 87.
30 LT, p. 86.
31 LT, p. 86. When an extract of 'The Mass on the World' was first published in an anthology, the symbolic passage on the 'offering' was chosen because of its universalist perspective; see S. Lemaiître, *Textes mystiques d'Orient et d'Occident*, Paris, 1955, pp. 295 ff.
32 Available either on record or cassette from Omega Recordings, The Croft, Portway, Wantage, Oxon.
33 See 'The Mystical Milieu' (1917), WTW, pp. 115-49.
34 MD, p. 16.
35 M. & E. Lukas, *Teilhard. A Biography*, London, 1977 and New York, 1977.
36 See H. de Lubac, *The Religion of Teilhard de Chardin*, London, 1967.

CHAPTER 2

1 See Françoise Teilhard de Chardin (1879-1911), *Lettres et Témoignages*, Paris, 1975.
2 Quoted in C. Cuénot, *Teilhard de Chardin*, London, 1965, p. 10, from an article in which Teilhard described his expedition to the El Faiyûm area south-west of Cairo; see his 'Huit Jours au Fayoum', originally published in *Relations d'Orient*, December 1907, pp. 276-8, reprinted in OSc I, pp. 31-8. Ibid., p. 35, he refers to some of the desert scenes as 'very biblical'.
3 Quoted in *Teilhard de Chardin Album*, London, 1966, p. 36. The original is found in 'The Heart of Matter' (1950).
4 H. Lammens (1826-1937) began to publish on Islam from 1906 onwards. He later became Professor of Arabic at St Joseph's University, Beirut. Among his many publications is the well-

known *Islam – Beliefs and Institutions*, London, 1929, reprinted in 1968. Information about Teilhard's years in Egypt can be gleaned from his *Lettres d'Egypte 1905-1908*, Paris, 1963.

5 H. C. Cairns, op. cit., p. 121. For references to the desert in Teilhard's early writings see WTW, pp. 29 & 31; *Journal*, pp. 42, 57, 58, 177, 178; MM. p. 159: 'the happy days when I felt the intoxication of the desert'.

6 See P. Teilhard de Chardin, *Lettres d'Hastings et de Paris 1908-1914*, Paris, 1965.

7 See Françoise Teilhard de Chardin, op cit., pp. 173 & 176.

8 *Lettres d'Hastings et de Paris*, pp. 82 & 127. His sister's letters refer to Teilhard's regular correspondence with several Jesuits in Shanghai; they also mention the presence of three Chinese novices at Hastings. See Françoise Teilhard de Chardin, op. cit., pp. 222 & 237.

9 'There was a great spiritual intimacy between brother and sister.' H. de Lubac, *The Religion of Teilhard de Chardin*, p. 367, n. 110.

10 MM, p. 288. For Teilhard's letters on the death of his sister see H. de Lubac, op. cit., p. 256 f.

11 See *Lettres d'Hastings et de Paris*, pp. 188, 191, 194.

12 Originally published in *Revue des Questions Scientifiques*, the article was later included in J. Maréchal, *Etudes sur la Psychologie des Mystiques*, Paris, 1924; English translation: London, 1927. For a reference to Teilhard's meeting of Maréchal see *Lettres d'Hastings et de Paris*, p. 182.

13 These notes are discussed in the APPENDIX. Surprisingly, no reference to Maréchal's importance is found in the new Teilhard biography by M. & E. Lukas. For a discussion of Maréchal's decisive influence on Teilhard's conceptual development see H. C. Cairns, op. cit., p. 126.

14 R. d'Ouince, *Un prophète en procès*, vol. 1, p. 52; confirmed in a personal interview with Father d'Ouince, Paris, March 1973.

15 H. de Lubac writes: 'In the Catholicism of the first half of the twentieth century, Père Teilhard was one of the rare thinkers to be deeply interested in the great spiritual systems that divide the world between them. In this we can no doubt see something of the influence of Père Léonce de Grandmaison, but it is even more due to reflection on his own mystical sense, sharpened by his contacts with the East.' *The Religion of Teilhard de Chardin*, p. 233.

16 Since its foundation in the 1830s one of the major French journals for the dissemination of Eastern thought. See R. Schwab, *La Renaissance Orientale*, Paris, 1950, p. 109.

17 Paris, 1913; a second, enlarged version was printed in 1916, and in 1952, a Spanish translation was published in Buenos Aires; see J. Huby ed., *Christus, Manual de Historia de las Religionas*. After an introduction by L. de Grandmaison, the book contains some excellent contributions on ancient and living religions, among others, L. Wieger on Chinese religions, and L. de la Vallé Poussin on Buddhism and Indian religions. To some extent, the book was meant to reply to S. Reinach's controversial *Orpheus*, Histoire générale des Religions, Paris, 1909; see *Christus*, p. 3, n. 1. Father Martindale, an English convert and one of Teilhard's friends at Hastings, also contributed a section to *Christus*; later he published *Lectures on the History of Religions*, London, 1910-1.

18 Personal communication from Father H. de Lubac. Father d'Ouince relates how the closely-knit group of friends at Hastings discussed their future contribution to the renewal of theology. They assigned philosophy to Valensin, the history of religions and theory to Huby, Rousselot, and Charles, and 'l'évangélisation des gentils' to Teilhard. See R. d'Ouince, op. cit., vol. I, p. 67.

19 For an account see F. Bouvier, A. Lemonnyer, eds, *Comptes rendus analytiques des Semaines d'Ethnologie religieuse de Louvain 1912-13*, Paris, 1913; B. Emonet, 'La Semaine d'Ethnologie Religieuse — Louvain 27.8-4.9.1912; *Etudes*, vol. 133, 1912, pp. 83-100. In the same journal, Bouvier had reported in 1908 on the History of Religions Congress at Oxford under the title 'La Science comparée des Religions comment elle se fait et se défait'.

20 OSc I, p. 75. Besides Teilhard, several of his friends attended the Louvain conference, i.e. the Jesuits Grandmaison, Huby, Charles, Valensin, and Lammens, as well as Pinard de la Boullaye. The latter was then already working on his famous survey *L'Etude Comparée des Religions*. In preparation since 1910, but first published in 1922, this is considered to be the most comprehensive survey of the development of the history of religions as a discipline up to that time. According to personal information from H. de Lubac, it is possible and even likely that Teilhard was familiar with this work although he would not have studied it in detail. Father Pinard de la Boullaye was then teaching at the Jesuit house at Enghien (Belgium)

which possessed an excellent library collection in the history of religions, now housed in the Jesuit library at Chantilly (France). In 1914, Pinard de la Boullaye was offered the Chair in the History of Religions at the Institut Catholique, Paris. The second Louvain conference in 1913 was also attended by the Islamicist Louis Massignon whom Teilhard knew well in later years.

21 'Pour fixer les traits d'un monde qui s'efface – La semaine d'ethnologie religieuse de Louvain', *Le Correspondant*, 10.11.1912; reprinted in OSc I, pp. 75-82. Ten years later, Teilhard still referred to these scholarly debates when reviewing a book on *Les Religions de la Préhistoire* for an anthropological journal. See OSc I, p. 416 f.

22 Personal communication from Father René d'Ouince.

23 C. Geertz, *Islam Observed. Religious Developments in Morocco and Indonesia*, New Haven, 1968, p. 44.

24 MM, p. 47.

25 MM, p. 125. For a similar description see *Journal*, p. 104.

26 WTW, p. 29.

27 See especially 'Nostalgia for the Front' (1917) and 'The Heart of Matter' (1950), both in HM, for comparable passages.

28 The journal *Le Lotus Bleu* was founded by Madame Blavatsky in 1887. Since then, it has regularly appeared in Paris as the joint publication of the theosophical societies of France, Belgium, and Switzerland. From its early days, it has published articles on Hindu mysticism. So far, there exists no conclusive evidence whether Teilhard knew this journal or not.

29 WTW, p. 29.

30 See the footnote in *Journal*, p. 53.

31 MM, p. 60.

32 MM, p. 97.

33 See the essay of this title in WTW, pp. 115-49, written in 1917.

34 London, 1904; French translation *L'Expérience religieuse*, Paris, 1906.

35 WTW, p. 189.

36 W. James, *Pragmatism, A New Name for some Old Ways of Thinking*, London, 1907.

37 A footnote in the *Journal*, added by Teilhard, mentions that these three paths equal the three first chapters of 'Cosmic Life'.

38 *Journal*, p. 266; my translation.

39 See lecture IV 'The One and the Many'.

40 W. James, op. cit., p. 151.

41 ibid., p. 153.

42 ibid., p. 262.

43 ibid., p. 274.

44 ibid., p. 292.

45 See *Journal*, p. 264.

46 See *Journal*, p. 270, p. 374; WTW, p. 301.

47 See *Journal*, p. 269, pp. 270-2.

48 P. Teilhard de Chardin, *Ecrits du temps de la guerre*, Paris, 1965, p. 371. The quotation is taken from the essay 'Note on the Presentation of the Gospel in a New Age' (1919), now published in HM, pp. 209-24.

49 E. Schuré, *Les Grands Initiés*. Esquisse de l'Histoire Secrète des Religions, Paris, 1889. An English translation first appeared in 1912. The book became immensely popular. By 1920, it had reached its 58th edition according to H. Pinard de la Boullaye, *L'Etude Comparée des Religions*, Paris, 1929, vol. I, p. 510, n. l. The latter also indicates that, together with R. Reinach's *Orpheus*, Schuré's book popularized the critical stance of B. Bauer. In 1926, L. Roure wrote a criticism of Schuré, *La Légende des Grandes Initiés*. Even today Schuré's book still enjoys popularity as it was recently reprinted in France. An English version was published in New York in 1961 and it is claimed that, since 1889, the book has gone through 220 editions.

50 MM, p. 267.

51 See LI, p. 109, n. 20, 12.

52 MM, p. 268. This remark may point to the essay 'Forma Christi' (1918), or even more 'The Universal Element (1919), both in WTW.

53 R. C. Zaehner, *Evolution in Religion*, Oxford, 1971, p. 6.

54 C. Schneider, 'P. Teilhard de Chardin et E. Schuré', *Cahiers d'études cathares*, vol. 13, 1962, pp. 31-5.

55 His stories on mysticism made such a deep impression on Teilhard that he wrote 'Three stories in the style of Benson', found in P. Teilhard de Chardin, *Hymn of the Universe*, pp. 39-55. As Teilhard's first degree had been a *licence-ès-lettres* (Caen, 1902), one need hardly be surprised that he was more inclined to seek the inspiration of poets and writers than the guidance of scholars in his reading on mysticism.

56 See *Journal*, p. 366, pp. 379-81, p. 386.

57 R. Garric in LZ, p. 9.

58 See the letter quoted in LI, p. 150, n. 31, 12.

59 My translation; see CE, pp. 58 & 60. The essay is 'Pantheism and Christianity' (1923); the expression recalls the 'initiates' of Schuré's book, read in 1918.

60 See P. Teilhard de Chardin – M. Blondel, *Correspondence*, ed. H. de Lubac, New York, 1967, discussed in Chapter five.

61 He had followed Bergson on the Chair of Philosophy at the College de France. Teilhard's influence can be discerned in several of Le Roy's works.

62 The first French woman to obtain a Doctorate of Philosophy in 1914, she was noted for her work on Plato. Teilhard corresponded with her later from China. Before 1918, she had stayed for some time in Egypt. See J. Baudry, *Dictionnaire des correspondants de Teilhard de Chardin*, Lille, 1974, pp. 153-6.

63 Quoted in LT, p. 26.

64 A point stressed in G. Baudry, *Qui était Teilhard de Chardin?* Lille, 1972, p. 30.

65 In 1928, he spent two months in Ethiopia and what was then French Somaliland; see LT, pp. 144-50.

66 C. Cuénot, op. cit., p. 10. For a list of Teilhard's years in the East see TABLE I in the APPENDIX.

CHAPTER 3

1 R. d'Ouince in LTF, p. 5.

2 See *Letters from a Traveller* (LT) and *Letters to Léontine Zanta* (LZ), both beginning in 1926, and *Lettres Intimes* (LI), begun in 1919. For a synopsis of Teilhard's years in the East see the APPENDIX, p. 235.

3 See C. Cuénot, 'Le Père Emile Licent SJ, un portrait', *Le ruban rouge* 19, Paris, 1963, pp. 36-45, and 'Le R. P. Emile Licent SJ', *Bulletin de la Société d'études indochinoises* 1, Saigon, 1966, pp. 9-83. It was Licent's hope to create a Jesuit educational centre for North China in Tientsin, comparable to the one the Jesuits had built up in Shanghai. This extraordinary man and his work deserve a separate study.

4 LI, p. 104.

5 LT, p. 73.

6 LI, p. 104.

7 Tientsin was a 'treaty-port' where nationals of other countries had been granted extra-territorial rights to live in 'concession' districts. Like other cities in the East, Tientsin was a 'dual' city, consisting of an indigenous Chinese and a foreign settlement,

at about two miles distance from the native city. By 1920, there existed seven different national 'concessions', housing a foreign population of over 11,000 (Europeans, Americans, Japanese, Russians), compared with a Chinese population of 837,000. The Jesuits were housed at the southern side of the British concession. By 1922, a museum had been built for the natural history collections gathered by Father Licent. In 1923, the Jesuits opened the High Institute of Commercial and Industrial Arts 'to give the young men of China a serious training in technical subjects which the economic development of the country renders necessary'. See O. D. Rasmussen, *Tientsin*. An Illustrated Outline History, Tientsin, 1925, p. 254; ibid., p. 256, refers to Teilhard's and Licent's forthcoming publication about their palaeontological expeditions to North China and Mongolia.

8 LZ, p. 51 f.

9 LT, p. 81.

10 C. Cuénot, op. cit., p. 116.

11 LZ, p. 52.

12 LT, p. 90.

13 LT, p. 101; 'Chooses Mongoles', written in October 1923, on his return from Mongolia to Tientsin, is found in LT, pp. 92-103.

14 LT, pp. 99-101 *passim.*

15 LT, p. 95.

16 LT, p. 101.

17 LT, p. 102.

18 LZ, p. 53; see also LZ, p. 57 f.

19 HM, p. 119. The literary history of 'The Mass on the World' has been researched into by Father Grootaers, Tokyo, who knew Teilhard in China. A new Japanese translation of 'The Mass on the World' by Grootaers has been prefaced by the essay 'When and where was the "Mass on the World" written?' (also in *The Teilhard Review*, vol. XII, 1977). According to Grootaers, it 'must have been written on days spent under the tent and inside the Ordos Desert (i.e. the region inside the Yellow River bend)'. Grootaers considers the essay 'The Priest' as the first version of the Mass, the main text as the second, to be followed by a third version, announced in a letter from Teilhard in 1929. However, this last project came to nothing.

20 M. Eliade, 'Cultural Fashions and the History of Religions', in J. M. Kitagawa, ed., *The History of Religions*, Chicago, 1967, p. 33 f.

21 See Lama Anandagarika Govinda, 'Die Weltanschauung Teilhard de Chardins im Spiegel des östlichen Denkens', in H. de Terra, ed., *Perspektiven Teilhard de Chardins*, München, 1966, pp. 124-53.

22 LT, p. 116 f.

23 See LZ, p. 64 f.; also LT, p. 108 f.

24 LZ, p. 65.

25 LT, p. 119.

26 LT, p. 110.

27 LI, p. 126.

28 R. d'Ouince in LTF, p. 5.

29 LT, p. 122.

30 MD, p. 107.

31 MD, pp. 103 f., 106, 107 f.

32 See LI, pp. 471-82: 'Les Révisions du Milieu Divin'. Further material is found in the letters after 1927, and in R. d'Ouince, *Un Prophète en Procès*; ibid., vol. I, pp. 207 ff. describes the polemic after the publication of *Le Milieu Divin* in 1957.

33 A close friend of Teilhard's since their student days in Hastings. In 1925, Teilhard wrote about Charles that 'Eastern questions fascinate him clearly more and more. His hobby-horse (excellent in my view) is that Hindu philosophies can be much more christianized than that of Aristotle' (LI, p. 128 f.). After visiting Ceylon in the early thirties, Father Charles published a monograph on the Buddhist monks of Ceylon which was read and criticized by Teilhard. See LI, p. 251.

34 LT, p. 154.

35 See LT, p. 138 f. & LTF, pp. 60 & 64. Whereas his former teacher and French director, Professor Marcellin Boule, was opposed to a fuller integration into Chinese organizations, Teilhard was emphatic in not wanting to prolong a separatist attitude. He shared this approach with the Swedish explorer Sven Hedin whom he urged 'to trust the Chinese and work with them'. The latter was grateful for this advice and gained 'the full confidence of even the most anti-foreign Chinese . . .' See LT, p. 154.

36 LTF, p. 65.

37 LT, p. 126.

38 Quoted in Cuénot, op. cit., p. 77.

39 G. Barbour, op. cit., p. 23.

40 LZ, p. 80.

41 LZ, p. 70.

42 LTF, p. 69.

43 LTF, p. 67.

44 See LT, p. 175. Already in 1927 Teilhard wrote, according to a letter, an article on the new China for a Catholic paper in India. In spite of repeated research, nobody has been able to locate this 'moderately pro-China' article so far, and it may possibly be lost; see LTF, p. 70. The complex question of Teilhard's attitudes towards contemporary Chinese political developments would provide a fascinating piece of research.

45 LT, p. 176.

46 Hu Shih, *My Credo and its Evolution*, New York, 1931, p. 40. Born in 1891, Hu Shih had received his postgraduate education in philosophy in the USA where he worked under Dewey. Later, Hu Shih became head of the Philosophy Department at Peking University and leader of a language reform group. In his numerous writings, he formulated a 'religion of social immortality' to replace traditional Chinese beliefs. His creed, strongly influenced by modern scientific concepts, was originally published in 1923. It provoked a public controversy in which every leading thinker in China took part. Stated in ten propositions, this creed was called 'Hu Shih's New Decalogue' by some Christian missionaries. In 1931, Hu Shih re-published the creed with an account of his own development, entitled *My Credo and its Evolution*, which is the autobiography referred to by Teilhard.

47 LT, p. 176 f.

48 LT, p. 177.

49 For the entire passage see LTF, p. 44.

50 LTF, p. 45.

51 LZ, p. 79.

52 HE, pp. 19-47.

53 C. Cuénot, op. cit., p. 77.

54 See the correspondence edited by P. Leroy, *Dans le sillage des sinanthropes*. Lettres inédites de P. Teilhard de Chardin et de J. G. Anderson, Paris, 1971.

55 Kashgar lies at the western end of the Tarim basin, at the crossroads of the southern and northern branch of the ancient Silk Road.

56 See G. Le Fèvre, *La Croisière Jaune*. Expédition Citroën Centre Asie. Paris, 1933, reprinted 1952. Additional information can be found in the special expedition issue of the journal *La Géographie*, vol. LVIII, Paris, 1932.

57 Quoted in *Teilhard de Chardin Album*, p. 114.

58 For a description of the Chinese delegation see G. Le Fèvre, op. cit., pp. 83-5.

59 *La Géographie*, p. 376.

60 J. Hackin was a well-known specialist on Buddhism in Central Asia. He had translated works from Tibetan and was able to communicate with the Tibetan monks encountered during the expedition. His particular specialization was comparative studies in iconography, and his reason for joining the 'Yellow Expedition' was to trace through Chinese Turkestan one of the ancient routes by which Buddhism had spread eastwards from India into China. Since the end of the nineteenth century, this particular route had raised much interest in the scholarly world, particularly through the earlier expeditions of von Lecocq, Paul Pelliot, and Sir Aurel Stein. Later, in 1938, during the International Exhibition of Chinese Art in London, Hackin was invited to deliver one of the official lectures on 'Buddhist Art in Central Asia: Indian, Iranian and Chinese Influences (from Bamiyan to Turfan)', chaired by Sir Francis Young-husband. See J. Hacklin et al., *Studies in Chinese Art and Some Indian Influences*, London, 1938.

61 See G. Le Fèvre, op. cit., pp. 270 f. & 254. The painter Jacovleff managed to produce a beautiful set of studies in colour of the various ethnic types. Only a limited edition of these exists, one of which is found in the family of Teilhard's younger brother.

62 First published in the journal *La Géographie*, pp. 379-90; reprinted in OSc IX, pp. 1697-1708.

63 See LT, p. 191. Similarly, the leader of the 'Yellow Expedition' pressed Teilhard to accompany the French group on their return expedition via Indo-China. He was unwilling to go, however.

64 See OSc XI, maps 10 and 11; also Teilhard's report 'Observations Géologiques à travers les déserts d'Asie Centrale de Kalgan à Hami', in OSc IV, pp. 1795-1831.

65 See G. Le Fèvre, op. cit., chap. XVI. A detailed traveller's account of the Muslim rising is found in M. Cable & F. French, *The Gobi Desert*, London, 1946, pp. 220-57: 'Revolt in the Gobi'.

66 G. Le Fèvre, op. cit., pp. 333-40; *La Géographie*, p. 256 f.

67 G. Le Fèvre, op. cit., p. 337.

68 Teilhard's younger brother Joseph thinks that Teilhard's health, especially his heart condition, was permanently affected by the physical and climatic conditions endured during the 'Yellow Expedition'.

69 In 1932, a big exhibition in Paris presented the results to the public. See *Album de la Croisière Jaune*, Paris, 1932, published on that occasion. A documentary film on the expedition is still available in France.

70 LT, pp. 180 & 186. Although the experience of the Gobi Desert and Sinkiang is only briefly documented in Teilhard's letters, his descriptions of the physical, social, political and cultural conditions are corroborated by contemporary accounts of other visitors to this region as, for example, Sven Hedin and Owen Lattimore.

71 See LT, p. 184. Their final version are the essays 'Sketch of a Personalistic Universe' (1936), HE, pp. 53-92, and 'Some Reflexions on the Conversion of the World (1936), SC, pp. 118-27. Contrary to the original intention, the latter is mainly concerned with Christianity rather than with 'various religions'.

72 See G. Baudry, *Qui était Teilhard de Chardin?* Lille, 1972, p. 37 f.: 'L'expédition eut aussi l'avantage de faire vivre ce prêtre en contact quotidien avec une équipe dynamique de techniciens et d'ingénieurs, symbole de la civilisation technicienne, symbole aussi de l'incroyance moderne, car peu de ces hommes avaient la foi chrétienne. Cette expérience humaine a renforcé Teilhard dans la conviction qu'il faut au christianisme une apologétique renouvelée qui parte des valeurs humaines et terrestres et qui, en les assimilant, manifeste leur orientation fondamentale vers le christianisme.'

73 See SC, p. 126.

74 LZ, p. 108.

75 TF, pp. 40-59.

76 LT, p. 204.

77 New York, 1965.

78 G. Barbour, op. cit., p. 40.

79 LI, p. 305.

80 LT, p. 219.

81 LT, p. 218 f.

82 Teilhard remained in contact with him in the following years. Patterson was a Fellow at Trinity College, Cambridge, and in 1938 became director of the Cambridge University Museum of Archaeology and Ethnology.

83 See LT, pp. 207-18 for his impressions of India.

84 H. de Terra, *Memories of Teilhard de Chardin*, London, 1964, p. 53.

85 ibid., p. 34.

86 See LT, p. 213.
87 LT, p. 216.
88 LT, p. 219.
89 H. de Terra, op. cit., p. 64 f.
90 ibid., p. 66.
91 ibid.
92 R. Speaight, *Teilhard de Chardin*, London, 1967, p. 216. This affinity is examined in B. Bruteau, *Evolution Toward Divinity*. Teilhard de Chardin and the Hindu Traditions, Wheaton, USA, 1974.
93 See LT, p. 222.
94 H. de Terra, op. cit., p. 113.
95 See LT, pp. 236-9; H. de Terra, op. cit., pp. 82-96; details of the itinerary are found in C. Cuénot, op. cit., p. 198, n. 1.
96 LT, pp. 236 & 237.
97 H. de Terra, op. cit., p. 97.
98 ibid., p. 84.
99 ibid., p. 102.
100 LT, p. 173.
101 Interview with Father Leroy, Versailles, February 1974.
102 H. de Terra, op. cit., p. 106.
103 PM, pp. 291-9.
104 PM, pp. 206-12.
105 PM, p. 211.
106 PM, pp. 211-12, *passim.*
107 See J. Needham's review of *The Phenomenon of Man* in the *New Statesman*, 7.11.59. He also writes there: 'to insist that "during historic time the principal axis of anthropogenesis has passed through the West" is simply to perpetuate a vulgar error'.
108 For a much more detailed historical study of this theme, see the authoritative work by W. H. McNeill, *The Rise of the West*. A History of the Human Community, Chicago, 1963.
109 See PM, pp. 237-53, 'The Collective Issue'.
110 His wide range of encounters and experiences are evident from the letters of this period and also from the writings of his friends, such as Lucile Swan, Malvina Hoffman, Claude Rivière, P. Leroy, Dominique de Wespin. See also the chapters on China in M. & E. Lukas, *Teilhard*, London, 1977.
111 New York, 1938.
112 See L. Swan, 'With Teilhard de Chardin in Peking', *The Month*, vol. 1, London, 1962, pp. 5-15.

113 ibid., p. 6.

114 Personal information. Apparently in 1933 Teilhard helped Helen Snow to arrange the first exhibition of works by Chinese left-wing artists in Paris. Similarly, Father d'Ouince knew of Chinese students whom Teilhard helped to come to France for their studies – incidents of little importance, but nevertheless illustrating Teilhard's concern for individual Chinese he met.

115 Teilhard refers to Marxism since the early 1920s when he met an active member of the French Communist Party, Ida Treat, who became a lifelong friend. It seems that extracts of the letters she received from Teilhard between 1926-52 are published in the first section of *Letters to Two Friends* without an indication of the addressee.

116 Paris, 1968. See especially chap. IX 'Attitude de Teilhard devant la guerre et l'indicible misère de la Chine'; chap. X 'Un essai d'explication de l'indifférence apparente de Teilhard devant la souffrance'; and chap. XIII 'Teilhard et les religions de la Chine'.

117 C. Rivière, op. cit., p. 128.

118 ibid., p. 221.

119 ibid., p. 142.

120 The general state of Buddhism in China, including the Buddhist renaissance movement, is described in detail in K. Ch'en, *Buddhism in China*, Princeton, 1964; H. H. Welch, *The Practice of Chinese Buddhism 1900-1950*, Cambridge, Mass., 1967 and *The Buddhist Revival in China*, Cambridge, Mass., 1968.

121 L. Swan, op. cit., p. 10.

122 See P. Leroy, 'L'Institut de Géobiologie à Pékin, 1940-1946. Les dernières années du P. Teilhard de Chardin en Chine'. *L'Anthropologie*, vol. 69, no. 3-4, 1965, pp. 360-7.

123 Cuénot lists 27 essays for the Peking period 1939-46; see the 'Chronological List of Works', HM, pp. 241-51.

124 Personal communication. See also P. Leroy, 'Teilhard de Chardin tel que je l'ai connu', translated as 'The Man', LT, pp. 15-47, and his personal notes in *Lettres Familières de Pierre Teilhard de Chardin mon ami 1948-1955* (LF).

125 See LF, pp. 15 & 32; C. Rivière, op. cit., p. 61.

126 This is well brought out in M. & E. Lukas, *Teilhard*, London, 1977.

127 It is impossible to gain a complete picture of Teilhard's reading as only three *carnets de lecture* are known to exist, the first two dealing with 1945, and the last with 1950.

Whether he took notes on reading in other years, is unknown. Valuable supplementary evidence can be found in the diaries from mid-1944 onwards. The earlier diaries (1925-44) were lost on his departure from China.

128 A list of representative titles is found in C. Cuénot, op. cit., p. 236 f.

129 The notes on Karl Barth are analysed in the doctoral thesis by Marc Faessler, *Homme Réel et Phénomiène Humain*, University of Geneva, 1967. To my knowledge, no other work has made use of the notes in the *carnets de lecture* which remain unpublished. A systematic analysis of their contents is still outstanding.

130 A detailed discussion of Teilhard's notes and comments on the two books is found in the APPENDIX, section IV, pp. 238-47.

131 *carnet de lecture II*, p. 59 comments on Beverley Nichols, *Verdict on India*, London, 1944. According to Teilhard, the author seems to favour Jinnah rather than Gandhi or Nehru.

132 *carnet de lecture II*, no page number. Teilhard indirectly referred to Huxley's book in an essay of 1947; see FM, p. 190, also TF, p. 200.

133 Paris, 1931. See *carnet de lecture*, II, p. 42 & *cahier XIV*, p. 5.

134 H. Delacroix, *Etudes d'histoire et de psychologie de mysticisme*, Paris, 1908; J. Baruzi, *St Jean de la Croix et la problème de l'expérience mystique*, Paris, 1924. Both are listed for further consultation in *carnet de lecture II*, p. 42, and are well-known reference works on the history of mysticism.

135 See LF, p. 127 f.; also C. Cuénot, op. cit., p. 246 f.

CHAPTER 4

1 See the interview 'Rencontre avec le Père Teilhard de Chardin' in *Les Nouvelles Littéraires*, 11.1.51.

2 The late diaries consist of nine exercise-books, *cahiers XIII-XXI*, dating from July 1944 to April 1955. They are kept in the Jesuit Archives at Chantilly.

3 See especially the valuable correspondence with his friend and former collaborator, Father Pierre Leroy, SJ, *Lettres Familières de Pierre Teilhard de Chardin mon ami 1948-1955*, Paris, 1976, hereafter abbreviated as LF.

4 In his general chronology of Teilhard's religious and philosophical essays, published in HM, pp. 241-51, C. Cuénot lists:

1916-22:	38 titles
1923-31:	19 titles
1932-45:	48 titles
1946-55:	92 titles

5 Among the religious and philosophical thinkers he met were Emmanuel Mounier, Gabriel Marcel, Nicolas Berdyaev, Louis Lavelle, Jean Hippolyte, Vladimir Lossky, and Abbé Pierre. At UNESCO, he met Julian Huxley and Joseph Needham. Ten years after his death, in 1965, UNESCO was to devote a symposium to both Teilhard's and Einstein's thought; see R. Maheu ed., *Science et synthèse*, Paris, 1966; translated *Science and Synthesis*, New York, 1971.

6 LI, p. 367. The only contemporary statement in public of Teilhard's ideas is found in the long interview accorded to Marcel Brion in early 1951 (see note 1 above). It inaugurated a new series of regular encounters with well-known intellectual figures through which the journal *Les Nouvelles Littéraires* presented their life and work to its readers. The interview with Teilhard was the first; it was followed by 'Recontre avec Jean-Paul Sartre', an indication of the equal importance accorded to both thinkers. This is also expressed in the comment of a student chaplain of that time: 'If you want to fill an auditorium, all you have to do is advertise that you have Teilhard or Jean-Paul Sartre'. Quoted in M. & E. Lukas, op. cit., p. 215.

7 LF, p. 39, quoted in C. Cuénot, op. cit., p. 268.

8 Letter to Father Martindale, 2.12.48.

9 C. Cuénot, op. cit., p. 261, mentions it only briefly. A longer account is found in J. Bacot, 'Autour du Congrès Universel des Croyants: Quelques Evocations', *Cahiers Pierre Teilhard de Chardin 2*, Paris, 1960, pp. 143-50. For a detailed discussion see U. King, 'Teilhard and the World Congress of Faiths', *The Teilhard Review*, vol. XI, no. 2, 1976, pp. 48-52.

10 J. Bacot, op. cit., p. 146.

11 One of his essays, written as early as 1929, already refers to Younghusband. See TF, p. 22, n. 4.

12 *cahier XIII*, p. 105.

13 *cahier XIV*, p. 11.

14 For the development of the French branch see J. Bacot, op. cit., and cyclostyled papers from the 'Union des Croyants', Paris: *Le Congrès Universel des Croyants – Historique 1946-1962*; S. Lemaître, *Le Père Teilhard de Chardin – Sa présence*, 1965; J.

F. Six, *Louis Massignon, prophète du dialogue entre croyants d'Orient et d'Occident*, 1958.

15 FM, pp. 185-92.

16 FM, p. 192.

17 *Le Congrès Universal des Croyants – Historique 1946-1962*, p. 2.

18 Available in cyclostyled form from 'Union des Croyants', Paris.

19 'Le Congrès Universal des Croyants' (1950), unpublished. The three talks are published as 'A Phenomenon of Counter-Evolution in Human Biology or the Existential Fear' (1949), AE, pp. 181-5; 'How may we Conceive and Hope that Human Unanimisation will be Realised on Earth' (1950), FM, pp. 281-8; 'The Zest for Living' (1950), AE, pp. 229-43. They are analysed in U. King, op. cit. Thus, six contributions can be clearly dated as addressed to the 'Union des Croyants' between 1947 and 1950: four published essays, one participation in a discussion, and one outline; the latter two only available in cyclostyled form. The biography by M. & E. Lukas, p. 221, wrongly describes the essay 'Ecumenism' (December 1946) as addressed to the 'Union des Croyants' before this movement had come into existence.

20 This idea was more fully developed in the subsequent lecture 'The Zest for Living' (1950); AE, pp. 229-43.

21 Personal communication from one of the secretaries, Mme d'Hauteville; also confirmed by Father Leroy who, after Teilhard's death, took the latter's place on the committee of the 'Union des Croyants' and still holds this position at present.

22 Briefly referred to by Teilhard in TF, p. 139, n. 2.

23 Personal communication from Swami Ritajananda, Gretz (France).

24 The correspondence, dating from June 1946 to March 1955, is still in the Lemaître family. When living in the United States, he also remained in touch with other members; for example, Louis Massignon saw Teilhard in New York in 1952; Dr Loriot, the treasurer of the movement, met him during a visit in London in 1954; see C. Cuénot, op. cit., pp. 311 & 366.

25 The meetings of the 'Union des Croyants' took place at the Musée Guimet until 1958.

26 Paris, 1955. See also her earlier books *Le Mystère de la Mort dans les religions de l'Asie*, Paris, 1943; *Abdul Baha – Une grande figure de l'unité*, Paris, 1952. Later publications include *Ramakrishna*, Paris, 1954, and *Hindouisme ou Sanâtana Dharma*,

Paris, 1957, published in English as *Hinduism*, London, 1959.

27 See P. Leroy, *'Les "Textes Mystiques d'Orient et d'Occident" '*, *Hommage à Solange Lemaître*, Union des Croyants, Paris, 1961.

28 See Teilhard's letter to S. Lemaître, 12.12.53: 'Ci-joint un projet de "notice" me concernant, – que je preférérais à celui que vous m'avez envoyé. Je n'ai pas d'objection sérieuse à ce que vous publiez quelques passages de la Messe sur le Monde, – bien que cela puisse faire peut-être se froncer les soucils de qq. supérieur'. In 1953, after reading Lemaître's work *Abdul Baha – Une grande figure de l'unité* (which devotes several pages to the work of the *World Congress of Faiths*), Teilhard described this book as 'those beautiful pages on unity' and he expressed the hope that Lemaître's forthcoming anthology of mystical texts would similarly embody the idea of unity as its major theme. See letter to S. Lemaître, 11.1.53.

29 Letter to Dr Loriot, 24.12.52.

30 Letter to S. Lemaître, 2.3.55.

31 He is reported to have said: 'Surtout . . . faites vivre l'Union des Croyants, c'est le Mouvement de Cîme de demain'. See S. Lemaître, *Le Père Teilhard de Chardin – Sa Présence*, Association des Amis de P. Teilhard de Chardin, Paris, 1965, p. 10.

32 René Grousset (1885-1952) is well known as historian of the Orient and the Crusades. See his *Histoire de la Philosophie Orientale*, 1923; *Histoire de l'Extrême-Orient*, 1929; *Les Civilisations de l'Orient*, 1929-30; *Les Philosophies Indiennes*, 1931; *Le Bilan de l'Histoire*, 1946; *Histoire des croisades et du Royaume franc de Jérusalem*, 1948; *L'Inde*, 1949. Teilhard referred to Grousset as early as 1934 (see LI, p. 274) but a closer study of his works seems to have occurred only after 1946. Unfortunately, his subsequent correspondence with Grousset appears to be lost.

33 See C. Cuénot, op. cit., p. 297, n. 1. Teilhard's contacts with René Grousset, Solange Lemaître, and the 'Union des Croyants' are discussed ibid., pp. 295-8. The readers' register of the Musée Guimet shows no record of Teilhard's borrowing of books. However, the former librarian thinks that he was known well enough to obtain books without going through the formality of signing the register. Personal communication.

34 TF, pp. 134-47.

35 See S. Lemaître, 'In Memoriam', *Réflexions sur le Bonheur*, *Cahiers P. Teilhard de Chardin 2*, Paris, 1960, p. 154.

36 Paris, 1938, reprinted 1966. Its subtitle is 'La Doctrine Morale

et Métaphysique de Ramanuja'. See *cahier XIV*, pp. 87 and 150, for Teilhard's references to Lacombe's book.

37 Personal communication from Mlle Jeanne Mortier who kindly allowed me to consult the letters dealing with Indian thought and also Teilhard's introduction to the correspondence.

38 C. Cuénot, op. cit., p. 297, n. 1.

39 See *Actes du XXI Congrès International des Orientalistes*, Paris 23.-31.7.48, published in 1949-50, p. 5.

40 London, 1943.

41 See *cahier XVI*, p. 5 ff.

42 Written in 1950, the theme of this essay is first announced in English on the 4.10.48 as 'the heart of matter', and on the 7.10.48 as 'The Golden glow'; see *cahier XVI*, pp. 4 & 5.

43 *cahier XVI*, p. 5. G. Dunbar, op. cit., vol. I, p. 163 writes in a section on 'Hindu religious movements' that, after the coming of the Moghuls, 'the fires of adversity had brought into greater prominence than ever before the doctrine of the essential unity of God, a doctrine which involves a belief that "every god accepted by Hinduism is elevated and ultimately identified with the central Reality which is one with the deeper Self of Man . . ."' Here and elsewhere he quotes Radhakrishnan's *The Hindu View of Life*, Oxford, 1927.

44 Letter to Solange Lemaître, 5.1.49. – The Neo-Confucian philosopher Chu Hsi of the twelfth century is sometimes described as 'both the Herbert Spencer and Thomas Aquines of China'. See J. Needham, *Within the Four Seas. The Dialogue of East and West*, London, 1969, p. 67, and *Science and Civilisation in China*, vol. 2, Cambridge, 1956, pp. 455 f.

45 The contact through Jacques Masui is definitely established but it may be that Teilhard first heard about Sri Aurobindo earlier from his friend Abbé Breuil. Apparently, the latter realized the similarities between the two thinkers and pointed them out to Aurobindo, in a letter written at the end of 1950. However, it only arrived after Aurobindo's death. See A. Monestier, *Teilhard et Sri Aurobindo*, Paris, 1963, p. 6. – Jacques Masui, who died in November 1975, was the editor of the review *Hermès. Recherches sur l'expérience spirituelle*. Its editorial committee included well-known scholars and writers on Eastern religions such as Benz, Conze, Murti, Tucci and Watts.

46 Personal communication from Jacques Masui. See also his monograph *In Memoriam: P. Teilhard de Chardin*, Bruxelles,

1955, which is probably the first printed comparison between Teilhard and Aurobindo.

47 Teilhard read several other titles in psychology. In *cahier XVII*, p. 48, he noted down a plan for a psychoanalytical study of Christianity.

48 Later, after meeting Northrop personally, Teilhard wrote that they held 'completely opposite positions'. See LF, p. 129.

49 The Maurice Lectures (King's College, London) for 1951; published London, 1952. Teilhard first learnt about this book through a review in *Time*. See LF, pp. 175 and 186.

50 Letter to S. Lemaître, 11.1.53.

51 Letter to S. Lemaître, 13.9.50.

52 See *cahier XVII*, pp. 6-9.

53 Perhaps his cousin Marguerite? However, the extract, dated 10.9.48, is not found in any of the published letters to her. This is not unusual, as can be seen from extracts of other letters, found in the *Journal*, but not elsewhere.

54 *cahier XVII*, p. 9.

55 See *cahier XIV*, p. 86 and also R. Grousset, op. cit., p. 121 f.

56 A comparison between Shiva and the cosmic Christ provides a fruitful line of enquiry. A contemporary tapestry, designed by an Indian Christian, shows Christ on the cross, surrounded by Indian symbols, as 'Lord of the Sacred Dance', a traditional epithet of Shiva. The wider analogies between the Indian tradition of a 'cosmic divinity' and Teilhard's 'cosmic Christ' are explored in B. Bruteau, *Evolution toward Divinity*. Teilhard de Chardin and the Hindu Traditions, Wheaton, 1974.

57 C. Cuénot, op. cit., p. 299.

58 Quoted in C. Cuénot, op. cit., p. 299.

59 LF, p. 67 f. The book is L. Jugnet, *L'Evolution Rédemptrice du P. Teilhard de Chardin*, Toulouse, 1950.

60 See LF, p. 93. The interview is found in Nouvelles Littéraires, 11.1.51.

61 See E. Maillart, *Oasis Interdites*. De Pékin au Cachemere, Paris, 1937; English translation: *Turkestan Solo*. One Woman's Expedition from the Tien Shan to the Kizil Khum, London, 1938. After reading this work, Teilhard wrote to the author: 'If your pilgrimage in Asia has only revealed to you the organic immensity of the world, your effort will have been amply rewarded, a hundred times more than through any so-called scientific results . . . The goal of all science is only to teach us to become conscious of the unity and movement of everything that surrounds us'. Letter of 21.6.37.

62 *cahier XVII*, p. 55. See also Teilhard's discussions on Indian religions reported by Maryse Choisy, *Teilhard et l'Inde*, Paris, 1964.

63 LF, p. 130.

64 LI, p. 368.

65 LF, p. 130.

66 LF, p. 140. This comment was made after hearing a sermon by Cardinal Fulton Sheen in New York.

67 See LF, p. 163.

68 LI, p. 463.

69 See LF, p. 123.

70 See LI, pp. 453 & 462 f.; LF, p. 242. Father Paul Henry SJ from Louvain had negotiated with a Swiss publisher to bring out a German translation of some of Teilhard's articles, already published in French. The Jesuit General withheld permission for publication in early 1955. Similarly, Teilhard learnt shortly before his death that he was not allowed to return again to France to participate in a scientific symposium.

71 See LF, pp. 36 & 213; M. & E. Lukas, *Teilhard. A Biography*, London, 1977.

72 LF, p. 225.

73 Stated in a brief biographical outline written in 1950; see HM, pp. 152-4.

CHAPTER 5

1 For a detailed examination of Teilhard's vocabulary see C. Cuénot, *Nouveau Lexique Teilhard de Chardin*, Paris, 1968; M. C. Deckers, *Le vocabulaire de Teilhard de Chardin*, Louvain, 1968.

2 See *Journal*, p. 295: 'My method'; also H. de Lubac, *The Religion of Teilhard de Chardin*, London, 1967, p. 161 f., 'A reversal of method'; E. Rideau, *La Pensée du P. Teilhard de Chardin*, Paris, 1965, pp. 49-59. For the early period, the transference of scientific images to religious thought has been studied by H. C. Cairns, op. cit.

3 D. Gray, *The One and the Many. Teilhard de Chardin's Vision of Unity*, London, 1969, p. 68. See his insightful discussion on 'Typology in Teilhard', pp. 68-71.

4 Father Leroy in LT, p. 34.

5 For a list of the early essays which discuss pantheism, monism and mysticism, see TABLE II in the APPENDIX, p. 236.

6   WTW, pp. 13-71.
7   WTW, pp. 115-49.
8   CE, pp. 56-75.
9   WTW, p. 28.
10 WTW, p. 101.
11 WTW, p. 29 f.
12 See WTW, p. 28 f. for a discussion of this theme.
13 MM, p. 58.
14 For the quotations from the diary see *Journal*, pp. 31, 177, 183 & 42.
15 ibid., p. 27.
16 WTW, p. 14.
17 *Journal*, p. 303.
18 ibid., p. 175.
19 MD, p. 138. This passage has been commented upon by J. A. T. Robinson, *Exploration into God*, Stanford, 1967, p. 132. By contrast, Teilhard's development of the sense of man is expressed in the essay 'The Rise of the Other' (1942), AE, pp. 59-75.
20 See WTW, p. 120 f.
21 ibid., p. 124 f.
22 ibid., p. 129.
23 London, 1976. The book is divided into I. The Way of Physics; II. The Way of Eastern Mysticism; III. The Parallels.
24 WTW, p. 130.
25 ibid., p. 135 f.
26 ibid., p. 122.
27 ibid., p. 137.
28 ibid., p. 148.
29 See 'The Universal Element' (1919), WTW, pp. 289-302.
30 Some of Teilhard's major writings on this theme are found in the collection of essays entitled *Science and Christ*. The christological perspective implied in this convergence has been dealt with at length in the studies of C. F. Mooney and D. Gray.
31 See G. M. Hopkins's poems 'God's Grandeur' and 'As Kingfishers Catch Fire, Dragonflies Draw Flame'.
32 See 'Creative Union' (1919), WTW, pp. 289-302. For an extensive discussion of this theory see D. Gray, *The One and the Many. Teilhard de Chardin's Vision of Unity*, London, 1969.
33 D. Gray, op. cit., p. 16.
34 For 'pan-Christism' see SC, pp. 59 & 124; HM, p. 55. Blondel's

use of 'pan-Christism' is discussed in TB, p. 58 f. For ' "pan-Christic" monism' see CE, p. 171, and for ' "pan-Christic" mysticism' HM, p. 47.

35 WTW, pp. 177-90.

36 HM, pp. 182-95.

37 See P. Teilhard de Chardin – M. Blondel, *Correspondence*, ed. H. de Lubac, New York, 1967 (TB), and the letters to Valensin in *Lettres Intimes*.

38 See H. de Lubac, *The Religion of Teilhard de Chardin*, p. 157, and TB, p. 10.

39 HM, pp. 67-77.

40 ibid., p. 75 f.

41 The first version of 'My Universe' (1918) is found in HM, pp. 196-208, the second in SC, pp. 37-85.

42 CE, pp. 56-75.

43 TB, p. 25.

44 MM, p. 302.

4⁻ See TB, pp. 52 & 120.

46 See TB, pp. 29 & 39.

47 CE, p. 68.

48 CE, p. 65.

49 See CE, pp. 58-60.

50 CE, p. 65.

51 CE, p. 72. The translation of 'le Tout' as 'the Whole' has been replaced by 'the All' throughout.

52 CE, p. 64.

53 CE, pp. 64-70, *passim*.

54 See especially chap. 9 'The element of novelty', & chap. 14 'God all in all'.

55 H. de Lubac, op. cit., p. 155.

56 C. Cuénot, *Nouveau Lexique Teilhard de Chardin*, Paris, 1968, pp. 145-55.

57 See C. Cuénot, op cit., p. 146 f.

CHAPTER 6

1 LZ, p. 53.

2 TF, pp. 40-59.

3 For a list of later writings which include specific comparisons with Eastern religions see TABLE III in the APPENDIX, p. 237.

4 LZ, p. 108. The theme had preoccupied him for some time;

see the reference to the 'Eastern' and 'Western' solution with regard to the problem of the One and the Many in a letter of 9.2.31, LI, p. 223 f.

5 TF, p. 40.
6 TF, p. 42.
7 See TF, pp. 42-5, *passim*.
8 TF, p. 137 f.
9 See SC, pp. 105-6, *passim*.
10 TF, p. 45.
11 TF, p. 44.
12 SC, p. 105.
13 As for example 'logically' (SC, p. 106; TF, p. 48; LI, p. 251 & p. 274), 'in strict logic' and 'in theory' (both TF, p. 45).
14 TF, p. 45.
15 TF, p. 46 f.
16 See TF, p. 47.
17 TF, p. 54. The original reads: 'le Christianisme, pour demeurer lui-même, doit embrasser, en la sauvant, la mystique occidentale'. One could understand this as meaning a marrying of the mystical with the institutional in religion.
18 TF, p. 55.
19 The notes were taken by C. Cuénot and J. Bousquet at the Ecole Normale Supérieure, Paris, where the lecture entitled 'Orient et Occident – la Mystique de la Personnalité' was given to a student society on 8.1.33. A brief summary is found in C. Cuénot, op. cit., p. 140 f., a fuller statement in C. Cuénot, *Ce que Teilhard a vraiment dit*, Paris, 1972, pp. 224-8.
20 C. Cuénot, *Ce que Teilhard a vraiment dit*, p. 226 f.
21 Teilhard had known Father de Lubac since 1922 and corresponded regularly with him from 1930 onwards; see *Lettres Intimes* and H. de Lubac, *Teilhard Posthume*. For H. de Lubac's works on Buddhism, see his *Aspects du Bouddhisme*, Paris, 1951; *La Rencontre du Bouddhisme et de l'Occident*, Paris, 1952; *Amida*, Paris, 1955.
22 Quoted in C. Cuénot, op. cit., p. 142. However, as de Lubac's letter remains unpublished, this question may have been inferred from Teilhard's answer.
23 LI, p. 251. Cuénot relates this passage wrongly to Monchanin. Since Teilhard's letters to de Lubac (LI) have been published, it seems that the initial criticism came from de Lubac himself.
24 See the essays on Hinduism and Christianity in J. Monchanin, *Mystique de l'Inde, mystère chrétien*, ed. S. Siauve, Paris, 1974.

On Monchanin see J. Mattam, *Land of the Trinity*, Bangalore, 1975, and H. de Lubac, *Images de l'Abbé Monchanin*, Paris, 1967, especially pp. 119-151: 'L'Abbé Monchanin et le Père Teilhard de Chardin'. Monchanin first met Teilhard in 1925 and greatly admired some of his privately circulated writings, in particular, the essays, 'The Phenomenon of Man' (1928) and 'The Spirit of the Earth' (1931). Later, after 1946, Teilhard read some of Monchanin's works (see LI, p. 252); Monchanin (1895-1957) was one of the earliest people to compare Teilhard's and Aurobindo's thought (in a lecture given in Pondicherry in 1955 or 1956).

25 H. de Lubac, *The Religion of Teilhard de Chardin*, p. 153.
26 LI, p. 273 f.
27 TF, pp. 134-47.
28 TF, pp. 163-208.
29 See TF, p. 200-1, *passim*.
30 AE, pp. 215-27.
31 TF, pp. 209-11.
32 TF, p. 209. The French has 'deux voies' instead of 'routes'. The English translation renders both 'voie' and 'route' by 'road'.
33 LI, p. 273.
34 See the essays 'The Grand Option' (1939) and 'The Heart of the Problem' (1949) in FM, pp. 37-60 and pp. 260-9.
35 Teilhard's emphasis on time is a special feature of his typological approach to historical data. Its newness is discussed in F. Bravo, *La Vision de l'Histoire chez Teilhard de Chardin*, Paris, 1970.
36 AE, p. 383.
37 See M. Weber, *The Sociology of Religion*, London, 1966, p. 166, and also the discussion in R. Bendix, *Max Weber. An Intellectual Portrait*, London, 1966, p. 201 ff.
38 C. Cuénot, *Teilhard de Chardin*, p. 141.

CHAPTER 7

1 *The Vision of the Past*, London, 1966, p. 75.
2 AE, p. 242.
3 TF, p. 47.
4 CE, p. 199.
5 CE, p. 121, n. 8.

6 See CE, p. 61 & AE, p. 157.
7 See TF, p. 209. The references to the Sufis date from 1950 and later. Perhaps Teilhard learnt more about the Sufis from Massignon, and also through his association with the French branch of the *World Congress of Faiths*.
8 AE, p. 219.
9 SC, p. 104 f.
10 SC, p. 105.
11 See LI, p. 274.
12 The numerous events and publications in connection with *The World of Islam Festival*, London, 1976, drew particular attention to this. The many activities and various branches of the Sufi movement are also much better known today. For a discussion of the general difficulties of Islam in the modern world see W. Cantwell-Smith, *Islam in Modern History*, Princeton, 1957.
13 G. Le Brun Kéris, 'Teilhard de Chardin et l'Islam', *La Croix*, 17.12.69.
14 The French translator of Iqbal's work *The Reconstruction of Religious Thought in Islam* published an article comparing Iqbal and Teilhard. See Eva Meyerovitch, 'Orient et Occident', *The New Morality* 1, 1963, pp. 49-68. Other similarities could be pointed out between Teilhard and the modern Islamic thinker Fathi Uhman from Egypt.
15 Eva Meyerovitch, op. cit., p. 66.
16 SC, p. 106.
17 H. de Lubac, *Images de l'Abbé Monchanin*, Paris, 1967, p. 150, n. 1.
18 See LZ, p. 58.
19 See LI, p. 274.
20 See CE, p. 122, n. 9.
21 See CE, pp. 121 & 122.
22 CE, p. 123.
23 SC, pp. 98-112.
24 CE, pp. 96-132.
25 The French title 'L'épreuve des religions' expresses the 'trial' situation more clearly than the English translation 'Religions put to the test'. See the sections in SC, pp. 104-6, CE, pp. 121-6.
26 Entirely concerned with this theme is the essay 'A Mental Threshold Across Our Path: From Cosmos to Cosmogenesis', AE, pp. 251-68.
27 See FM, pp. 260-2, *passim*. The translation is partly my own.
28 TF, p. 21. Written in 1929, Teilhard's affirmation of man

'become adult' long antedates that of Bonhoeffer and more recent theologians.

29 SC, p. 101 f. A fuller discussion of this theme is found in 'Modern Unbelief – Its Underlying Causes and Remedy' (1933), SC, pp. 113-17.

30 SC, p. 103.

31 AE, p. 240. See the letter of 16.3.54: 'Our age is one of *atheism*. – No, I would say, on the contrary, it is an age of the obscure adoration of a "God Ahead".' LF, p. 232.

32 See, for example, SC, p. 108; HM, p. 96; LF, p. 232.

33 CE, p. 126.

34 SC, p. 103; see also LI, p. 251.

35 TF, p. 134.

36 SC, p. 103.

37 TF, pp. 134-47.

38 TF, p.135.

39 TF, p. 136. In J. Needham's opinion, it is impossible to over-estimate the importance which the Buddhist rejection of the world and the doctrine of *maya* had in Chinese Buddhism. Irreconcilable with Taoism and Confucianism which, in their different ways, both accept the world, it helped to inhibit the development of Chinese science. He refers to a fifth century AD Chinese observer who considered Buddhism as suitable for Indians but not for Chinese and quotes him as saying that 'for Confucius and Laotse the regulating of the things in this world is the main objective, but for the Buddhists the objective is the escape from this world'. See J. Needham, *Science and Civilisation in China*, vol. 2, Cambridge, 1956, p. 403 ff.

40 See TF, p. 139.

41 See TF, p. 140.

42 See TF, p. 141. 'God and his transcendence' refers to Indian spirituality. Stressing the 'religious character of Indian thought', H. Nakamura has pointed out that Indian languages have an extraordinarily rich vocabulary for the idea of God, in contrast to Western classical languages. See his *Ways of Thinking of Eastern Peoples – India – China – Tibet – Japan*, Hawaii, 1964, pp. 157 & 159.

43 See TF, pp. 144 & 142.

44 TF, pp. 141 & 143, *passim*.

45 Title of the last subsection of the essay; see TF, pp. 145-7 for the following quotations.

46 See TF, p. 144 where Teilhard refers to 'the humanism of a Tagore'. He may have read Tagore in Peking; his diary of 1944

quotes an extract from Tagore's *Gitanjali*. See *cahier XIII*, p. 59.

47 TF, p. 146.

48 See J. Needham, 'The Roles of Europe and China in the Evolution of Oecumenical Sciences', *British Association for the Advancement of Science*, September 1967, pp. 83-98, especially p. 95. Elsewhere Needham uses the image of different 'rivers' flowing into modern science, just as Teilhard talks about the different 'rivers' of religion coming together; see TF, p. 145 f.

49 Letter to S. Lemaître, 11.1.53. Teilhard also expressed his concern that the newly founded Centre for World Religions at Harvard might risk to pursue 'a lowest common denominator – rather than a new God . . . except if it may give birth to someone like Newman'. See *cahier XVIII*, p. 137.

50 New York, 1971.

51 R. E. Whitson, op. cit., p. 52. See especially the chapters on 'Convergence of Religions', pp. 35-53, and 'Convergence and Commitment', pp. 166-87.

52 AE, p. 239.

53 SC, p. 112.

54 CE, p. 125.

55 See CE, p. 208. The axial role of Christianity is discussed in detail in 'The Christian Phenomenon' (1950), CE, pp. 199-208. See also the epilogue of the same title in *The Phenomenon of Man* (1940), pp. 291-9.

56 CE, p. 199.

57 LZ, p. 79.

58 CE, p. 130.

59 See CE, pp. 125, 126 & 128, *passim*, for quotations from 'How I Believe'.

60 HE, p. 91. He also described Christianity in terms of a 'personalistic universe' wherein the personal represents the highest form of the spiritual. See 'Sketch of a Personalistic Universe' (1936), HE, pp. 53-92, and 'Some General Views on the Essence of Christianity' (1939), CE, pp. 133-7; also the section on 'The Personal Universe' and 'The Personalising Universe' PM, pp. 257-64.

61 CE, p. 128.

62 CE, p. 130; see the entire section on 'The Universal Christ and the Convergence of Religions', CE, pp. 126-30.

63 SC, p. 112.

64 CE, p. 130.

65 SC, p. 118.
66 *The Vision of the Past*, p. 205.
67 PM, p. 239.
68 TF, p. 145.
69 He distinguished clearly between the coil and a true, converging spiral. In *cahier XIV*, p. 128, the difference is shown in the following diagram:

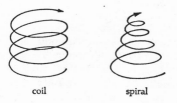

coil   spiral

70 R. E. Whitson, op. cit., p. 22. See his chapter on 'The Unity of Civilization'.
71 LF, p. 187. Interestingly, C. Cuénot's *Nouveau Lexique Teilhard de Chardin*, Paris, 1968, has an entry on 'convergence', but not on 'confluence'.
72 See C. Cuénot, op. cit., pp. 15 and 48. R. E. Whitson, op. cit., p. 21 f., indicates as an example: 'Our most forceful specification of convergence in process is probably that of biological generation, in which the offspring is clearly a new reality not identifiable singly with parents. It is not simply an addition of their characteristics, but something quite different; yet in origin of individual existence it is in complete continuity with them: it embodies them in the greater effect of their convergence.'
73 See PM, pp. 114 f.
74 SC, p. 110.
75 SC, p. 197.
76 I have discussed this further in 'Exploring Convergence: The Contribution of World Faiths', The Third Francis Younghusband Lecture, *World Faiths* 106 (1978), pp. 1-16. An extensive exploration of convergence is found in R. E. Whitson, op. cit.

CHAPTER 8

1 PM, p. 219; see also 'The Basis and Foundations of the Idea of Evolution' (1926) in *Vision of the Past*, pp. 116-42, and 'The Human Rebound of Evolution and its Consequences' (1947), FM, pp. 193-213.

2 WTW, p. 87. The importance of evolution for a comparative study has been recognized by R. C. Zaehner, *Evolution in Religion*. A Study in Sri Aurobindo and Pierre Teilhard de Chardin, Oxford, 1971, although he does not explore the theme of evolution in any depth. – For the place of evolution in the reinterpretation of Christianity see Teilhard's collection of essays in *Christianity and Evolution* (CE).

3 HE, p. 43.

4 SC, pp. 98, 99 & 100, *passim*.

5 AE, p. 237.

6 *The Vision of the Past*, p. 140.

7 These ideas are more fully developed and set in a comparative context in U. King, 'The One and the Many: The Individual and the Community from a Religious Perspective', *The Teilhard Review*, vol. XI, no. 1, 1976, pp. 9-15.

8 TF, pp. 23 & 24, *passim*.

9 See the discussion on secularization in the preface of CE, pp. 9-13. N. M. Wildiers writes there that Teilhard's 'religion of the earth' and secularization 'cover, in fact, the same ideological and sociological reality'; ibid., p. 9.

　　R. J. Zwi Werblowsky, *Beyond Tradition and Modernity*. Changing Religions in a Changing World, London, 1976, p. 6, argues 'that Western religion has undergone changes that are, to some extent, paradigmatic for all other religions'. This does not imply, however, 'that Western experience sets the standard by which all other developments have to be measured'. Nor does it mean an 'inevitable transcultural or intercultural convergence on the Western model'.

10 TF, p. 25.

11 See *cahier XVII*, p. 104; also HM, p. 53: 'All around us, and within our own selves, God is in process of "changing", . . .'. These two texts of 1950 may be compared with earlier passages, such as the sections on 'The Future of the Spirit' and 'The Arising of God', written in 1931; see HE, pp. 38-47.

12 See letter to Dr Loriot, 24.12.52, and also Teilhard's papers on 'The God of Evolution' (1953) and 'My Litany' (1953), CE, pp. 237-45. For a discussion of process theology see the contributions in E. H. Cousins, ed., *Process Theology*, New York, 1971.

13 Only found in C. Cuénot, *Teilhard de Chardin*, p. 216 f., from which all quotations are taken. The same ideas were expressed in more detail in the subsequent essay 'How I Believe' (1934), CE, pp. 96-132.

14 MM, p. 58.

15 *The Vision of the Past*, p. 173; partly my translation.

16 HE, p. 44; see also SC, p. 102. 'The Spirit of the Earth' is found in HE, pp. 19-52.

17 SC, p. 100.

18 HE, p. 100; see the entire essay 'The Phenomenon of Spirituality' (1937), HE, pp. 93-112.

19 SC, p. 104.

20 AE, pp. 229-43.

21 See AE, pp. 232 & 238.

22 AE, p. 236. See also FM, p. 204 f. where he writes under the title 'The Spiritual Nourishment of Human Endeavour' that if 'we accept the idea of a reflective rebounding of evolution, it is not enough to reckon the future of the world in terms of reserves of mechanical energy and food supplies, or the probable longevity of the earth . . . the evolutionary vigour of Mankind can wither away although it be surrounded by mountains of coal, oceans of petroleum and limitless stocks of corn; it can do so as surely as in a desert of ice, if Man should lose his impulse, or worse, develop a distaste for ever-increased growth "in complexity and consciousness" '.

23 PM, pp. 64 & 42.

24 See the subtitle in AE, p. 240.

25 AE, p. 240.

26 CE, pp. 123 & 124, *passim*.

27 AE, p. 241.

28 Recognized by Huxley, too. The latter stated in his introduction to *The Phenomenon of Man* that 'he and I were on the same quest' (PM, p. 11). Elsewhere, he wrote about meeting Teilhard: 'I realized that I had found not only a friend, but a partner in the intellectual and spiritual adventure' (quoted in R. Speaight, op. cit., p. 297). In the judgment of a fellow-scientist, George Gaylord Simpson, who knew Teilhard well, 'Huxley and Teilhard could hardly differ more as regards

theories of evolution, attitudes towards science, and conclusions as to theology, but they both have proposed systems in which, in quite different ways and proportions, science and mysticism are involved' (*This View of Life*, New York, 1964, p. 215). In 1941, after reading Huxley's *The Uniqueness of Man*, Teilhard noted: '. . . in a way so parallel to my own ideas (though without integrating God as the term of the series) that I feel greatly cheered'. Referring to his own work, he expressed at the same time the regret that 'there is nothing being published to give a constructive, dynamically Christian interpretation of what's happening' (LT, p. 284).

Teilhard and Huxley had personal contacts from 1946 onwards. In 1951, the latter asked for a conribution to a book, and Teilhard wrote 'The Transformation and Continuation in Man of the Mechanism of Evolution' (AE, pp. 297-309), dedicated to Huxley. However, the contribution was not accepted as it did not fit in with 'the tone of the other communications' (LF, p. 126) Huxley was editing.

The similarities between Teilhard's and Huxley's thought are discussed in M. Gex, 'Vers an humanisme cosmologique'. *Revue de Théologie et de Philosophie*, vol. 3, 1957, pp. 186-205. However, a fuller comparison, taking into account the references in Teilhard's correspondence with Father Leroy (LF) and his unpublished letters to Huxley, is still outstanding.

29 For references to Huxley see LF, pp. 92, 97 & 166 f.

30 Letter to J. Huxley, 8.9.52; see also LI, p. 412.

31 HM, p. 91.

32 AE, pp. 241 & 242, *passim*.

33 AE, p. 242; slightly different translation.

34 'Le goût de vivre'. This is the French title of the essay under discussion, translated as 'The Zest for Living'.

35 See the postscript in AE, p. 243: 'Religious "contact" = Initiation of the 3rd *reflection* . . . = *neo-zest made explicit: Love* (higher form of zest ! !)'.

36 OSc IX, p. 3936.

37 CE, pp. 118 & 119, *passim*.

38 See 'On the Possible Bases of a Universal Human Creed' (1941), FM, p. 76-81, described as 'Remarks on a New York Congress of Science and Religion'. Teilhard here presents some reflections on convergence as a 'personal testimony, the fruit of thirty years spent in close and sincere contact with scientific and religious circles in Europe, America and the Far East.

39 FM, p. 76 f. This theme is more fully developed in 'The Heart

of the Problem' (1949), FM, pp. 260-9: at the source of the modern religious crisis lies 'a conflict of faith between upward and forward'.

40 FM, p. 81.

41 FM, p. 185-92.

42 See the short note on 'Ecumenism' (1946), SC, pp. 197-8.

43 FM, p. 189.

44 SC, p. 198.

45 See SC, pp. 197 & 198.

46 *cahier XVII*, p. 87; Teilhard used the English 'spearhead' here.

47 Such an integration would require a theological development going beyond Teilhard. In 1945, his *carnet de lecture* included some extracts on Shiva and Kali, taken from Ch. Autran, *Mithra, Zoroaster et la Préhistoire aryenne du Christianisme*, Paris, 1935. Apart from this, only the diaries of 1949-50 carry some references to Shiva, together with extracts from R. Grousset, *Bilan de l'Histoire*. There he found South Indian hymns quoted, praising the cosmic forces of Shiva. It is the Shiva of the cosmic dance, the universal divine energy pulsating through the universe, manifesting itself at times as blind force which, he felt, has not been integrated into the Christian notion of God.

48 AE, p. 48.

49 TF, p. 105.

50 FM, p. 23.

51 AE, p. 49.

52 See CE, p. 120.

53 Personal communication from Father Leroy.

54 B. Bruteau, *Evolution toward Divinity*. Teilhard de Chardin and the Hindu Traditions, Wheaton, 1974, p. 76. This is the first comparative study of its kind and deserves high commendation. The author thinks that Teilhard's basic insights find more or less close parallels in various strands of traditional Hindu thought as well as in contemporary reinterpretations, such as that of Sri Aurobindo. In particular, she points to a common vision of God in the cosmos and God as energy, and a similar approach to the problem of action and the conquest of evil. As Teilhard himself was unaware of such similarities, and to some extent inimical to the Hindu outlook, the study aims to refute his criticisms and to show how the Hindu world-view would have been helpful to the development of his own, had he taken the trouble to study it. The book highlights the similarities rather than the differences between Teilhard and

Indian thought. However, it does not examine whether, given certain premisses, particular data are really comparable.

55 *carnet de lecture II*, p. 10.

56 See *carnet de lecture II*, p. 8. The difference between emanation and Teilhard's understanding of creation is examined in R. B. Smith, *Towards the Discovery of God*, Ph.D thesis, University of Exeter, 1968.

57 See *carnet de lecture II*, pp. 10 & 9.

58 These differences were first clearly formulated in a lecture given at Pondicherry in 1956, published in note form in 1974. See 'Teilhard et Sri Aurobindo', in J. Monchanin, *Mystique de l'Inde, mystère chrétien*, Paris, 1974, p. 31 f.

59 The difference between Aurobindo's and Teilhard's understanding of involution and evolution is discussed in J. Feys, *The Philosophy of Evolution in Sri Aurobindo and Teilhard de Chardin*, Calcutta, 1973, on whose arguments I have mainly drawn here. This book is a very detailed philosophical study of the theme of evolution in Teilhard and Aurobindo, the most comprehensive work on the subject in existence. R. C. Zaehner's *Evolution in Religion* and other books notwithstanding, a fully comprehensive and critical comparison of all aspects of the two thinkers has still to be undertaken.

60 PM, p. 61.

61 J. Feys, op. cit., p. 108. Feys relates Aurobindo's view of involution and evolution to the Indian *sat-karya-vada* theory of causation which considers the effect in essence as always pre-existent in the cause.

62 J. Feys, p. 231 f. Unfortunately, Feys's important study on evolution does not recognize the implications of Teilhard's evolutionary perspective for his understanding of religion, especially with regard to the further evolution of religion.

63 This fundamental difference has been completely overlooked by B. Bruteau, *Evolution toward Divinity*. For the relationship between the transcendent and immanent in Teilhard's thought, see H. de Lubac's essay ' "Ascent" and "Descent" in the Work of Teilhard de Chardin', TB, pp. 143-68.

64 See R. Bellah, 'Religious Evolution', in *idem, Beyond Belief. Essays on Religion in a Post-Traditional World*, New York, 1970, pp. 20-50.

65 See Huxley's preface to G. B. Barbour, *In the Field with Teilhard de Chardin*, New York 1965, p. 8 f.

66 See CE, p. 222 f.

67 C. Cuénot, op. cit., p. 262.
68 Already announced in PM, p. 283.
69 See J. O'Manique, *Energy in Evolution – Teilhard's Physics of the Future*, London, 1969.
70 See LF, pp. 188 & 193.
71 Teilhard wrote these remarks in English. See C. Cuénot, 'Un inédit de Pierre Teilhard de Chardin', *Etudes Teilhardiennes* 1, 1968, pp. 57-60.
72 CE, p. 93.
73 LF, p. 193.
74 SC, p. 112.
75 He found this expression in J. V. L. Casserley, op. cit., and was so delighted with this formula that he quoted it in several letters; see letter to Solange Lemaître, 11.1.53; LI, p. 422; LF, p. 186.
76 LI, p. 460; also LI, p. 450.
77 AE, pp. 226 & 227.
78 *Christianity and the Encounter of the World Religions*, New York, 1963, p. 30.
79 FM, p. 79.
80 London, 1971. Dobzhansky calls Teilhard 'one of the most profound religious philosophers of our time' and points out that his 'writings belong really to a class by themselves; an understanding of their singularity is essential for a comprehension of their contents' (ibid., pp. 95 & 114).
81 See ibid., pp. 109 & 110.

CHAPTER 9

1 CE, p. 68.
2 See especially 'The Mystical Milieu' (1917), 'The Mass on the World' (1923), 'My Universe' (1924), *Le Milieu Divin* (1927), 'How I Believe' (1934), 'The Phenomenon of Spirituality' (1937), 'My Fundamental Vision' (1948), 'The Heart of Matter' (1950), and 'The Christic' (1955).
3 See the works of H. de Lubac, M. Barthélemy-Madaule, Ch. Mooney, and F. Nemeck listed in the BIBLIOGRAPHY. The late Professor R. C. Zaehner, well known for his contribution to the study of mysticism, turned from initial enthusiasm to

a subsequent rejection of Teilhard but he still granted at the end that the latter was a mystic. Earlier, he had called him 'one of the greatest mystics of all time' (*The Teilhard Review*, vol. II, no. 2, 1967, p. 42).

4 The most recent critical discussions are found in S. T. Katz, ed., *Mysticism and Philosophical Analysis*, 1978, and F. Staal, *Exploring Mysticism*, 1975. Other publications taking different approaches are R. C. Zaehner, *Mysticism Sacred and Profane*, 1957; *Hindu and Muslim Mysticism*, 1960. W. T. Stace, *Mysticism and Philosophy*, 1960. F. C. Happold, *Mysticism: A Study and Anthology*, 1970. W. Johnston, *The Still Point*, 1971, and *The Inner Eye of Love*, 1978. A. C. Danto, *Mysticism and Morality*, 1976. G. Parrinder, *Mysticism in the World's Religions*, 1976. See also A. Ravier, ed., *La Mystique et les mystiques*, Paris, 1965.

5 Emphasized by H. de Lubac in his commentary on the Teilhard-Blondel Correspondence (TB); see also his *The Religion of Teilhard de Chardin*, chap. 9 'The element of novelty'.

6 Protagonists of the essential unity of all religions can be found in both West and East. Apart from the well-known views of the Neo-Vedanta in this matter see, among others, the works of A. Huxley, F. Schuon, and some recent writings on Sufism, especially by S. H. Nasr.

7 Teilhard's synthesis between a personal and universal approach is analysed in M. Barthélemy-Madaule, *La Personne et le drame humain chez Teilhard de Chardin*, Paris, 1967. The importance of a convergent structure is discussed in A. Glässer, *Konvergenz – die Struktur der Weltsumme P. Teilhard de Chardins*, Kevalaer, 1970.

8 CE, p. 102.

9 TF, pp. 209-11, from which all quotations are taken.

10 See the title of the essay under discussion, and also 'A Clarification: Reflections on Two Converse Forms of the Spirit', AE, pp. 215-27.

11 AE, p. 223; see the similar remark, made in 1954, quoted above in chapter 5, n. 57.

12 Discussed in Zaehner's article 'Teilhard and Eastern Religions', *The Teilhard Review*, vol. II, no. 2, 1967-68, pp. 41-53

13 ibid., p. 43.

14 The diagram in this form is my own but it is adapted from a similar diagram found in FM, p. 269. For a discussion of the *via tertia*, see AE, p. 56.

15 See MD, parts I and II.

16 See A. Ravier, 'Teilhard de Chardin et l'expérience mystique d'après ses notes intimes' in *Terre Promise*, Cahier VIII, Fondation et Association Teilhard de Chardin, Paris, 1974, pp. 212-32.

17 *cahier XIII*, pp. 113, 96 & 90, *passim*.

18 A point also stressed by M. Barthélemy-Madaule, *Bergson et Teilhard de Chardin*, Paris, 1963, pp. 475-93: 'La Vie Mystique'.

19 Cyclostyled discussion of the 1948 conference, Union des Croyants, Paris, pp. 30, 37 & 38.

20 LTF, p. 115.

21 HM, p. 88.

22 TF, p. 143.

23 See the section on *shakti* in B. Bruteau, *Evolution toward Divinity*, pp. 122 ff.

24 *Journal*, p. 204.

25 *carnet de lecture II*, p. 42. The criticism relates to R. Bastide, *Le Problème de la Vie Mystique*, Paris, 1931.

26 TF, pp. 117 & 120.

27 TF, p. 205.

28 It would require a detailed philosophical investigation to decide how far the positing of a self can only be done in contra-distinction and relation to the other, i.e. how far the personal self is a relational concept.

It has been argued that the Upanishadic *tat tvam asi* cannot provide a basis for a personal I-Thou relationship, and that Indian philosophy is undeveloped with respect to the relational concept of love. See P. T. Raju, 'The Inward Absolute and the Activism of the Finite Self', in S. Radhakrishnan & J. H. Muirhead, eds, *Contemporary Indian Philosophy*, London, 1952 p. 532 f. For a philosophical critique of Teilhard's understanding of the person, see Ch. Winckelmans de Cléty, *The World of Persons*, London, 1967, pp. 391-7 & 407-19. The author wrongly assumes, however, that Teilhard thinks in pluralistic terms whereas he is primarily a monist. It is in fact the attempt to combine a pluralistic and monistic perspective in a process of unification which characterizes Teilhard's synthesis as convergent.

29 HM, p. 89.

30 CE, p. 183.

31 CE, p. 184: 'Christian charity is forthwith both dynamized, universalized and (if I may be allowed the word . . .) "pantheized".' In his diary he distinguishes two forms of Christian charity: one seeks to 'supernaturalize' man, the other implies

the effort to 'superhumanize' him. See *cahier XV*, p. 89.

32 Quoted by C. Cuénot, 'Un inédit de Pierre Teilhard de Chardin'. *Etudes Teilhardiennes* 1, 1968, p. 57. With reference to the comparison between Christian and Buddhist love, see the remarks found in P. Tillich, op. cit., pp. 70-2, especially the contention that Buddhist compassion lacks the will to transform individual and social structures.

33 *cahier XIV*, p. 86, & *cahier XV*, p. 77.

34 See Teilhard's notes on reading Maréchal in the APPENDIX. The central place given to love by Teilhard is highlighted in an anecdote reported in C. Rivière, *En Chine avec Teilhard*, p. 204: It seems the Cartesian axiom 'I think, therefore I am' was changed by the philosophers Blondel and Valensin (both well known to Teilhard) into 'I will, therefore I am' which Teilhard then turned into 'I love, therefore I am'.

35 F. K. Nemeck, *Teilhard de Chardin et Jean de la Croix. Les 'passivités' dans la mystique teilhardienne comparées à certains aspects de la 'nuit obscure' de saint Jean de la Croix*, Montréal, 1975.

36 See ibid., p. 133.

37 Swami Siddheswarananda, *Pensée Indienne et Mystique Carmélitaine*, Centre Védantique Ramakrichna, Gretz, 1974. These comparisons, first developed in a lecture series given at the Sorbonne in the late 1940s, are perhaps little known outside the Ramakrishna-Mission. The publication contains five studies dealing with St John of the Cross, plus a general essay on Indian thought and Carmelite spirituality. But in spite of certain similarities between the mysticism of St John and *jnana-yoga*, Swami Siddheswarananda seems to think that there is really no genuine *jnanin* to be found in Europe. The Christian search for man's union with the Divine is more like the royal path of the *raja-yogin*, and he affirms without hesitation that St John of the Cross is 'like the Patanjali of the West'; see ibid., p. 156.

38 'The Spiritual Contribution of the Far East' (1947) bears the following editorial footnote: 'In 1946, during an interview with Siddheswarananda, . . . Père Teilhard was at pains to obtain more accurate information about the various forms of yoga, and to confirm that in India the highest ecstasy corresponded to final loss of consciousness in an impersonal whole'. TF, p. 139, n. 2.

39 TF, p. 201. Some months before, Teilhard referred to the Swami in a letter as 'a very honorable man', but remarked that 'one lets him naively take a disproportionate and ridiculous

amount of room. I find it humiliating that one lets him give twelve lectures at the Sorbonne (to a private group) to disseminate a nebulous and certainly "infra-western" mysticism whilst nothing is said or published where the gentiles might appreciate the "terrific" (sic) spiritual energy which is accumulating in the Christian "neo"-mysticism'. (LI, p. 368). This strong reaction must be related to Teilhard's difficult personal situation on his return from China: he was not allowed to speak publicly on a religious topic.

40 TF, p. 105.

41 See his article 'Teilhard and Eastern Religions', *The Teilhard Review*, vol. II, no. 2, 1967-68, pp. 41-53. Zaehner makes much of *Bhagavad-Gita* 11.13: 'Then did the son of Pandu see the whole [wide] universe in One converged, there in the body of the God of gods, yet divided out in multiplicity'. See his commentary *The Bhagavad-Gita*, Oxford, 1969. The similarities with the *Bhagavad-Gita* are also pointed out by B. Bruteau, op. cit.

42 R. C. Zaehner, *Evolution in Religion*, Oxford, 1971, p. 3.

43 See F. von Hügel, *Selected Writings*, London, 1964, for a modern parallel to Teilhard's understanding of religion and mysticism.

44 This affinity has been explored in the stimulating study by Marie-Ina Bergeron, *La Chine et Teilhard*, Paris, 1976.

45 HM, p. 100.

46 R. Robertson, *The Sociological Interpretation of Religion*, Oxford, 1970, p. 90; emphasis added.

47 See *cahier XIII*, p. 100, and *cahier XIV*, pp. 11 & 40.

48 See PM, p. 42 where energy is defined as 'a capacity for action or, more exactly, for interaction'.

49 SC, p. 221 which reproduces a letter to the personalist philosopher E. Mounier in which Teilhard refers to a 'theology of modern science'.

50 See HM, p. 95.

51 F. C. Happold, *Mysticism. A Study and an Anthology*, London, 1971, p. 395.

52 These are the subtitles of the three parts of the essay 'My Fundamental Vision' (1948), TF, pp. 163-208.

53 W. Johnston, *The Inner Eye of Love*. Mysticism and Religion, London, 1978, p. 179.

EPILOGUE

1 C. G. Jung, *Psychology and Religion: West and East*, collected works, vol. 11, London, 1969, pp. 557 & 537.
2 J. Kelley, 'Personal Recollections of Teilhard', *The Teilhard Review*, vol. X, 1975, p. IX.
3 See H. Dumoulin, 'Die geistige Vorbereitung des Abendlandes für den Dialog mit Asien', *Stimmen der Zeit* 177, 1966, pp. 13-8.
4 J. Dunne, *The Way of all the Earth – An Encounter with Eastern Religions*, London, 1973, p. 220.
5 A. Curle, *Mystics and Militants. A Study of Awareness, Identity and Social Action*, London, 1976.

APPENDIX

1 In 1945, Teilhard read and commented upon three lectures by Karl Barth published under the title *God in Action*, New York, 1936. The notes in the *carnet de lecture* relating to Karl Barth are reproduced and analysed in the thesis of M. Faessler, *Homme Réel et Phénomène Humain* – Essai sur les fondements christologique et cosmologique de l'anthropologie à partir des oeuvres de K. Barth et de P. Teilhard de Chardin, University of Geneva, 1967.
2 First published in 1924, a second, enlarged edition appeared in two volumes, Louvain, 1937-38. *Studies in the Psychology of the Mystics*, London, 1927, is a translation of the 1924 edition. Teilhard's extracts from the second volume of the French edition are found in *carnet de lecture I*, pp. 87-92.
3 J. Maréchal, op. cit., vol. II, pp. 409-83; Engl. trl., pp. 284-344.
4 See J. Maréchal, op. cit., p. 421.
5 ibid., pp. 423-31; English translation, pp. 294-300.
6 ibid., p. 426.
7 J. Maréchal, op. cit., p. 431 ff.
8 See *cahier XIII*, p. 139 (16.7.45).
9 2 vols, Louvain, 1923-33, commented upon in *carnet de lecture II*, pp. 1-10.
10 Father Pierre Johanns, SJ, (1882-1955), studied Sanskrit at Oxford, obtaining a B.Litt. He spent 17 years in India (1921-38), teaching in Jesuit houses in Calcutta and Kurseong. For a detailed discussion of Johanns's work see J. Mattam, *Land of the*

Trinity. A Study of Modern Christian Approaches to Hinduism, Bangalore, 1975, chap. I.

11 Published from Calcutta, 1922-46, in association with Father Dandoy who, after Johanns's return to Belgium in 1938, became its sole editor.

12 In a modern bibliographical survey on Hinduism, Johanns's volume on Vallabha is still listed and described as combining a 'lucid summary in Western terms with a liberal Christian critique'. N. Hein, 'Hinduism', in C. J. Adams, ed., *A Reader's Guide to the Great Religions*, New York, 1965, p. 67.

BIBLIOGRAPHY

I WORKS BY PIERRE TEILHARD DE CHARDIN

The philosophical and religious essays of Pierre Teilhard de Chardin have been published in a series of thirteen volumes entitled *Oeuvres* (Editions du Seuil, Paris). Their titles are listed below, followed by the English translation, published first by Collins, London and then in the United States by Harcourt Brace Jovanovich, New York, or Harper & Row, New York. A list of abbreviations for the most frequently used titles will be found on the first page of the NOTES.

A Books

Vol.

1	*Le Phénomène Humain*	1955	*The Phenomenon of Man*	1959
2	*L'Apparition de l'Homme*	1956	*The Appearance of Man*	1965
3	*La Vision du Passé*	1957	*The Vision of the Past*	1966
4	*Le Milieu Divin*	1957	*Le Milieu Divin*	1960
5	*L'Avenir de l'Homme*	1959	*The Future of Man*	1964
6	*L'Energie Humaine*	1962	*Human Energy*	1969
7	*L'Activation de l'Energie*	1963	*Activation of Energy*	1970
8	*La Place de l'Homme dans la Nature*	1963	*Man's Place in Nature*	1966
9	*Science et Christ*	1965	*Science and Christ*	1968
10	*Comment Je Crois*	1969	*Christianity and Evolution*	1971
11	*Les Directions de l'Avenir*	1973	*Toward the Future*	1975
12	*Ecrits du Temps de la Guerre 1916-1919*	1976	*Writings in Time of War*	1968[1]
13	*Le Coeur de la Matière*	1976	*The Heart of Matter*	1978

[1] This translation is based on an earlier French edition of the war essays, published by Editions Grasset, Paris, 1965.

Hymne de l'Univers, Paris 1961; trl. as *Hymn of the Universe*, London, 1965, New York, 1969.

Journal, tome I (cahiers 1-5 : 26 aout 1915-4 janvier 1919). Texte intégral, eds N. & K. Schmitz-Moormann, Paris, 1975.

L'Oeuvre Scientifique, 11 volumes, eds N. & K. Schmitz-Moormann, Olten, 1971.

Let Me Explain. Texts selected and arranged by J.-P. Demoulin, London, 1970, New York, 1972.

B Letters

Dans le sillage des sinanthropes. Lettres inédites de P. Teilhard de Chardin et de J. G. Anderson (1926-1934), ed. P. Leroy, Paris, 1971.

Génèse d'une Pensée, eds A. Teillard-Chambon & M. H. Begouen, Paris, 1961; trl. *The Making of a Mind*. Letters from a Soldier-Priest (1914-1919), London, 1965.

Lettres d'Egypte (1905-1908), ed. H. de Lubac, Paris, 1963.

Lettres d'Hastings et de Paris (1908-1914), eds A. Demoment & H. de Lubac, Paris, 1965.

Lettres Familières de Pierre Teilhard de Chardin Mon Ami. Les dernières années (1948-1955), ed. P. Leroy, Paris, 1976.

Lettres Intimes à Auguste Valensin, Bruno de Solages, Henri de Lubac, André Ravier (1919-1955), ed. H. de Lubac, second edition, Paris, 1974.

Letters from a Traveller (1923-1955), ed. C. Aragonnès, London, 1966.

Letters to Two Friends (1926-1952), ed. R. d'Ouince, London, 1970.

Letters to Léontine Zanta (1923-1939), eds R. Garric & H. de Lubac, London, 1969.

Pierre Teilhard de Chardin — Maurice Blondel Correspondence (1919), ed. H. de Lubac, New York, 1967.

C Unpublished material

Cahiers XIII-XXI (diaries 1944-1955); Jesuit Archives, Chantilly.

Carnets de lecture I & II; Jesuit Archives, Chantilly.

Correspondence with Madame Solange Lemaître; private collection.

Unpublished letters, especially to J. Huxley, Dr Loriot, Ella Maillart, Father Martindale, Mlle Mortier, Dr Needham, Father d'Ouince; Fondation Teilhard de Chardin, Paris.

II WORKS ON TEILHARD DE CHARDIN

A Bibliographies and journals

BAUDRY, G., *Pierre Teilhard de Chardin – Bibliographie*, Lille, 1972.

JARQUE, J. E., *Bibliographie génerale des Oeuvres et Articles sur Pierre Teilhard de Chardin parus jusqu' à fin décembre 1969*, Fribourg, 1970.

L'ARCHEVEQUE, P., *Teilhard de Chardin: Index analytique*, Quebec, 1967.

L'ARCHEVEQUE, P., *Teilhard de Chardin: Nouvel index analytique*, Quebec, 1972.

POLGAR, L., *Internationale Teilhard Bibliographie 1955-1965*, München, 1965.

POULAIN, D., *Teilhard de Chardin, Essai de Bibliographie (1955-1965)*, Quebec, 1966.

Acta Teilhardiana, München.

Etudes Teilhardiennes, Bruxelles.

Perspektiven der Zukunft, Freiburg.

Revue internationale Pierre Teilhard de Chardin, Bruxelles.

The Teilhard Review, London.

B Biographies

ALBUM based on publications and letters of P. Teilhard de Chardin, and on papers preserved at the Fondation Teilhard de Chardin, Paris. Designed by J. Mortier & M. L. Aboux, London, 1966.

CUENOT, C., *Teilhard de Chardin. A Biographical Study*, London, 1965.

LUKAS, M. & E., *Teilhard. A Biography*, London, 1977.

RAVEN, C. E., *Teilhard de Chardin: Scientist and Seer*, London, 1962.

SPEAIGHT, R., *Teilhard de Chardin. A Biography*, London, 1967.

C Books on Teilhard's Thought

BARBOUR, G., *In the Field with Teilhard de Chardin*, New York, 1965.

BARTHELEMY-MADAULE, M., *Bergson et Teilhard de Chardin*, Paris, 1963.

BARTHELEMY-MADAULE, M., *La Personne et le drame humain chez Teilhard de Chardin*, Paris, 1967.

BAUDRY, G., *Qui était Teilhard de Chardin?* Introduction à sa vie et son oeuvre, Lille, 1972.

BAUDRY, G., *Dictionnaire des correspondants de Teilhard de Chardin*, Lille, 1974.

BERGERON, M.-I., *La Chine et Teilhard*, Paris, 1976.

BRAVO, F., *La Vision de l'Histoire chez Teilhard de Chardin*, Paris, 1970.

BRAYBROOKE, N. ed., *Teilhard de Chardin. Pilgrim of the Future*, London, 1966.

BRUTEAU, B., *Evolution toward Divinity*. Teilhard de Chardin and the Hindu Traditions, Wheaton, USA, 1974.

CHOISY, M., *Teilhard et l'Inde*, Paris, 1964.

CORBISHLEY, T., *The Spirituality of Teilhard de Chardin*, London, 1971.

CUENOT, C., *Nouveau Lexique Teilhard de Chardin*, Paris, 1968.

CUENOT, C., *Ce que Teilhard a vraiment dit*, Paris, 1972.

DAECKE, S. M., *Teilhard de Chardin und die evangelische Theologie*. Die Weltlichkeit Gottes und die Weltlichkeit der Welt, Göttingen, 1967.

DECKERS, M. C., *Le Vocabulaire de Teilhard de Chardin*, Louvain, 1968.

DELFGAAUW, B., *Evolution, The Theory of Teilhard de Chardin*, London, 1961.

FARICY, R. L., *Teilhard de Chardin's Theology of the Christian in the World*, New York, 1967.

FENEBERG, R., *Die Phänomenologie bei Teilhard de Chardin*, Meisenheim, 1968.

FEYS, J., *The Philosophy of Evolution in Sri Aurobindo and Teilhard de Chardin*, Calcutta, 1973.

GLASSER, A., *Konvergenz. Die Struktur der Weltsumme P. Teilhard de Chardins*, Kevalaer, 1970.

GOSZTONYI, A., *Der Mensch und die Evolution*. Teilhard de Chardins philosophische Anthropologie, München, 1968.

GRAY, D., *The One and the Many*. Teilhard de Chardin's Vision of Unity, London, 1969.

HAAS, A., *Teilhard de Chardin Lexikon*, 2 vols, Freiburg, 1971.

HANSON, A. ed., *Teilhard Reassessed*, London, 1970.

HEMLEBEN, J., *Teilhard de Chardin in Selbstzeugnissen und Bilddokumenten*, Hamburg, 1966.

JARQUE, J. E., *La Foi en l'Homme*. L'apologétique de Teilhard de Chardin, Paris, 1969.

JUGNET, L., *L'Evolution Rédemptrice du P. Teilhard de Chardin*, Toulouse, 1950.

LIGNEUL, A., *Teilhard and Personalism*, New York, 1968.

LUBAC, H. de, *The Faith of Teilhard de Chardin*, London, 1965.

LUBAC, H. de, *The Religion of Teilhard de Chardin*, London, 1967.

LUBAC, H. de, *Teilhard Posthume*. Réflexions et souvenirs, Paris, 1977.

MAHEU, R. ed., *Science and Synthesis*. An International Colloquium organized by UNESCO on the tenth anniversary of the death of A. Einstein and P. Teilhard de Chardin, New York, 1971.

MONESTIER, A., *Teilhard et Sri Aurobindo*, Paris, 1963.

MOONEY, C.F., *Teilhard de Chardin and the Mystery of Christ*, London, 1966.

NEMECK, F. K., *Teilhard de Chardin et Jean de la Croix*. Les 'passivités' dans la mystique teilhardienne comparées à certains aspects de la 'nuit obscure' de saint Jean de la Croix, Montréal, 1975.

O'MANIQUE, J., *Energy in Evolution*. Teilhard's Physics of the Future, London, 1969.

OUINCE, R. de, *Un prophète en procès*, vol. I: *Teilhard de Chardin dans l'Eglise de son temps*; vol. II: *Teilhard de Chardin et l'avenir de la pensée chrétienne*, Paris, 1970.

RIDEAU, E., *Teilhard de Chardin. A Guide to his Thought*, London, 1969.

RIVIERE, C., *Teilhard, Claudel et Mauriac*, Paris, 1963.

RIVIERE, C., *En Chine avec Teilhard*, Paris, 1968.

SCHELLENBAUM, P., *Le Christ dans l'Energétique Teilhardienne*, Paris, 1971.

SCHMITZ-MOORMANN, K., *Das Weltbild Teilhard de Chardins*, Opladen, 1966.

SIMPSON, G. Gaylord, *This View of Life*. The World of an Evolutionist, New York, 1964; see chap. 11 'Evolutionary Theology: The New Mysticism'.

TEILHARD DE CHARDIN, F., *Lettres et Témoignages*, Paris, 1975.

TERRA, H. de, *Memories of Teilhard de Chardin*, London, 1964.

TERRA, H. de, ed., *Perspektiven Teilhard de Chardins*, München, 1966.

WILDIERS, N. M., *An Introduction to Teilhard de Chardin*, London, 1968.

ZAEHNER, R. C., *Evolution in Religion*. A study in Sri Aurobindo and Pierre Teilhard de Chardin, Oxford, 1971.

D Articles

ANANDAGARIKA GOVINDA, 'Die Weltanschauung Teilhard de Chardins im Spiegel des östlichen Denkens' in H. de Terra ed., *Perspektiven Teilhard de Chardins*, München, 1966, pp. 124-53.

ALDWINCKLE, R. F., 'Science and mysticism in Teilhard de Chardin', *Canadian Journal of Theology* 12, 1966, pp. 184-93.

BARTHELEMY-MADAULE, M., 'Milieu Mystique et Milieu Divin', *Le Message Spiritual de Teilhard de Chardin*, Colloque de Milan, ed. C. Cuénot, Paris, 1969, pp. 36-45.

BARTHELEMY-MADAULE, M., 'Mystique et recherche scientifique' *Etudes Teilhardiennes* 1, 1968, pp. 91-106.

BARTHELEMY-MADAULE, M., 'Croire et Penser', *Etudes Teilhardiennes* 3, 1970, pp. 5-14.

BRION, M., 'Recontre avec le Père Teilhard de Chardin', *Les Nouvelles Littéraires*, 11.1.1951.

COLIN, F., 'Contribution du P. Teilhard de Chardin à la formulation de la mystique d'Occident', *Académie des sciences, belles-lettres et arts de Besançon, Procès-verbaux et mémoires, 175,* 190-1, pp. 85-101.

CUENOT, C., 'Le Père Emile Licent SJ, un portrait', *Le ruban rouge* 19, Paris, 1963, pp. 36-45.

CUENOT, C., 'Le R. P. Emile Licent SJ', *Bulletin de la Société d'études indochinoises* 1, Saigon, 1966, pp. 9-83.

CUENOT, C., 'Un inédit de Pierre Teilhard de Chardin', *Etudes Teilhardiennes* 1, 1968, pp. 57-60.

DEMOULIN, J.-P., 'Foi au Monde et vérité scientifique', *Etudes Teilhardiennes* 1, 1968, pp. 107-42.

DELETIE, H., 'Teilhard de Chardin et la philosophie traditionelle de l'Extrême-Orient', *Recontre Orient-Occident* 4, 1962, pp. 13-18.

DUMOULIN, H., 'Die geistige Vorbereitung des Abendlandes für den Dialog mit Asien', *Stimmen der Zeit* 177, 1966, pp. 275-88.

GEX, M., 'Vers un humanisme cosmologique', *Revue de Théologie et de Philosophie*, 3, 1957, pp. 186-205.

GRAY, W., 'Oomoto and Teilhard de Chardin, Two case studies in revitalization', *Japanese Religions* 8, 1974, pp. 19-27.

GROOTAERS, W. A., 'When and where was the "Mass on the World" written?', *The Teilhard Review*, 12, 1977, pp. 91-4.

HUXLEY, J., 'Introduction' to P. Teilhard de Chardin, *The Phenomenon of Man*, London, 1959, pp. 11-28.

HUXLEY, J., 'Foreword' to G. Barbour, *In the Field with Teilhard de Chardin*, New York, 1965, pp. 7-9.

KING, U., 'The Phenomenology of Teilhard de Chardin', *The Teilhard Review* 6, 1971, pp. 33-45.

KING, U., 'Religion and the Future; Teilhard de Chardin's Analysis of Religion as a Contribution to inter-religious Dialogue, *Religious Studies* 7, 1971, pp. 307-23.

KING, U., ' "The Death of God – the Rebirth of God" '. A Study in the Thought of Teilhard de Chardin', *The Modern Churchman* 18, 1974, pp. 18-30.

KING, U., 'Teilhard's Comparison of Western and Eastern Mysticism', *The Teilhard Review* 10, 1975, pp. 9-16.

KING, U., 'Teilhard and the World Congress of Faiths', *The Teilhard Review* 11, 1976, 48-52.

KING, U., 'Teilhard's Fundamental Vision', *Ampleforth Journal* 83, 1978, pp. 11-21.

KELLY, J., 'Personal Recollections of Teilhard', *The Teilhard Review*, 10, 1975, pp. IX-XI.

LE BRUN KERIS, G., 'Teilhard de Chardin et l'Islam', *La Croix*, 17.12.1969.

LEMAITRE, S., 'In Memoriam', *Cahiers Pierre Teilhard de Chardin* 2, 1960, pp. 151-8.

LEMAITRE, S., *'Le Père Teilhard de Chardin. Sa Présence'*, monograph, Association des Amis de Pierre Teilhard de Chardin, Paris, 1965.

LEROY, P., 'Les "Textes Mystiques d'Orient et d'Occident" ', *Hommage à Solange Lemaître*, cyclostyled, Union des Croyants, Paris, 1961.

LEROY, P., 'L'Institut de Géobiologie à Pékin 1940-1946. Les dernières années du P. Teilhard de Chardin en Chine', *L'Anthropologie* 69, 1965, pp. 360-7.

LEROY, P., 'Teilhard tel que je l'ai connu', trl. 'The Man' in P. Teilhard de Chardin, *Letters from a Traveller*, London, 1966, pp. 15-47.

MASUI, J., *In Memoriam: P. Teilhard de Chardin*, monograph, Bruxelles, 1955.

MEYEROVITCH, E., 'Orient et Occident', *The New Morality* 1, 1963, pp. 49-68.

NEEDHAM, J., 'The Phenomenon of Man', *New Statesman*, 7.11.59.

OUINCE, R. de, *'L'épreuve de l'obéissance dans la vie du P. Teilhard de Chardin'* in L'Homme devant Dieu, Mélanges offerts au Père Henri de Lubac, vol. 3, Paris, 1964, pp. 331-446.

OUINCE, R. de, 'Prologue' in P. Teilhard de Chardin, *Letters to Two Friends*, London, 1970, pp. 1-19.

RAVIER, A., 'Teilhard de Chardin et l'expérience mystique d'après ses notes intimes' in *Terre Promise*, Cahier VIII, Fondation et Association Teilhard de Chardin, Paris, 1974, pp. 212-32.

SCHNEIDER, C., 'P. Teilhard de Chardin et E. Schuré', *Cahiers d'études cathares* 13, 1962, pp. 31-5.

STIERNOTTE, A. P., 'An Interpretation of Teilhard as reflected in Recent Literature', Zygon. *Journal of religion and science* 4, 1968, pp. 377-425.

SWAN, L., 'With Teilhard de Chardin in Peking', *The Month* 1, 1962, pp. 5-15.

WILDIERS, N. M., 'La Religion Universelle', *Cahiers Pierre Teilhard de Chardin* 5, 1965, pp. 113-20.

ZAEHNER, R. C., 'Teilhard and Eastern Religions', *The Teilhard Review* 2, 1967-68, pp. 41-53.

E   *Unpublished theses*

CAIRNS, H.C., *The Identity and Originality of Teilhard de Chardin*, Ph.D thesis, University of Edinburgh, 1971.

DUVALL, M. V., *Man's Concept of His Religious Fulfillment*: A Cross-Cultural Study of Major Perspectives in Teilhard de Chardin and Classical Hindu, Buddhist, and Confucian Thought, Ph.D thesis, Fordham University, New York, 1966.

FAESSLER, M., *Homme Réel et Phénomène Humain*. Essai sur les fondements christologique et cosmologique de l'anthoropologie à partir des oeuvres de K. Barth et de P. Teilhard de Chardin, Doctorate in Theology, University of Geneva, 1967.

KRAMLINGER, T., *The Sacred and Salvation* – A Study of Teilhard de Chardin's Religious Experiences in Evolutionary Being and Time and their Relation to Contemporary Religious Experiences, Ph.D thesis, University of Tübingen, 1971.

MARINI, C., *Via dell'Est via dell' Ovest nel Pensiero di Teilhard de Chardin*, Tesi di lauréa, University of Urbino, 1969.

SMITH, R. B., *Towards the Discovery of God*. A Study in the Thought of Teilhard de Chardin, Ph.D thesis, University of Exeter, 1968.

III   WORKS ON RELATED SUBJECTS

A   *Books cited or consulted*

ABHISHIKTANANDA, *Saccidananda*. A Christian Approach to Advaitic Experience, Delhi, 1974.

ACTES du XXI Congrès International des Orientalistes, Paris, 1949-50.

AUTRAN, C., *Mithra, Zoroaster et la Préhistoire aryenne du Christianisme*, Paris, 1935.

BARTH, K., *God in Action*, New York, 1936.

BARUZI, J., *St Jean de la Croix et le problème de l'expérience mystique*, Paris, 1924.

BELLAH, R. N., *Beyond Belief*. Essays on Religion in a Post-Traditional World, New York, 1976.

BENDIX, R., *Max Weber*. An Intellectual Portrait, London, 1966.

BERDYAEV, N., *Solitude and Society*, London, 1938.

BERDYAEV, N., *Spirit and Reality*, London, 1939.

BOUVIER, F. & LEMONNYER, A. eds, *Comptes rendus analytiques des Semaines d'Ethnologie religieuse de Louvain 1912-1913*, Paris, 1913.

CABLE, M. & FRENCH, F., *The Gobi Desert*, London, 1946.

CANTWELL-SMITH, W., *Islam in Modern History*, Princeton, 1957.

CAPRA, F., *The Tao of Physics*, London, 1976.

CASSERLEY, J., *The Retreat of Christianity from the Modern World*. The Maurice Lectures, King's College, London, for 1951, London, 1952.

CH'EN, K., *Buddhism in China*, Princeton, 1964.

CHAUDHURI, H. & SPIEGELBERG, F., *The Integral Philosophy of Aurobindo*, London, 1960.

COUSINS, E. H. ed., *Process Theology*, New York, 1971.

CURLE, A., *Mystics and Militants*. A Study of Awareness, Identity and Social Action, London, 1976.

DANTO, A. C., *Mysticism and Morality*. Oriental Thought and Moral Philosophy, London, 1976.

DELACROIX, H., *Etudes d'histoire et de psychologie de mysticisme*. Les grands mystiques chrétiens, Paris, 1908.

DOBZHANSKY, T., *The Biology of Ultimate Concern*, London, 1971.

DUNBAR, G., *History of India*, 2 vols, London, 1943.

DUNNE, J., *The Way of all the Earth*. An Encounter with Eastern Religions, London, 1973.

GEERTZ, C., *Islam Observed*. Religious Developments in Morocco and Indonesia, New Haven, 1968.

GHOSE, Aurobindo, *The Life Divine*, third edition, New York, 1965.

GRAHAM, A., *The End of Religion*, New York, 1971.

GRAHAM, A., *Contemplative Christianity*. An approach to the Realities of Religion, London, 1974.

GRIFFITH, B., *Return to the Centre*, London, 1978.

GROUSSET, R., *Histoire de la Philosophie Orientale*, Paris, 1923.

GROUSSET, R., *Histoire de l'Extrême-Orient*, Paris, 1929.

GROUSSET, R., *Les Civilisations de l'Orient*, Paris, 1929-30.

GROUSSET, R., *Les Philosophies Indiennes*, Paris, 1931.

GROUSSET, R., *Le Bilan de l'Histoire*, Paris, 1946.

GROUSSET, R., *L'Inde*, 1949.

HACKIN, J. et al, *Studies in Chinese Art and Some Indian Influences*, London, 1938.

HAPPOLD, F. C., *Mysticism: A Study and an Anthology*, London, 1971.

HICK, J. ed., *The Myth of God Incarnate*, London, 1977.

HUBY, J., *Christus. Manuel d'Histoire des Religions*, Paris, 1913.

HUGEL, F. von, *Selected Writings*, London, 1954.

HU SHIH, *My Credo and its Evolution*, New York, 1931.

HUXLEY, A., *Perennial Philosophy*, London, 1945.

IQBAL, M., *The Reconstruction of Religious Thought in Islam*, Oxford, 1934.

JACOVLEFF, A., *Dessins et Peintures d'Asie* exécutées au cours de l'expédition Citroën Centre-Asie, Paris, n.d.

JAMES, W., *Pragmatism. A New Name for some Old Ways of Thinking*, London, 1907.

JAMES, W., *The Varieties of Religious Experiences*, New York, 1967; first edition London, 1904; French trl. *L'expérience religieuse*, Paris, 1906.

JOHANNS, P., *Vers le Christ par le Vedanta*, 2 vols, Louvain, 1932-33.

JOHANNS, P., *La pensée religieuse de l'Inde*, Namur, 1952.

JOHNSTON, W., *The Still Point. Reflections on Zen and Christian Mysticism*, New York, 1971.

JOHNSTON, W., *Christian Zen*, New York, 1974.

JOHNSTON, W., *Silent Music. The Science of Meditation*, London and New York, 1974.

JOHNSTON, W., *The Inner Eye of Love. Mysticism and Religion*, London and New York, 1978.

JUNG, C. G., *Psychology and Religion: West and East*, London, 1973.

KATZ, S. T. ed., *Mysticism and Philosophical Analysis*, London, 1978.

KLOSTERMAIER, K., *Hindu and Christian in Vrindaban*, London, 1970.

LACOMBE, O., *L'Absolu selon le Vedanta*, Paris, 1938, repr. 1966.

LAMMENS, H., *Islam. Beliefs and Institutions*, London, 1929, repr. 1968.

LE FEVRE, G., *La Croisière Jaune*, Paris, 1933.

LEMAITRE, S., *Le Mystère de la Mort dans les religions de l'Asie*, Paris, 1943.

LEMAITRE, S., *Abdul Baha. Une grande figure de l'unité*, Paris, 1952.

LEMAITRE, S., *Textes mystiques d'Orient et d'Occident*, 3 vols, Paris, 1955.

LEMAITRE, S., *Ramakrishna*, Paris, 1954.

LEMAITRE, S., *Hindouisme ou Sanatana Dharma*, Paris, 1957; trl. *Hinduism*, London, 1959.

LUBAC, H. de, *Aspects du Bouddhisme I*, Paris, 1951.

LUBAC, H. de, *La rencontre du Bouddhisme et de l'Occident*, Paris, 1952.

LUBAC, H. de, *Aspects du Bouddhisme II – Amida*, Paris, 1955.

LUBAC, H. de, *Images de l'Abbé Monchanin*, Paris, 1967.

MAILLART, E., *Oasis Interdites. De Pékin au Cachemere*, Paris, 1937; trl. *Turkestan Solo*, One Woman's Expedition from the Tien Shan to the Kizil Khum, London, 1938.

MARECHAL, J., *Etudes sur la Psychologie des Mystiques*, Paris, 1924; trl. *Studies in the Psychology of the Mystics*, London, 1927. Enlarged second edition, 2 vols, Louvain, 1937-38.

MATTAM, J., *Land of the Trinity*. A study of Modern Christian Approaches to Hinduism, Bangalore, 1975.

McNEILL, W. H., *The Rise of the West*. A History of the Human Community, Chicago, 1963.

MERTON, T., *Zen, Tao et Nirvana*, Paris, 1970.

MERTON, T., *The Asian Journal of Thomas Merton*, New York, 1973.

MOFFITT, J., *Journey to Gorakhpur*. Reflections on Hindu Spirituality, London, 1972.

MONCHANIN, J., *Mystique de l'Inde, mystère chrétien*. Ecrits et inédits, Paris, 1974.

NAKAMURA, H., *Ways of Thinking of Eastern Peoples: India – China – Tibet – Japan*, Honolulu, 1964.

NASR, S. H., *Ideals and Realities of Islam*, London, 1971.

NEEDHAM, J., *Science and Civilisation in China*, vol. 2, Cambridge, 1956.

NEEDHAM, J., *Within the Four Seas. The Dialogue of East and West*, London, 1969.

NORTHROP, F. S. C., *The Meeting of East and West*. An Inquiry concerning World Understanding, New York, 1946.

OTT, E., *Thomas Merton. Grenzgänger zwischen Christentum und Buddhismus*, Würzburg, 1977.

OTTO, R., *Mysticism East and West*, London, 1932, repr. 1970.

PANIKKAR, R., *The Intra-Religious Dialogue*, New York, 1978.

PARRINDER, G., *Asian Religions*, London, 1975.

PARRINDER, G., *Mysticism in the World's Religions*, London, 1976.

PINNARD DE LA BOULLAYE, H., *L'Etude Comparée des Religions*, Paris, 1922.

RADHAKRISHNAN, S., *The Hindu View of Life*, Oxford, 1927.

RADHAKRISHNAN, S., *East and West in Religion*, London, 1933.

RADHAKRISHNAN, S., *Eastern Religions and Western Thought*, London, 1939.

RADHAKRISHNAN, S., *East and West: Some Reflections*, London, 1955.

RADHAKRISHNAN, S., & MUIRHEAD, J. H., eds, *Contemporary Indian Philosophy*, London, 1952.

RADHAKRISHNAN, S., & RAJU, P. T. eds, *The Concept of Man. A Study in Comparative Philosophy*, London, 1966.

RASMUSSEN, O. D., *Tientsin. An Illustrated Outline History*, Tientsin, 1925.

RAVIER, A. ed., *La Mystique et les Mystiques*, Paris, 1965.

ROBERTSON, R., *The Sociological Interpretation of Religion*, Oxford, 1970.

ROBINSON, J. A. T., *Exploration into God*, Stanford, 1967.

ROLLAND, R., *Prophets of the New India*, London, 1930.

SCHIMMEL, A., *Gabriel's Wing. A study into the religious ideas of Sir M. Iqbal*, Leiden, 1963.

SCHWAB, R., *La Renaissance Orientale*, Paris, 1950.

SCHURE, E., *Les Grands Initiés. Esquisse de l'Histoire Secrète des Religions*, Paris, 1889.

SIDDHESWARANANDA, *Pensée Indienne et Mystique Carmélitaine*, Gretz, France, 1974.

SMART, N., *The Yogi and the Devotee. The Interplay between Upanishads and Catholic Theology*, London, 1968.

SMART, N., *The Religious Experience of Mankind*, London, 1971.

SMART, N., *The Phenomenon of Religion*, London, 1973.

SMITH, D. H., *Chinese Religions*, London, 1968.

SNOW, E., *Red Star over China*, New York, 1938.

SNOW, H., *Inside Red China*, New York, 1939.

SPEER, A., *The Secret Diaries*, London, 1976.

STACE, W. T., *Mysticism and Philosophy*, London, 1960.

STAAL, F., *Exploring Mysticism*, London, 1975.

SUZUKI, D. T., *Mysticism Christian and Buddhist*, London, 1957.

TILLICH, P., *Christianity and the Encounter of the World Religions*, New York, 1963.

WEBER, M., *The Sociology of Religion*, London, 1966.

WEBER M., *The Religion of India: The Sociology of Hinduism and Buddhism*, New York, 1958.

WELCH, H. H., *The Practice of Chinese Buddhism 1900-1950*, Cambridge, Mass., 1967.

WELCH, H. H., *The Buddhist Revival in China*, Cambridge, Mass., 1968.

WERBLOWSKY, R. J. Z., *Beyond Tradition and Modernity*. Changing Religions in a Changing World, London, 1976.

WHITSON, R. E., *The Coming Convergence of World Religions*, New York, 1971.

WINCKELMANS DE CLETY, C., *The World of Persons*, London, 1967.

ZAEHNER, R. C., *Mysticism Sacred and Profane*, Oxford, 1957.

ZAEHNER, R. C., *Hindu and Muslim Mysticism*, London, 1960.

ZAEHNER, R. C., *The Bhagavad-Gita*, Oxford, 1969.

ZAEHNER, R. C., *Concordant Discord*: the interdependence of faiths, Oxford, 1970.

B   Articles

AUCLAIR, M., 'Solange Lemaître' in M. Auclair, *A la grace de Dieu*, Paris, 1973, pp. 95-103.

BACOT, J., 'Autour de Congrès Universal des Croyants: Quelques Evocations', *Cahiers Pierre Teilhard de Chardin* 2, Paris, 1960, pp. 143-50.

BULLETIN CITROEN, *Numéro Spécial* consacré à l'Exposition des Expéditions Citroën Centre-Asie et Centre-Afrique, Paris, 1932.

CUTTAT, J. A., 'L'expérience chrétienne est-elle capable d'assumer la spiritualité orientale' in A. Ravier ed., *La Mystique et les Mystiques*, Paris, 1965.

DUMOULIN, H., 'Welt and Selbst in der östlichen Meditation' in H. Kunn et al., *Interpretation der Welt*. Würzburg, 1965, pp. 472-96.

ELIADE, M., 'Cultural Fashions and the History of Religions' in J. M. Kitagawa ed., *The History of Religions*, Chicago, 1967, pp. 21-38.

ELIADE, M., 'Foreword' to T. N. Munson, *Reflective Theology: Philosophical Orientations in Religion*, New Haven, 1968.

EMONET, B., 'La Semaine d'Ethnologie Religieuse – Louvain 27.8.-4.9.1912', *Etudes* 133, 1912, pp. 83-100.

GEOGRAPHIE, LA, Special number devoted to the 'Yellow Expedition', vol. 58, Paris, 1932.

HEIN, N. J., 'Hinduism', in C. J. Adams ed., *A Reader's Guide to the Great Religions,* New York, 1965, pp. 45-82.

KING, U., 'The One and the Many: The Individual and the Community from a Religious Perspective'. *The Teilhard Review* 11, 1976, pp. 9-15.

KING, U., 'Exploring Convergence: The Contribution of World Faiths', The Third Francis Younghusband Lecture, *World Faiths* 106, 1978, pp. 1-16.

KLOSTERMAIER, K. K., 'Hindu-Christian Dialogue: Its Religious and Cultural Implication', *Sciences Religieuses/Studies in Religion* 1, 1971, 83-97.

NEEDHAM, J., 'The Roles of Europe and China in the Evolution of Oecumenical Sciences', *British Association for the Advancement of Science,* 1967. pp. 83-98.

PETTAZZONI, R., 'The Formation of Monotheism' in W. A. Lessa & E. Z. Vogt, *Reader in Comparative Religion,* Evanston, 1958, pp. 40-6.

RAJU, P. T., 'The Inward Absolute and the Activism of the Finite Self', in S. Radhakrishnan & J. H. Muirhead eds, *Contemporary Indian Philosophy,* London, 1952.

SIX, J. F., 'Louis Massignon, prophète du dialogue entre croyants d'Orient et d'Occident', cyclostyled, Union des Croyants, Paris, 1958.

SMART, N., 'Interpretation and Mystical Experience', *Religious Studies* 1, 1965, pp. 75-87.

SMART, N., 'Sri Aurobindo and History', in *Sri Aurobindo 1872-1972 – A Centenary Symposium,* Sri Aurobindo Society of Great Britain, London, 1972, pp. 15-22.

UNION DES CROYANTS, 'Le Congrès Universal des Croyants, Historique 1946-1962', cyclostyled, Paris, 1962.

UNION DES CROYANTS, *Hommage à Solange Lemaître,* monograph, Paris, 1969.

INDEX

(This index refers only to the main text and not the notes)

b